YALE STUDIES IN ENGLISH, 190

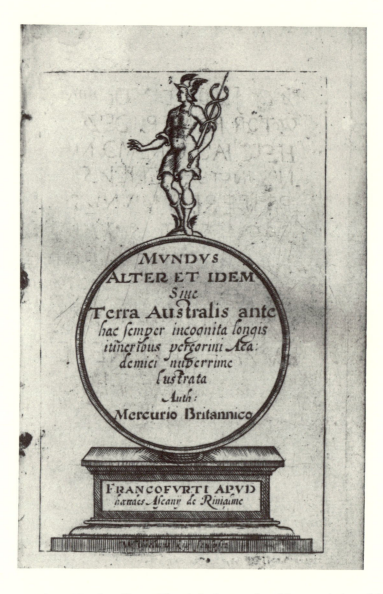

MVNDVS
ALTER ET IDEM
Siue
Terra Australis ante
hac semper incognita longis
itineribus peregrini Aca:
demici nuperrime
lustrata
Auth:
Mercurio Britannico

FRANCOFVRTI APVD
haeraes Ascanij de Rinialme

Title page from *Mundus Alter et Idem* (1605), reproduced by permission of the
Folger Library.

ANOTHER WORLD AND YET THE SAME

Bishop Joseph Hall's
Mundus Alter et Idem

TRANSLATED AND EDITED BY
JOHN MILLAR WANDS

NEW HAVEN AND LONDON
YALE UNIVERSITY PRESS

Published with the assistance of the Elizabethan Club
from the foundation established in memory of
Oliver Baty Cunningham of the Class of 1917, Yale College.

Designed by James J. Johnson
and set in Baskerville type.
Printed in the United States of America by
The Alpine Press, Stoughton, Mass.

Library of Congress Cataloging in Publication Data

Hall, Joseph, Bp. of Norwich, 1574-1656.
    Another world and yet the same.

    (Yale studies in English, 190)
    Bibliography: p.
    Includes index.
    I. Wands, John Millar, 1946- .
II. Title. III. Series.
PA8523.H4M813 1981   873'.04   81-4998
ISBN 0-300-02613-7   AACR2

10 9 8 7 6 5 4 3 2 1

*To the memory of Dick Sylvester,
who leads us still*

CONTENTS

ILLUSTRATIONS

ACKNOWLEDGMENTS

This edition came about from my desire to make an undeservedly neglected work better known, but it would never have progressed to completion in its present form without the encouragement and aid of a large group of scholars. Most important in moving it beyond the idea I first entertained in the spring of 1976 was the interest shown by Dick Sylvester, who patiently answered my questions and helped me choose the present format. Only once did a query to him return unanswered; later I found that the radiation therapy he was undergoing had affected his eyesight. The unfailing generosity he showed to me and other young scholars stands as an enduring monument to his greatness.

Other colleagues who provided special expertise include Bart Giamatti and Larry Manley, who read the introduction in an earlier version; Paula Johnson, who read both the introduction and the translation, making elaborate suggestions for improving the phrasing; Clarence Miller and Elizabeth McCutcheon, who advised me on matters utopian; Katharine Pantzer, who aided me in establishing the chronology of the early editions and thus in selecting the copy text; Father Germain Marc'hadour and John Kazazis, who helped with problems in translating the Greek and Latin; and Fred Sochatoff, who compared my translation against the original, correcting a number of errors and offering many suggestions for improvement.

Most of my research was done at Yale, and I owe a special debt of gratitude to Marjorie Wynne and the staff at Beinecke Library for cheerfully providing me with the hundreds of books I needed to consult. I also want to thank Dennis Marnon and the staff at the Houghton Library, John Aubrey and the staff at the Newberry, and the staffs at Princeton,

Columbia, the British Library, and the Bibliothèque Nationale for the help they rendered—which was in several instances quite extraordinary.

My initial interest in Joseph Hall was stimulated by my dissertation director, Will Jewkes, and though he did not play an active role in this book, it is inevitable that some of his influence should appear in my approach to the subject. John Hart, Peggy Knapp, and Ann Hayes from Carnegie-Mellon University gave me encouragement, as well as sound stylistic advice, as did Henry Sams and Elmer Borklund from Penn State.

The movement from manuscript to finished book could not have occurred without the diligence of Dorothee Metlitzki, who assumed the guidance of Yale Studies in English after Dick Sylvester's death. Throughout this process she has continually displayed the graciousness and fairness one always hopes to find in professors of the humanities. I also wish to thank George deF. Lord and John Hollander, who read my manuscript for the committee, as well as Gene Waith and Louis Martz, who were instrumental in eliciting the aid of the Elizabethan Club to support the printing of this book, which otherwise would have been a far more risky undertaking. I must also thank the Committee for Yale Studies in English and Ellen Graham and Charlotte Dihoff from the Press for the assistance they have given.

In the final stages of the manuscript, Georges Edelen, the reader for the Press, went over it with scrupulous care and made numerous suggestions for improvement, saving me—in not a few cases—from error. Professor Edelen served as an excellent reader, sympathetic to the aims of the project and demanding in his standards. I want to thank him for the time he expended on all aspects of the manuscript; any mistakes that remain, however, are mine alone.

I am grateful to the Folger Library for permission to reproduce the title page of the first edition of *Mundus Alter et Idem* (1605). The maps and other illustrations are reproduced from the second edition (1607) by kind permission of the Newberry Library.

My thanks, finally, to two grants from the A. Whitney Griswold Fund for Research in the Humanities in Yale College, which covered much of the cost of preparing the manuscript for Yale Studies in English, and to Dottie Nelson, Wanda Fiak, and David and Priscilla De Wolf for their expert typing. During the academic year 1979–80, Carnegie-Mellon University provided me with a research assistant, Paul Kravits, who proofread the manuscript carefully and enthusiastically. Toward the end I also pressed my mother and aunt into the job of proofreading, which they did cheerfully, although not without questioning the morality of the work. But for their aid and that of my wife, Frances Terpak, who abandoned her dissertation for several months to type the text and corrections into the CMU computer, I would still be far from finished.

INTRODUCTION

AUTHORSHIP

In 1605 a small Latin volume entitled *Mundus Alter et Idem* appeared in London. Purportedly written by Mercurius Britannicus and published in Frankfort, this work describes an imaginary voyage to *Terra Australis Incognita* and the people and governments discovered there. Though relatively little known today, in its own time the book was quite popular, going through two Latin editions, two editions of the English translation, and one edition of the German within ten years of its appearance. Despite its success, however, the book was never claimed by either of the two men advanced as its author. For this reason, the evidence for assigning authorship to Joseph Hall (1574-1656), bishop of Norwich, must be examined.[1]

The other person plausibly advanced is Alberico Gentili (1552-1608), an Italian refugee educated at the University of Perugia who settled in England in the later 1570s. Incorporated at Oxford in 1581 as a Doctor of Canon Law and appointed Regius Professor of Civil Law in 1587, he moved his residence to London in 1590 (*DNB*, 7, 1003-06). The arguments in Gentili's favor are assembled by E. A. Petherick in his article "Mundus alter et idem,"[2] but they are principally these:

---

1. Huntington Brown surveys the problem in the introduction to his edition of *The Discovery of a New World*, pp. xxviii-xxxiv, but ignores some of the available internal evidence. On several points my discussion parallels his.

2. *Gentleman's Magazine*, 281 (1896), 66-87. Petherick, without examining the internal evidence that favors Hall, and apparently ignorant of Milton's attribution of the work to him, feels Gentili is the more likely author.

The traveller [Mercurius Britannicus] is identified with . . . Gentili in the table of contents (at the heading of Book II, chapter ii) of the Hanau edition of the *Mundus* (1607) and in certain uncorrected copies of the Frankfort edition (c. 1605); Gentili is named as the author on the title page of the German translations of 1613 and 1704, and again on that of the Utrecht edition of the Latin edition (1643); and he is accepted as the author by an unknown contributor to the *Universal Lexikon* of J. P. von Ludewig (1732-1748).[3] The *Mundus* was dedicated to the Earl of Huntingdon and published at the expense of Ascani[us] Rinialme, both of whom were fellows of Gentili's at Gray's Inn, and the Hanau edition bears the same imprint as four other of his acknowledged works. (Brown, *Discovery*, pp. xxvii-xxviii)

These points would be strong evidence for Gentili's authorship were there not even stronger evidence for Hall's.

Hall is first clearly specified as the author of the *Mundus* in *An Apology* (1642), one of the pamphlets written by John Milton in the war against episcopacy begun by Smectymnuus.[4] Hall, one of the most respected bishops in England, was the person selected by William Laud, the Archbishop of Canterbury, as the defender of episcopacy. Milton's tendency to attack personalities rather than philosophies leads him to criticize Hall for his earlier secular works—works unsuited to the dignity of a churchman—and he calls *Mundus Alter et Idem*

that wretched pilgrimage over *Minshews* Dictionary, . . . the idlest and paltriest Mime that ever mounted upon banke. Let him ask *the Author of those toothless Satyrs*[5] who was the maker, or rather the anticreator of that universall foolery, who he was, who like that other principle of the *Maniches* the *Arch evill* one, when he had look't upon all that he had made and mapt out, could say no other but contrary to the Divine Mouth, that it was very foolish. . . . Cer-

3. The article in the *Universal Lexikon* is on "Pamphagonia"; under "Hall, Joseph" in the same lexicon, however, the *Mundus* is attributed to Hall.

4. An acronym formed from the initial letters of the five moderate Puritan divines (Steven Marshall, Edmund Calamy, Thomas Young, Matthew Newcomen, and William Spurstow) who, in a series of pamphlets, called for church reform.

5. The first three books of *Virgidemiae* were subtitled "Tooth-lesse Satyrs." I follow Arnold Davenport's practice of using *Virgidemiae* (the nominative plural form) in preference to *Virgidemiarum* (the genitive plural form governed by the English words "Sixe Bookes") used on the title page of the original edition. See Davenport, ed., *The Poems of Joseph Hall*, p. 159.

tainly he that could indure with a sober pen to sit and devise laws
for drunkards to carouse by, I doubt me whether the very sobernesse
of such a one, like an unlicour'd *Silenus,* were not stark drunk.
(*Works,* 3, 294-95)

Several pages later—stung by Hall's assertion that using the word
"sleekstone" (slang for a trollop) to refer to *Virgidemiae* shows that
Milton "can be as bold with a prelate as familiar with a Laundresse,"[6]—
Milton turns the jibe about knowing loose women back on Hall:

What if I had writ as your friend the author of the aforesaid *Mime,*
Mundus alter & idem, to have bin ravisht like some young *Cephalus*
or *Hylas,* by a troope of camping Huswives in *Viraginia,* and that
he was there forc't to sweare himselfe an uxorious varlet, then after a
long servitude to have come into *Aphrodisia* that pleasant Countrey
that gave such sweet smell to his nostrils among the shamelesse
Courtezans of *Desergonia?* surely he would have then concluded me
as constant at the Bordello, as the gally-slave at his Oare. (*Works,* 3,
300)

Significantly, neither Hall, who normally answers Milton's accusation
point by point, nor his son, who is believed to have written the later
pamphlets against Milton beginning with *A Modest Confutation,* re-
futes Milton's attribution of the work.

Besides Milton's testimony we have the testimony of John Healey
who translated *Mundus Alter et Idem* into English as *The Discovery of a
New World* (1609). The first edition of *The Discovery* contains the translator's preface headed "I. H. the Translator, vnto I. H. the Author" (¶4r).
Healey's preface to the second edition (c. 1613-14) calls the author "that
Reuerend man" (¶1r), and William Knight's preface to the *Mundus* says
that the author is devoted to "the sacred calling of Theology."[7] Neither
the initials nor the title would apply to Gentili; they both fit Hall.
Though such references cannot be conclusive, when supplemented by
internal evidence and by correspondences between the *Mundus* and
Hall's other works, there can be little doubt concerning Hall's authorship.

The work, signed at the end in the Latin 1605 edition as "Peregrinvs

6. Hall (?), *A Modest Confutation* (1642), C1r.
7. *Mundus,* p. 4 below. Hall was ordained in 1603 and received his D.D. in 1612.

quondam Academicus," is signed in *The Discovery of a New World* as "The Cambridge Pilgrime." In both versions the author says: "These men, these customs, and these cities I gazed upon, was astonished by, and laughed at; and after 30 years, weakened by so much labor of traveling, I returned to my homeland." Hall was educated at Cambridge, but Alberico Gentili was affiliated only with Oxford. Moreover, Gentili's native land was not England but Italy, a land he never returned to (*DNB*, 7, 1004).

Several other statements in the *Mundus* support Hall's authorship and disqualify Gentili. In Book 1, the narrator Mercurius compares the dispute for supremacy between Artopolis and Creatium to that quarrel between "the two most learned academies in the whole world [which] are constraining themselves from that same most disgraceful dispute with difficulty—both of them my mother, and one of them even my wet nurse, true sisters." Though he does not name the two universities, there is little doubt which ones a *British* Mercury would mean: Cambridge and Oxford. Hall received his B.A., M.A., B.D., and D.D. from Cambridge and was incorporated at Oxford 11 July 1598.[8] Gentili also attended two famous universities, Perugia and Oxford (*DNB*, 7, 1004), but these institutions had no close kinship, nor did they dispute with one another in any way resembling the long-standing rivalry between Oxford and Cambridge.

Despite the incorporation of Gentili's name in the index of the Hanau edition, there are further clues tying Hall to the *Mundus*. The tomb of Vortunius in Moronia Mobilis has a cryptic inscription modeled on one beginning "Alia Loelia Crispis..." in Jerome Turler's *Traueiler*.[9] But the author of the *Mundus* alters the name of the monument's erector from "Lucius Agatho Priscius" to "H. I.," once again Hall's initials, though in reverse order.

Finally, as Huntington Brown notes in the introduction to his edition of *The Discovery of a New World*, "the most telling evidence of all is the large number of comparatively recondite images and allusions in the *Mundus* which occur in both earlier and later acknowledged writings of Hall, [and] the occurrence of details which show an intimate knowledge of the estate of Sir Robert Drury at Halsted [Hawstead]" (p. xxviii). In particular, the *Mundus* contains sayings and descriptions from scenes painted on Robert Drury's walls that only a person who had

---

8. *Alumni Cantabrigienses*, part 1, vol. 2, 287; *Alumni Oxonienses*, 1 (early series), 633.

9. Fol. A8r. Hall knew this work; see pp. xlviii–xlix below.

visited the place could know about.[10] Though we have nothing to connect Gentili with Hawstead, we know Hall lived there from 1601 to 1608. Moreover, more than a dozen passages in the *Mundus* echo similar passages in *Virgidemiae*; only a person intimately acquainted with this work would be likely to borrow from it so extensively. A similar perusal of Gentili's works written in this period reveals none of these correspondences.

The only remaining puzzle is why, in addition to the edition surreptitiously printed in London, Hall's work should be printed by Gentili's publisher, Wilhelm Antonius, in Hanau and contain Gentili's name in the index. Petherick assumes some "uncorrected" Frankfort copies also contain Gentili's name. But what Petherick assumes are Frankfort copies are actually a reissue of 1607 combining Frankfort and Hanau signatures with the Frankfort title page printed on Hanau preliminaries, as I note in the section "Publication Data," below. As we investigate the chain of friendships necessary to convey the work from Joseph Hall to Wilhelm Antonius we discover, as did Petherick, that Gray's Inn appears to be the crucial link among most of the principals involved. But this link in no way disqualifies Hall as the author. The *Mundus* was dedicated to Henry Lord Hastings, the fifth Earl of Huntingdon, who succeeded to his title in 1604. Two other of Hall's works—*Heaven upon Earth* (1606) and *Contemplations* (1612)—were also dedicated to him, and in his dedication to the *Contemplations* Hall describes Hastings as a "bountiful favourer of all good learning" and "the first patron of my poor studies" (*Works*, 1, 96). In addition, Hall's father had been a minor officer in the employ of Huntingdon's granduncle, the third Earl, who had helped to see that Hall was elected to his fellowship at Emmanuel College (*Works*, 1, xix). Presumably the fifth Earl was a good friend of Hall's and a person likely to commend his work to others.

Hastings, then heir apparent to the Earl of Huntingdon, was admitted to Gray's Inn on 17 March 1597/98, according to Edward Petherick ("Mundus alter et idem," p. 76). Significantly, Ascanius Rinialme, whose heirs underwrote the first two editions of the *Mundus*, had been a member of Gray's Inn, having been admitted 3 August 1592. Finally, Alberico Gentili was admitted on 14 August 1600. So, of the four people besides Hall whose names are somehow involved in the book's publication, all but William Knight, the supposed author of "To the Reader, Greetings" (pp. 3–5, below), belonged to the same Inn of Court, and one

10. In particular, see pp. 96, 110 below.

was a close friend of Hall's. Given the direct connection between the Earl of Huntingdon and Gray's Inn, Joseph Hall could very well have known Gentili.

Once Gentili is seen as having been involved not in the writing but in the publication of the *Mundus,* the appearance of his name in the Hanau edition becomes comprehensible. When Gentili transmitted the work to Germany with the order to have it printed anonymously, the printer may very well have believed the work to be Gentili's and—whether out of playfulness or forgetfulness—stuck in his name anyway. Or perhaps the insertion was an attempt to mislead the reader about the true author and thereby protect Hall from any speculation that may have surfaced in England after the appearance of the Frankfort edition.

Though almost no one writing on Hall in the last hundred years has questioned his authorship, the elaborate shielding to keep Hall from becoming known as the author has misled some commentators on the *Mundus.* One problem has been whether the statements in the prefatory section entitled "To the Reader, Greetings," signed by William Knight, were really written by him and whether they can be believed.[11] For example, William Knight claims Hall "could not be induced by any entreaties whatever to permit [it] to be printed." I think we must discount this, since disclaimers of authorial involvement in the publication of manuscripts are frequent in the Renaissance,[12] and for several other reasons as well. Knight's assertion that the *Mundus* was one of Hall's exercises composed "for his own training and amusement in a youthful and leisurely academic period" is—in fact—untrue. Though the *Mundus* may well have been partially written at Cambridge, there are too many esoteric details in the work that must have come from an intimate knowledge of Sir Robert Drury's home in Hawstead for us to believe that Hall did not continue to work on the text after he left Cambridge in 1601. Nor is it possible to believe that Hall would have been ignorant of the whereabouts of the manuscript as it was being readied for printing.

The so-called Frankfort edition was printed in London by Humphrey Lownes, the printer of three editions of Hall's *Meditations and vowes* (*STC* 12679-81). And the entry of the *Mundus* in the *Stationers' Register* on 2 June 1605 was to John Porter, bookseller, who just four months earlier had been assigned the work Lownes printed. If Knight had undertaken surreptitious publication on his own, against Hall's

11. Ronald James Corthell, "The Early Literary Career of Joseph Hall," pp. 96-99, is also skeptical that Hall was reluctant to publish the *Mundus.*

12. See, for example, the similar disclaimer prefacing Donne's *Ignatius His Conclave* (1611).

wishes, surely he would have made a more judicious selection of publisher and bookseller. Moreover, Hall's Epistle to William Knight written
about 1608, commending his "unusual variety of tongues; style of arts,
. . . and, which is worth all, a faithful and honest heart" (*Works*, 6, 276),
demonstrates that if any break in their friendship occurred because of the
Mundus's publication it was neither severe nor long lasting. Thus I am
convinced that Hall was intimately involved in its publication from
beginning to end.

One can readily understand why Joseph Hall and his friends would
want to suppress the work's place of publication and authorship. Hall's
only previous satiric work, *Virgidemiae,* had come under the scrutiny of
Richard Bancroft, the Bishop of London, and John Whitgift, the Archbishop of Canterbury. Along with Cutwode's *Caltha Poetarum,* Mars-
ton's *Pigmalion* and *Scourge of Villanie,* Guilpin's *Skialetheia, Micro-
Cynicon,* Davies's *Epigrams,* Marlowe's *Elegies,* and all the Harvey-
Nashe controversial pamphlets, Hall's satires were called in to be burned.
Though they, along with Cutwode's work, were "staid" (not burned) at
the last minute (Arber, *Transcript*, 3, 678), the order of 1 June 1599 pro-
hibited the further printing of any satires, English histories, or plays:

> That thoughe any booke of the nature of theise heretofore expressed
> shalbe broughte vnto yow vnder the hands of the Lord Archebisshop
> of CANTERBURYE or the Lord Bishop of LONDON yet the said
> booke shall not bee printed vntill the master or wardens haue
> acquainted the said Lord Archbishop, or the Lord Bishop with the
> same to knowe whether it be theire hand or no. (Arber, *Transcript*,
> 3, 677)

This strongly worded order was apparently only partly effective, for
while the majority of the books on the Archbishop's list are quite scarce,
various books of satires and epigrams did appear in the next ten years,
and part 1 of *Virgidemiae* was reprinted in 1602 (Davenport, *Poems*, p.
xxvii). Yet the order must have discouraged some, for the tremendous
outpouring of satire in the 1590s died down to a trickle in the early seventeenth century. For Hall, now a minister, authorship of another satire
might have seemed not only out of keeping with the dignity of his office
but perhaps even a challenge to his ecclesiastical superiors. Anonymous,
ostensibly foreign publication would circumvent these problems and
help safeguard the English publisher from being fined or otherwise
punished.

Though "To the Reader, Greetings" displays a style radically dif-

ferent from the rest of the *Mundus* and may very well have been written
by Knight, the sentiments expressed seem likely to have come from Hall
and the others involved in safeguarding him from discovery. As the supposed editor of the work, Knight has also occasionally been thought to
have provided the marginal notes.[13] This attribution has always been
made in ignorance of the fact that Hall, not Knight, must have arranged
for publication. More importantly, the marginalia fit exactly with the
text both in style and in content; the books cited are ones Hall was well
acquainted with, and the sentiments expressed echo those in his other
works.

HALL'S LIFE

Joseph Hall died in 1656 at the age of 82. He had lived through a difficult
time in English history. Oliver Cromwell had less than two years to live;
England had less than four years left before the return to Stuart kings.
But even though he lived most of his life in the seventeenth century and
entered into its many controversies, Hall is clearly a child of the Age of
Elizabeth. The style of his writings, with its pleasant mixture of the
hyperbolic and the paradoxical balanced by the aphoristic and the direct,
is Elizabethan. Likewise, his belief in the absolute supremacy of the
episcopacy and the monarchy belongs to an earlier age. But above all,
Hall's moral stance, his abhorrence of all extremes in an age when
extremity seems to have been the norm, aligns Hall clearly with sixteenth-
century figures like Hooker, More, and Erasmus rather than with seven-
teenth-century figures like Laud, Milton, or Prynne. Bishop Hall's studied
moderation is well known to students of the Puritan-Anglican controversies of the 1640s. Yet, to students of literature, Hall is a hazy if not an
invisible figure. He wrote two remarkable secular works, *Virgidemiae*
(1597–98) and *Mundus Alter et Idem* (1605), and then turned his energies
to the Anglican church, producing predominantly religious writings
thereafter. Although his career breaks into two distinct periods, Hall's
concerns as a clergyman are the same as Hall's concerns as a satirist—
mankind's reform. What we know about Bishop Hall helps to illuminate
Joseph Hall the satirist.

Hall was born 1 July 1574 at Bristow Park, within the parish of
Ashby-de-la-Zouch, a town in the north of Leicestershire.[14] Both parents

13. Harold Ogden White, *Plagiarism and Imitation in the English Renaissance*,
p. 122.
14. For an extended treatment of Hall's life, see Joseph Hall, "Observations of Some

were strict Calvinists, especially his mother, who used to recount to her son the agonies of her struggles with the devil. Hall's rearing in a strict Calvinist and Puritan milieu continued when he attended university, for he enrolled in Emmanuel College, Cambridge, the "recognized academic centre of Puritanism" (Lewis, p. 28). Hall proceeded to the B.A. in 1592/93 and by 1596 was of sufficient standing for the M.A. At this same time he received a university fellowship, which he held for six or seven years, and was elected for two consecutive years to the University Lectureship in Rhetoric. What we know about Hall's later years at Cambridge (from 1595 to 1601) suggests that Hall was not nearly so strait-laced as many of his classmates at Emmanuel College.

In 1597 and 1598 he published the first and second parts of *Virgidemiae*, his books of satires, which added to his reputation and initiated the rash of satires marking the last years of the decade. By 1598, Francis Meres in *Palladis Tamia* mentions him twice as one of the foremost English satirists (fols. 277v, 283v). These satires show the direction Hall's writings will follow throughout his life. They ridicule anything either extreme or newfangled. In opposition, Hall cultivates what Aristotle would term the normal and the natural. Fops and Puritans are both ridiculed: the first for an excess of dress and decoration, the second for a defect of both. Effeminate youth are ridiculed because nature does not intend men to perfume and paint; people who crave burial in elaborate tombs are ridiculed because honor is gained not by great tombs but by just deeds. Hall's philosophy of moderation extends even to literature, for he disapproves of writers who violate probability or poetic decorum. Romance, for example, angers him because some of the invention employed by the poets strains one's belief, while the long narrative passages strain one's endurance.

In the last few years of the sixteenth century Hall was also writing *Mundus Alter et Idem* and probably even taking some interest in the dramatic activities of the university. Arnold Davenport, the editor of his poems, speculates that Hall may have helped compose the *Parnassus Plays*, since "it is demonstrable that the writer, whoever he was, knew *Virgidemiae* with suspicious intimacy and shared Hall's critical views. . . . In his *Apology*, etc. (1642, sigs. B3r sqq.), Milton drags in a reference to clergymen, or those soon to be clergymen, acting in College plays, and

---

Specialties in the Life of Joseph Hall, Bishop of Norwich" (*Works*, 1, ix-xlvii); John Jones, *Bishop Hall, His Life and Times*; George Lewis, *A Life of Joseph Hall, Bishop of Exeter and Norwich*, cited hereafter as "Lewis"; and Frank Livingstone Huntley, *Bishop Joseph Hall*.

seems to be hinting that his opponent [Hall] had been responsible for such activities" (Davenport, *Poems*, p. xviii, n. 1). *Mundus Alter et Idem* continued Hall's attack on extremity and perversion. This book, built upon the conceit of an imaginary voyage to Antarctica, presents a "world upside down" (Colie, *Paradoxia Epidemica*, p. 45), a nightmare world in which all vices are called virtues, in which any moderation is suppressed by extremity, any normal behavior by perversion. Gluttony, drunkenness, thievery, cowardice, and idiocy are the rule in this world, "another" world, and yet very much "the same" as the Europe of Hall's time. In fact, *Mundus Alter et Idem* is prophetic of the way in which extremity will increasingly displace moderation in the coming century.

Several years before Hall was ordained in 1603 he began to preach both in the university and in the villages around Cambridge while he waited for a benefice. Hall's sudden abandonment of literature for the ministry and almost total silence about these youthful productions have led some critics to speculate that he repented of having written them. This is incorrect. Some years later, in a letter written to Samuel Burton, the Archdeacon of Gloucester, accompanying ten of David's psalms that he had—as Hall terms it—"metaphrased" into English, he defends his youthful poetry: "Indeed my poetry was long sithence out of date, and yielded her place to graver studies: but whose vein would it not revive to look into those heavenly songs? I were not worthy to be a divine, if it should repent me to be a poet with David, after I shall have aged in the pulpit" (*Works*, 9, 683).

At the end of 1601 Hall was offered the rectory of Hawstead in Suffolk by Lady Anne Drury (Cullum, *History of Hawstead*, p. 64). He accepted, but his tenure at Hawstead proved difficult. Hall was beset by detractors; the rectory was falling into ruin; and Sir Robert Drury refused to grant Hall some ten pounds he felt belonged to him. Conditions were so bad that Hall complained: "I was forced to write books to buy books" (*Works*, 1, xxxiv). Two years later, about the time the *Mundus* initially appeared, Hall visited the Continent for the first time, with Sir Edmund Bacon, brother of Lady Drury. Above all, he was most eager to see firsthand "the state and practice of the Romish church, the knowledge whereof might be of no small use to me in my holy station" (*Works*, 1, xxix).

On his return to England Hall was introduced to the court of Prince Henry where, despite his pleading "indisposition of body," he preached a Sunday sermon and—at the request of the Prince—another three days later, with the result that the Prince had him installed as one of his domestic chaplains. On this same visit Lord Denny, impressed with Hall's behavior, soon thereafter offered him the donative of Waltham Holy Cross where Hall made his home from 1607 to 1628 (*Works, 1,* xxxiii–xxxv). In 1608 he published *Characters of Virtues and Vices,* significant as an indication of Hall's continued moderation and his concern with evil in the world. His vices are, as in his earliest writings, the vices of excess: hypocrisy, inconstancy, malcontentment, flattery, sloth. And the virtues, which Hall does not treat directly in his earlier works, are clearly the virtues of moderation: humility, faithfulness, patience, valor. In his preface, Hall confesses that he is deeply indebted to the heathen moralists, those "divines" of the ancient world who "bestowed their time in drawing out the true lineaments of every virtue and vice, so lively, that they who saw the medals might . . . learn to know virtue, and discern what to detest" (*Works,* 6, 89–90). His moderation is essentially Aristotle's "Golden Mean" Christianized.

Several times during his stay at Waltham Holy Cross, Hall was asked to preach before the court by King James. So valued was Hall's preaching that one of these requests occurred on the tenth anniversary of James's accession to the throne. In addition, he was several times called upon to perform state business. In 1616 he was sent to France with the embassy led by Viscount Doncaster. The next year he was ordered to accompany the king northward to Scotland in James's attempt to impose prelacy and the Anglican usages and liturgy on the Church of Scotland. Hall's moderation made him popular with the Scottish ministers, but accusations of Puritan sympathies from his fellow clerics induced King James to command Hall to write a defense of the five points then being urged upon the Church of Scotland. From the study he did preparatory to writing his defense Hall emerged as a tough-minded but tolerant Anglican who did not believe that adherence to the essential doctrines of the church necessarily meant conformity in every minute detail. Moreover, he learned to buttress his position on church matters by resorting to the practices of the early Church: practices ancient and free from the corruption of tradition, practices he considered the essence of Christianity.

During the next ten years Hall came into prominence as a writer of moderate Anglican treatises, and he tried to reconcile the factions of the now widening schism in the church: "It grieved my soul to see our own church begin to sicken of the same disease which we had endeavored to cure in our neighbours" (*Works*, 1, xliii). Even though Archbishop Laud still suspected him of harboring Puritan tendencies, in 1627 Hall became Bishop of Exeter and discharged his duties successfully.

In 1639 Hall published *Christian Moderation*, a comprehensive tract urging moderation in all areas of thought and action, but it was then too late for moderation in anything. By 1640 he was embroiled with the Smectymnuans, having defended episcopacy in his 1639 work *Episcopacy by Divine Right*. He did not ignore the abuses episcopacy had engendered, but he believed that reform, not abolition, was the proper remedy. He did expect that all men should worship within the Church of England, but within this broad unity he felt that some variety of beliefs and customs was not only inevitable but healthy. While the Smectymnuans, by and large, showed courtesy and restraint in their combat with Hall, when Milton entered the fray courtesy and restraint left. Milton had some hard things to say about Hall's poetry and *Mundus Alter et Idem*; Hall's son Robert, zealous for his aged father's honor (the Bishop was imprisoned in the Tower of London at the time), undertook his defense, and in a pamphlet called *A Modest Confutation of a Slanderous and Scurrilous Libel entitled Animadversions upon the Remonstrant's Defense against Smectymnuus* suggested, among other things, that Milton associated with loose women.

In November 1641, the King translated Hall to Norwich, but before he could take up residence there, he and 12 fellow bishops were insulted by the London mob, declared guilty of high treason by the Commons, and imprisoned in the Tower from 30 December 1641 until 5 May 1642. When released, Hall immediately went to Norwich where he was received with respect (Lewis, p. 395). The diocese Hall now headed was among those most noted for Puritanism: "Perhaps no bishop in England was better calculated to be successful, had success been possible, than was Hall; but the time for compromise was passed" (Lewis, p. 396).

Hall did enjoy peace until 1643, but then he and his family were turned out of the episcopal palace on short notice. Parliament refused to grant Hall the £400 given to him by the local committee and would allow only the "fifth" granted to the destitute wives of "malignants" (*Works*, 1, lxv). Hall and his wife then moved to a small house in Higham, a suburb of Norwich. His writings at this time still suggested the possibilities for reconciliation between Anglicans and Puritans (*The Peacemaker*), or suggested remedies for troubled souls in these unsettled times: *The Balm of Gilead, or the Comforter*; *Satan's fiery darts Quenched*; *Select Thoughts, or Choice Helps for a Pious Spirit*. Though Hall's works now had to be screened by a censor, they were readily approved.

His biographer, George Lewis, notes that Hall, "ever an indefatagible preacher, was always ready to occupy the pulpits of the Norwich churches, and to give the people the benefit of his rich and varied experience" (Lewis, p. 421). To the very end he preached often; still extant are two sermons preached in 1655, when Hall was 81. At this time Hall was even ordaining clergy into the Anglican church. Simon Patrick, influenced by the Cambridge Platonists, "decided to seek episcopal ordination from Bishop Hall, who ordained him 'in his own parlour at Higham about a mile from Norwich, April 5th 1654'" (McAdoo, *Spirit of Anglicanism*, p. 191). Doubtless others made the journey as well.

Lewis writes that Bishop Hall seemed almost insensible to the loss of his estate "and though often heard to bewail the spoiling of the Church, very rarely even mentioned his own misfortunes.... Stripped of wealth and left comparatively poor, he was not unmindful of those who were still poorer; every week to his dying day he distributed sums of money out of his own means to certain of the widows of the parish in which he lived. When confined to his bed, and almost overcome by weakness, he administered the rite of confirmation to such as desired it" (Lewis, pp. 421-22). A humble and moderate man to his death, Hall requested that his body be interred "without any funerall pompe," outside the walls of the church, for "I do not hold God's house a mete repositorie for the dead bodyes of the greatest Saint" (*Works*, 1, lxxviii). He died 8 September 1656.

MUNDUS ALTER ET IDEM AND MENIPPEAN SATIRE

In the history of literature *Mundus Alter et Idem* occupies a special place as a work with few descendants until the twentieth century, without even a name until 1952 when J. Max Patrick "coined" the word *dystopia*,[15]

15. Glenn Negley and J. Max Patrick, eds., *Quest for Utopia* (New York, 1952), pp. 297-98: "*Mundus Alter et Idem* is the opposite of *eutopia*; it is a *dystopia* if it is permissible to coin a word." Actually, according to *A Supplement to the OED* (1972), John Stuart Mill coined the word in 1868. Both Lyman Tower Sargent, *British and American Utopian Literature, 1516-1975*, p. 3, and Michael Winter, *Compendium Utopiarum Typologie und Bibligraphie*, 1, 43-46, see the *Mundus* more as a satire than as a dystopia. However, trying to determine when a particular work should be called a satire rather than a eutopia or a dystopia is difficult, for as Robert C. Elliott, *The Shape of Utopia*, pp. 23-24, reminds us, "satire is a necessary element of 'utopia.' . . . I suspect that we distinguish between *Utopia* as 'a utopia' and *Gulliver's Travels* as 'a satire' primarily because of the different distribution of positive and negative elements in the two works." I consider the *Mundus* both a dystopia and a satire because it not only describes a bad place but also uses these descriptions to satirize European habits. In his introduction, pp. ix-xix, Sargent provides useful definitions of "utopia," "eutopia," "dystopia," and "satire."

meaning "bad place," in opposition to the *eutopia* (or "good place") that Anemolius claims Utopia is in his Hexastichon (More, *Utopia*, p. 20). Yet, when studied in relation to Menippean satire, Hall's work readily discloses its artistic heritage. My desire, therefore, is to provide a short sketch of this genre from Lucian to Swift and note some of the important borrowings that link Hall with these other works in intent and execution. Tracing Hall's debt to his predecessors is made surer by his marginal references to earlier satirists, most importantly Aristophanes, Lucian, More, and Erasmus,[16] but none of these predecessors can be pointed to as *the* inspiration for this work in the way that Juvenal and Horace can be linked to Hall's *Virgidemiae*.[17]

A search for sustained attempts at dystopian writing in classical literature discloses nothing but brief descriptions of bad places inserted in longer works: the land of the Cyclops, where Odysseus and his men are imprisoned and devoured, the underworld where people such as Sisyphus and Ixion are punished, the land of Circe where men are turned to swine. What we do find instead are extended satiric treatments of supposedly perfect places, of travels made to find them, and of people who claim to be more honest, more clever, more intelligent than the norm. In these anti-utopian, anti-travel, anti-sophist writings of antiquity we find the satiric predecessors of *Mundus Alter et Idem.*

The first serious discussion of the principles for an ideal society occurs in Plato's *Republic*. The requirements Socrates sees as essential to any ideal commonwealth are wisdom, courage, self-control, and justice—virtues present in most utopias ever since. On the heels of its success appeared the first anti-utopian satire, Aristophanes' *Ecclesiazusae*, which disputes the central assumptions of Plato's work, specifically that people will necessarily be wise, self-controlled, or just. Aristophanes imagines the takeover of the government of Athens by women who intend to abolish poverty and create a reign of plenty. All citizens will be required to relinquish their private property. This accomplished, everyone's needs will be satisfied from the public coffers. Though the satire eventually degenerates into a farce about how the young men will be apportioned to satisfy the sexual longings of the women, young and old

---

16. Sandford M. Salyer, "Renaissance Influences in Hall's *Mundus Alter et Idem*," pp. 321–24, would include Rabelais in this list, but I find most of his suggestions of specific parallels between Rabelais and Hall unconvincing.

17. Arnold Stein, "The Second English Satirist," pp. 273–78; idem, "Joseph Hall's Imitation of Juvenal," pp. 315–22; Arnold Davenport, "Interfused Sources in Joseph Hall's Satires," pp. 208–13; and idem, Introduction to *Poems*, pp. xxiv–xxv.

alike, *The Ecclesiazusae* demonstrates the difficulty of getting everyone to agree to the idea of all things being held in common, something Plato assumes can be easily handled. Aristophanes also deflates Plato's ingenuity by depicting a much more attractive society. Unlike Plato's ideal state, poetry, music, eating, and lovemaking are all plentiful in Praxagora's commonwealth; whatever its defects, this play reveals the difficulty of maintaining a society too rigidly and intellectually conceived.

Lucian, however, is the most important writer to provide Hall with ammunition to bombard man's pride in himself and in his visionary schemes. In 1605 Isaac Casaubon classified Lucian as a "Menippean" satirist because of the mixture of prose and verse found in his dialogues and because Menippus, the Cynic philosopher, appears in two of them:

> Another factor which led to that classification was Lucian's claim to have invented the Comic Dialogue by uniting the serious connotations of philosophical dialectic with the wit and fantasy of Aristophanic comedy, a claim which Casaubon associated with Strabo's description of Menippus as *spoudogeloios*. (Duncan, *Ben Jonson*, p. 10)

Erasmus and More embraced the concept of *spoudogeloios*, "blending jest with earnest," in their writings, and in the *Mundus* so did Hall. There is Hall's delight in words and their etymologies, in the flying monster RUC who devours elephants at a gulp, and in the ridiculousness of the alchemists and their esoteric vocabulary. These are balanced by Hall's serious attacks on the corruption of the Catholic church, on the Spanish Inquisition, and on heretical sects. Hall even observes Lucian's intermixture of verse and prose, where the verse normally serves as parody. The silly epitaphs on the tombs in Yvronia and Moronia, the satiric verse from Hesiod to explain the meaning of the Sin-obran Plain, and the poem in mockery of alchemy extend Hall's ridicule one step further.

Another constant factor in Lucian's work, and according to Frye the hallmark of Menippean satire, is that the dramatic interest lies in a conflict of ideas rather than of character. People act "as mouthpieces of the ideas they represent," and evil and folly represent not social diseases but "diseases of the intellect" (Frye, *Anatomy*, p. 309). As I mention later (pp. xliii–xliv), Hall's characters are never fully drawn; rather, each personality is consumed by its particular vice. Some of the stock figures exposed by Lucian—sham doctors in *Philopseudes*, the *morosophoi* in

Alexander, the misers in *Charon* and *Timon*, the superstitious in *Philo-pseudes*—reappear in the *Mundus*, and though it would be wrong to say that Hall has merely copied from Lucian, the one-dimensionality of the types and the ironic tone with which Hall approaches and undercuts their beliefs are nonetheless in the spirit of Menippean satire.

Also significant in Lucian is the key metaphor of the detached ob-server who belittles human concerns by seeing them from a great height. In *Icaromenippus*, Menippus, who has despaired of hearing the truth about anything on earth and is on a flight to the throne of Zeus, pauses on the moon and gazes down on the activities of men, swarming about like ants. With the help of Empedocles, and an eagle's eye, Menippus is able to see "everything on earth—the men, the animals and very nearly the nests of the mosquitoes" (*Icaro.*, 12). The acts of the nobility afford him "rare amusement," but "those of the common people were far more ridiculous" (*Icaro.*, 16): "If I saw any man pluming himself on gold because he had eight rings and four cups, I laughed heartily at him too, for the whole of Pangaeum, mines and all, was the size of a grain of millet" (*Icaro.*, 18). Though Hall's narrator is never explicitly given so remote a vantage point, a Mercury (whether British or otherwise) can of course fly, and he does offer descriptions that sweep from city to city or from rivers to mountains to valleys in a sentence, as though he were perched aloft somewhere. Even when he is in the actual presence of the inhabitants, Mercury uses disguises, the cover of night, and friendly acquaintances who hide him so that he may observe the customs of the lands he visits unencumbered by the need to participate in them. Even his language, heavily dependent on litotes, generates aesthetic distance by allowing him to back away from straightforward utterances. Inhabi-tants are characterized as "no less dignified," conduct as "not unworthy," conversations as "not unpleasant." Such descriptions are not unhelpful in establishing a narrator not a little amused by and no less removed from his subject.

But Lucian's *True Story* is the work closest in spirit and content to the *Mundus*. Ridiculing the implausible journeys of his age, just as Hall ridicules those of Munster and Mandeville, Lucian announces that he will tell his tale merely because it makes a good story, for he has seen that others, with no better reason, have "written about imaginary travels and journeys of theirs, telling of huge beasts, cruel men and strange ways of living" (*Ver. Hist.*, 1, 3). Lucian freely admits that his stories are pure invention, having himself had no interesting experiences in real life, and he even boasts: "my lying is far more honest than [that of my predecessors], for though I tell the truth in nothing else, I shall at least be truthful in saying that I am a liar" (*Ver. Hist.*, 1, 4). In fact, he is not at all concerned about such lying, for he realizes that this "was already a common practice even among men who profess philosophy" (*Ver. Hist.*, 1, 3–4), a slap at Plato's *Republic* that suggests Lucian has no more patience with ideal commonwealths than Aristophanes has.

Like Hall with his men who travel on all fours and his amphibian pirates who stick fast to boats and capsize them, Lucian, by exaggerating his adventures beyond the limits of believability, casts doubt less on himself than on those authors from whom he borrows his material. Before we have turned to the third page of the narrative Lucian has satirized the exploits of earlier travelers by sailing past the farthest spot that Hercules and Dionysus had supposedly explored. His tale is a splendid parody of earlier works, the absurdities of each heightened and extended. As in the *Mundus,* there are frequent shifts of location, which afford us "a high degree of the ridiculous" (Frye, *Anatomy*, p. 43). A journey past the sun is followed by a visit to a community of lamps, followed by a twenty-month sojourn in the belly of a whale. Eventually he reaches the Island of the Blest, where all the philosophers dwell. Lucian easily punctures the pretensions of each: "Socrates . . . used to protest that he was above suspicion in his relations with young persons, but everyone held him guilty of perjury. In fact, Hyacinthus and Narcissus often said that they knew better" (*Ver. Hist.*, 2, 19). Only Plato ("He was living in his imaginary city under the constitution and laws that he himself wrote" [*Ver. Hist.*, 2, 17]) and the Stoics ("They were said to be still on the way up the steep hill of virtue" [*Ver. Hist.*, 2, 18]) are absent— a gibe at the severity and absurdity of their ideals, since all the other philosophers are content with the Elysian fields, as perfect a dwelling place as anyone might wish.

While Hall might not be in complete agreement with Lucian's characterization of the Stoics, being a neo-Stoic himself, the relentlessly skeptical tone of Lucian's narrative, a skepticism that questions the supposed honesty, virtue, and common sense of everyone—philosophers, heroes, statesmen, and poets alike—seems to strike a sympathetic chord in Hall. In the *Mundus,* Pythagorean philosophers, Roman Catholic churchmen, and such well-known scholars as Julius Caesar Scaliger and Justus Lipsius are weighed and found wanting by these same standards.

Other Lucianic techniques repeated in the *Mundus* are Hall's juggling with myths, his punning on etymologies, and his quoting of

ancient authors in strange contexts. But, above all, it is Lucian's lack of
patience with the outlandish tales and the outlandish beliefs of his
predecessors that leads him to debunk travel literature and ridicule
visionary schemes—and thereby gain Hall's admiration. Considering
the number of direct borrowings he makes—glass houses, inhabitants
who live on smoke, fish that spout wine—it is certain Hall knew *A True
Story* well.

As we move toward Hall's own time through More and Erasmus, we
find that Lucian moves right along with us, for together Erasmus and
More were responsible for some 30 of the Latin translations by which
Lucian reached Renaissance scholars. Erasmus's admiration for Lucian
is demonstrated by his long series of *Colloquies* in imitation of him:

> [Lucian] possesses such grace of style, such felicity of invention,
> such a charming sense of humour, and such pointedness in satire;
> his sallies arouse such interest; and by his mixture of fun and earnest,
> gaiety and acute observation, he so effectively portrays the manners,
> emotions, and pursuits of men . . . that whether you look for plea-
> sure or edification there is not a comedy, or a satire, that challenges
> comparison with his dialogues. (*Correspondence*, 2, 116)

High praise of this sort, singling out the blend of jest and earnest as the
means by which Lucian surpasses stage comedy and verse satire, might
well have enticed Hall—who had already practiced both these literary
forms in *The Parnassus Plays*[18] and *Virgidemiae*—to try his hand at
Lucianic satire. In his *Translations of Lucian,* More likewise tells us
that Lucian "everywhere reprimands and censures, with very honest and
at the same time very entertaining wit, our human frailties. And this he
does so cleverly and effectively that although no one pricks more deeply,
nobody resents his stinging words" (p. 3). James K. McConica stresses
the essentially Lucianic character of both writers when he says:

> In the early Erasmus, and especially the Erasmus who is the com-
> panion of More, the vein of Lucianic satire cannot be dissociated
> from the reforming motive. The greatest fruits of their collabora-
> tion, including those which have achieved immortality, are essen-
> tially Lucianic: *Moriae encomium,* the *Utopia,* the *Colloquia,* and

---

18. All or part of the *Parnassus Plays* are generally ascribed to Hall although he never
claimed to have written them; see Huntley, *Bishop Joseph Hall,* pp. 29-45.

their own translations of Lucian's dialogues. (*English Humanists,* p. 15)

Erasmus preserves Lucian's dialogue form in his *Colloquies* but seems to soften the bite of Lucian's humor slightly, shifting the balance toward more edification and less satire. Yet the fact that the Sorbonne censured the *Colloquies* in May 1526, "denouncing sixty-nine passages as 'erroneous, scandalous, or impious' and describing their author as 'a pagan who mocks at the Christian religion and its sacred rites and customs'" (Craig Thompson in *Colloquies of Erasmus,* p. xxx), should remind us how biting Erasmus's satires on the abuses of religion were perceived to be at the time. Though Hall abandons the dialogue form, his sympathy with the content of Erasmus's attacks is evident. Erasmus had praised the contemporary relevance of Lucian's *Alexander,* saying that it "gives us an object-lesson for detecting and refuting the impostures of those who even to-day pull wool over the eyes of the mob with their hocus-pocus miracles, false relics, bogus pardons, and such-like trickery." [19] Hall demonstrates his agreement with Erasmus by mocking the same subjects: exorcism, alchemy, religious pilgrimages, saints' relics, ostentatious funerals, self-seeking piety, and ridiculous monks. Though few of the actual incidents from *The Colloquies* reappear in the *Mundus,* Hall's tone diverges widely from the asperity found in much of *Virgidemiae* and approaches the more detached play of wit cultivated by Erasmus. In certain places, namely, the Parliament of Women in Viraginia and the religious pilgrimages of Moronia Pia, Hall names Erasmus directly. But the greatest debt Hall owes to Erasmus is to his *Praise of Folly,* a work that delights in verbal and intellectual display of the sort found in Rabelais, Swift's *Tale of a Tub,* and Book 3 of the *Mundus.*

Like *Mundus Alter et Idem* and *Utopia, The Praise of Folly* is a work of jesting seriousness, ironically praising man's dullness and yet sympathetically understanding the limits of reason in human beings. In this work Folly asks who but Folly ever drew people into civil society and in proof of this claim notes that no state "has ever accepted the laws of Plato or Aristotle or the teachings of Socrates" (*Moria,* tr. p. 40). And scholars, "who believed that anything as vague and empty as fame was worth so many sleepless nights, so much sweat, must be the greatest fools of all" (*Moria,* tr. pp. 41–42). Adopting the lofty vantage point of

19. Erasmus's letter to the bishop of Chartres, *Opera Omnia,* 1, 229–30, quoted in Douglas Duncan, *Ben Jonson and the Lucianic Tradition,* p. 28.

Lucian's *Charon* or *Icaromenippus*, Folly notes that if men could see life's calamities as clearly as Lynceus, the certainty of death would drive them to suicide (*Moria*, tr. pp. 46–48). But folly is infinitely pleasurable; pastimes like alchemy, gambling, hunting, praying to statues, or arranging one's funeral are so entertaining that there is no one in the world "who is not subject to some kind of madness" (*Moria*, tr. p. 60). By the time Folly is done the whole world has come under her spell: lawyers, logicians, scientists, theologians, preachers, kings, even Christ himself.

In Moronia, Hall provides a similar kaleidoscope. He starts by saying that no country in the world is as populous as Moronia (a direct borrowing from Cicero and from Erasmus) and proceeds to show the varieties: inconstant fools, hotheaded fools, credulous fools, fortunate fools, pious fools. Their most constant feature—as Folly has predicted—is their happiness. The Pazzivillans debate about what will bring their town the greatest fame: the erection of new bell towers on every roof, or the construction of a new mountain with a bridge attached for citizens to promenade on. Morosophers walk along planting their feet on the ground in such a way that they form the sign of the cross at every pace. In the summer, Moronians dress warmly to keep out the heat, in the winters lightly to let the cold escape. They speak to themselves, light candles in the daytime, shave their heads lest their celestial meditation be threatened. Hall solemnly presents their absurdities one after another, letting his imagination run free. Many of his descriptions are far more specific and biting than Erasmus's: slaps at the recognizable follies of specific nationalities and religious groups. Yet, on the whole, Hall preserves the jesting seriousness of his source.

Until recently, the place More's *Utopia* occupies in the tradition of Menippean satire has been little investigated, and the work has been viewed predominantly as a political treatise in which the Utopians and their state emerge as essentially admirable, though not ideal: "The underlying thought of *Utopia* always is, *With nothing save Reason to guide them, the Utopians do this; and yet we Christian Englishmen, we Christian Europeans . . . !*"[20] Alternately, it has been seen as "a holiday work, a spontaneous overflow of intellectual high spirits, a revel of debate, paradox, comedy and (above all) of invention, which starts many hares and kills none."[21] More himself, in his prefatory letter to Peter

20. R. W. Chambers, *Thomas More*, p. 128; P. Albert Duhamel, "Medievalism of More's *Utopia*," p. 238; and Edward Surtz, S.J., *Utopia, the Praise of Pleasure*, pp. 5–6, 193–99.

21. C. S. Lewis, *English Literature in the Sixteenth Century, Excluding Drama*, p. 169.

Giles, suggests rather a blend of the two: the joking seriousness we have seen in Erasmus and Lucian. He debates whether to publish *Utopia* or not, "something that may bring profit or pleasure to others" (*Utopia*, p. 43), and seems to be alluding to the Horatian maxim about the twofold aim of poetry. He especially worries about its reception, reasoning that "some [people] are so dull-minded that they fear all satire as much as a man bitten by a mad dog fears water" (*Utopia*, p. 45).

A. R. Heiserman, followed by an increasing number of critics,[22] has demonstrated what More hints at—the essentially satiric nature of the work—and Warren Wooden has pointed out the serious limitations of the ideals of the Utopians when they are viewed as absolutes to guide Europeans in their behavior ("Satiric Strategy," pp. 1-9). For example, they exalt marriage but allow divorce for all but the most trivial of reasons; they have supposedly abolished the death penalty for robbers but have instituted it for the far less serious crime of a slave accepting money from a free man; they claim to abhor war, but to find space for new colonies of Utopians they will instigate wars themselves, ruthlessly conduct them, and dispossess the losers. Though the fictional "Thomas More" grants the truth of many of Hythloday's arguments in Book 1 about the evils of England, at the end of Book 2 he has, understandably, many doubts, not only about the Utopians'

> method of waging war, their ceremonies and religion, as well as their other institutions, but most of all . . . [about] their common life and subsistence—without any exchange of money. . . . I knew, however, that [Hythloday] was wearied with his tale, and I was not quite certain that he could brook any opposition to his views. . . . I therefore praised their way of life and his speech and, taking him by the hand, led him in to supper. (*Utopia*, p. 245)

As Richard Sylvester argues, this last gesture seems to indicate that Hythloday, "once so proudly independent, so all-knowing and so all-seeing, now needs a helping hand quite desperately. Blinded by his absorption in his own vision . . . he can no longer find his own way back to reality" ("'Si Hythlodaeo Credimus,'" p. 300).

If these and other practices among the Utopians cannot be held up

22. A. R. Heiserman, "Satire in the *Utopia*," pp. 163-74; Elliott, *Shape of Utopia*, pp. 25-49; Edward Surtz, Introduction to Saint Thomas More, *Utopia*, pp. cxlvii-cliii; T. S. Dorsch, "Sir Thomas More and Lucian: An Interpretation of *Utopia*," pp. 345-63; and Brian Vickers, "The Satiric Structure of *Gulliver's Travels* and More's *Utopia*," pp. 233-57.

as admirable in themselves, they must exist for some other reason. One plausible explanation is that, like the four countries in Hall's southern continent, Utopia exists as a foil to Europe, and its practices show how barbarous Europeans are in contrast to artificially erected standards. A. R. Heiserman explains the rules in *Utopia* as being formulated by a method of subtraction: "since [More's] principal satiric object is the rule of money and property, he constructs a state from which money and property are banished and shows how other evils—tyrannical lust for money and freedom—disappear as a result" ("Satire in the *Utopia*," p. 170).

For example, because wars are generally long and often deadly to the common folk who are pressed to serve in the armies, More satirizes European practices by having the Utopians shorten their wars. They employ trickery, use bribery to persuade enemy soldiers to turn against their own leaders, hire mercenaries to free as many Utopians from service as possible, and send whole families into battle to stimulate their side to fight as valiantly as possible. Or, as Heiserman argues, when Hythloday describes how "incurably ill Utopians may choose to die, he does so in order to comment that in Utopia (though not in Europe) no sick man dies by negligence or against his will, thus using euthanasia to make his satiric point" ("Satire in the *Utopia*," p. 173).

Hall's normal method is not to subtract from or invert European practices, as More does, but to amplify and extend them. Thus European concern for the body instead of the mind is exaggerated into a land where all merit is determined by the size of one's stomach, European competitiveness is exaggerated into a land where everyone tries to beggar everyone else, and so on. In consequence, many of the practices of his dystopia are essentially opposite to those in *Utopia*; yet they function toward the same satiric end: to demolish man's pride in himself. While Hall's process of addition results in practices that cannot be viewed as anything but grotesque, More's process of subtraction is much more subtle in its effect on a modern audience, since the process of subtraction so alters European vices that they may seem to be metamorphosed into virtues. Euthanasia, for example, may seem to us a kindness for those incurably ill, but death inflicted by man is unlikely to have met with More's approval except insofar as it can be used to satirize the brutal way Renaissance Europe treats the sick. Utopian religious toleration may meet with our approval as enlightened behavior, but More's angry reaction to Luther, like Hall's to the Puritans, suggests *not* that religious schism is good but that it can be tolerated better than religious warfare if

it is kept private and does not threaten the commonwealth—something
not the case in Europe.[23]

Hall's technique of addition seldom allows us to mistake where he
stands. Whatever we may think about the monotonous sameness in the
lives of the Utopians (shared meals, shared entertainments, subdivision
housing) as a solution to the lack of community in Europe, the solution
of the Lavernians in the *Mundus* to band together into families of
robbers, and that of the Moronia Asperans to live a hermitlike existence,
never saying hello to anyone "except on Thursday," clearly present
worse alternatives. The solution *Utopia* offers to the changeability of
European political assemblies and the laws they enact is to have nothing
decided without a three-day discussion in the senate (*Utopia*, p. 123) and
to debate nothing on the first day it is proposed, "lest anyone, after
hastily blurting out the first thought that popped into his head, should
afterwards give more thought to defending his opinion than to support-
ing what is for the good of the commonwealth" (*Utopia*, p. 125). Whether
we applaud this or not, we are unlikely to prefer the practice of the
Viraginians in the *Mundus* who hold a continual parliament "because
of the uncertainty of the laws." It is permissible to retract any new law
the day after it is enacted; "it is not allowed the same day, lest they might
seem too inconstant."

At times when Hall seems to be borrowing from More it is often
difficult to know whether he has him in mind or is instead merely exaggerating the vices of contemporary Europe. In some cases we can be
certain, as when he names a river Sans-eau in honor of More's waterless
river Anydrus, or a forest Anylos, or the only admirable region in his
entire work Eugynia (from εὐ, "good," plus γῠνή, "woman") in imitation of Anemolius's Hexastichon that names the island of Utopia "Eutopia" (*Utopia*, p. 20). Similarly, Hall names his pseudophilosophers
Morosophers. Although the term originates in Lucian, More also uses
the word (*Utopia*, p. 64), and Hall might well have found it there.

Other practices in the *Mundus* may well parody More's descriptions: in Utopia soldiers go to battle surrounded by their wives, children,
and relatives, while in Lavernia robbers go out to plunder in the same
way; in Book 1 of *Utopia* Hythloday notes that European soldiers need
to cut men's throats lest "the hand or the mind through lack of practice
become dulled" (*Utopia*, p. 65), while in Lavernia Mercurius notes that
children are taught to steal something every day, "lest they grow inept

---

23. It is well to remember that "if a person contends too vehemently in expressing his
[religious] views, he is punished with exile or enslavement" (More, *Utopia*, p. 221).

from lack of practice"; in *Utopia* citizens are not allowed to accustom themselves to the butchering of animals, but they do wear leather work clothes (*Utopia,* p. 133), while in Crapulia magistrates are also dressed in leather, but the garment must be made from "the skin of whatever animal that person can devour at one sitting." These apparent borrowings could be explained as typical extensions of European vices by Hall, rather than as conscious inversions of More. Yet, taken as a whole, in the work of a person well acquainted with *Utopia,* they suggest at least an occasional backward glance.

But it is when Hall abandons his normal satiric technique of adding to European vices and follows More's process of subtracting from them that he seems to be employing conscious imitation. In Europe marriage is normally undertaken with the man unable to see more than a fraction of his intended bride. The solution in Utopia, as in Pamphagonia, is to remove all clothes. But while the Utopians look for lack of deformity (*Utopia,* p. 189), the Pamphagonians look to make sure that the bride's "hanging chins have reached [her] breasts." Unlike European states where, as Hythloday tells us, public offices are "put up for sale" (*Utopia,* p. 105), Utopia and Crapulia both promote people impartially, gauging them by qualities directly tied to the state's foremost concerns. In *Utopia,* where good government is most highly prized, the magistrates are virtuous, humble, and hardworking, elected by secret ballot, and any man who solicits votes "is deprived completely of the hope of holding any office at all" (*Utopia,* p. 193). In Crapulia, where gluttony is most highly prized, senators are promoted "not—as elsewhere—because of prudence, or riches, or the abundance of their beards, but because of the size of their stomachs; and the more one gains, the more highly he is promoted." Both the *Mundus* and *Utopia* sketch educational programs meant to instill in children's minds "opinions which are also useful for the preservation of their commonwealth" (*Utopia,* p. 229), implying that European nations are careless at this task. But instruction by the priesthood of *Utopia* is altered to instruction by gluttons in Crapulia, by Morosophers in Moronia, and by thieves or mountebanks in Lavernia, ensuring that vice will be as long-lived as virtue. All these reversals strike deeply at European practices, for they imply the haphazard results that must ensue when the state is run without anticipation of the consequences.

I have so far stressed the essential seriousness of both works; I should also stress that More and Hall inherit from Lucian an essentially playful and ironic attitude. In More some of this resides in the Greek place-names that constantly undercut the surface seriousness by denying the reality of the very people and places that their naming seems to affirm. For example, Nonsense (Hythloday) reports back to us about Noplace (Utopia) and the people of Much Nonsense (the Polyerites). Likewise, in Hall a lying thief (Mercury) is carried by an apparition ("The Phantasia") to the unknown southern continent where he visits the Province of Nonsense (Baveria, from the French *baver*, "to talk drivel"), where the people think themselves most wise, and to the Province of Eat-everything (Pamphagonia), established once-upon-a-time by a giant named Stomach (Omasius, from the Latin *omasum*, "stomach"). Litotes also plays an important ironic role in the *Utopia* by undercutting its seriousness and making it difficult for the reader to know exactly where he stands (McCutcheon, "Denying the Contrary," rpt. pp. 263–74). It is significant that Hall should seem to follow More's lead, using litotes no fewer than 150 times himself. Together these techniques help us keep our balance, never taking things seriously enough to descend into the misanthropy of Hythloday; yet at the same time they make us wonder just how fantastic is the voyage Mercurius makes, just how nonsensical is the tale Hythloday relates.

At times More and Hall even display an exuberant delight in the absurd. In Lucian's *Icaromenippus* the Cynic Menippus cuts off one wing of an eagle and one of a vulture and attaches them to his arms so that he can discover if what the poets say about heaven is true. Such an impossible feat finds its counterpart in More where "a whole forest has been uprooted in one place . . . and planted in another. Herein they were thinking not so much of abundance as of transport, that they might have wood closer to the sea or the rivers or the cities themselves" (*Utopia*, p. 179). In the *Mundus* not only do some of the inhabitants fly, but mountains are used to fill valleys, rivers are diverted into new channels, cities are on wheels so they "can be wheeled about here and there like a chariot," and a proposal is debated about bringing the sea through the middle of the mountains, since "other cities [are] wonderfully enriched by the sea's proximity."

With such a variety of techniques, the effects of both works on the reader are manifold, ranging from horror to indignation to disbelief to puzzlement to amusement to laughter to admiration. Though Hall's work more often elicits horror and laughter than More's, and More's more often admiration than Hall's, both are concerned with the optimum state of society, and both measure man's imperfection by the ever-changing distance between artificially erected extremes and the real world.

Swift called More "the only man of true virtue that ever England produced" (*Prose Works*, 5, 247), and significantly More is the only post-classical figure to be praised by Gulliver as he questions noble men in Laputa. A number of recent studies compare *Utopia* and *Gulliver's Travels*,[24] but except for Michael Winter's brief treatment in his bibliography of utopias (*Compendium Utopiarum*, 1, 43-46), no writer has done more than mention the possibility that the *Mundus* provides another satiric source for Swift. While we know that Swift owned a copy of *Utopia* (Vickers, "Satiric Structure," p. 233), he did not own a copy of the *Mundus* (Williams, *Dean Swift's Library*, pp. 88, 92). Nonetheless, he knew it well enough to incorporate a description from Moronia in *A Tale of a Tub* (p. 195), and his remarks in his "Ode to the Honorable Sir William Temple" where he calls virtue "a *Utopian* Ground," a "*Terra Incognita*" (*Poems*, 1, 26), suggest that both works remained in his mind.

All three men—More, Hall, and Swift—admired Lucian as a person who demolished man's pride in himself and his accomplishments, and all three saw man's pride as the main obstacle to his regeneration. Hythloday claims that men would have long ago adopted the laws of Utopia had they not been restrained by the monster Pride: "This serpent from hell entwines itself around the hearts of men and acts like a suck fish in preventing and hindering them from entering on a better way of life" (*Utopia*, pp. 243-45). Hall and Swift relentlessly continue this attack. In his sermon, "The Fall of Pride," Hall says:

> What is the best flesh and blood but a pack of dust made up together into a stirring heap, which in the dissolution moulders to dust again? *When I consider the heavens, and see the sun, the moon, and the stars, as they stand in their order, Lord, what is man, that thou regardest him?* what a worm! what an ant! what a nothing! . . . In short, when all is done, after all our cost and care, what is the best hide but *saccus stercorum*, as Bernard speaks; which if we do not find noisome, others shall? . . . *Why is* this *earth and ashes proud*, though it were as free from sin as it is from perfection? (*Works*, 5, 323-24)

24. John Traugott, "A Voyage to Nowhere with Thomas More and Jonathan Swift," pp. 534-65; Vickers, "Satiric Structure," pp. 233-57; Elliott, *Shape of Utopia*, pp. 50-67; and W. E. Yeomans, "The Houyhnhnm as Menippean Horse," pp. 258-66.

In *Gulliver's Travels* Swift has Gulliver say:

> When I behold a Lump of Deformity, and Diseases both in Body
> and Mind, smitten with *Pride*, it immediately breaks all the Mea-
> sures of my Patience; neither shall I ever be able to comprehend how
> such an Animal and such a Vice could tally together. (*Gulliver's
> Travels*, p. 296)

"Lump of Deformity," "pack of dust," "worm," "ant," "*saccus
stercorum*"—all degrading metaphors, all meant to deflate man's self-
image. But while Hall's method of exaggeration creates images of man
at his worst, Swift goes one step further and shows that even when man is
behaving at his best he is still an obnoxious creature. In the four books of
Gulliver's Travels we observe mankind from a variety of unflattering
angles. No matter how man is viewed, his pride in himself is misplaced:
in Books 1 and 2 he is a foul, lumbering oaf or a noisome, insignificant
insect; in Books 3 and 4 his reason is not only deficient but merely the
thinnest veneer over a beastly, irrational core. Each shift of perspective
leads Gulliver one step closer to his misanthropic conclusion, and even
if we are unwilling to identify man as Gulliver does, we cannot help but
be chastened by what we read.

Hall, like Swift, begins by focusing on the first of man's two great
sources of pride: his body. In Crapulia, Hall demonstrates how ugly our
bodies and our bodily functions can be: the Pamphagonians devour live
animals, gain no honor until their bellies hang down to their knees, and
parade around naked—except for a spoon and knife attached to their
wrists—to show off their corpulence. The dead are not burned but eaten,
since their bodies are "a combination of the most select kinds of food."
At the banquets of the Pamphagonians all are forced to eat until they
cannot exit through the door they entered and are then let out another
way. The Pamphagonians eat so much that their rivers are blocked with
excrement; the Yvronians drink so much that they need two chamberpots at their banquets—one for urine and one for vomit.

These disgusting descriptions have their counterparts in Swift in
the various embarrassments Gulliver encounters in Lilliput. Two men
have to work all day to carry off his excrement; like the monster RUC in
the *Mundus*, Gulliver eats whole animals at one bite and tosses off a full
hogshead in several gulps; he can enter but one building in Lilliput, and
then only by creeping in. He is told that his body odor is sometimes
offensive but is surprised when the queen cannot tolerate the royal

chambers on which he has urinated to extinguish a fire. In Book 2 Gulliver discovers firsthand the ugliness of human beings by being placed in
the same relationship to the Brobdingnagians as the Lilliputians were to
him. Their corpulence terrifies him. He sees that even the smoothest skin
is coarse and mottled when enlarged twelve times; he experiences their
offensive body odors himself; he sees skin cancers so large that he could
have crept into the holes, and lice crawling over people's bodies, using
their swinelike snouts to burrow into the skin, a sight that "perfectly
turned my Stomach" (*Gulliver's Travels*, p. 113).

Unlike Hall, Swift moves beyond bodily matters to political ones
and places Gulliver in the position of Menippus in Lucian's *Icaromenippus*, a detached observer of people one twelfth his size. Their
antics—walking a tightrope to gain preferment, arguing about which
end of an egg to crack—are not unrelated to European practices but
strike us as laughable when performed by people the size of chipmunks.
It is not until he finds himself in the land of Brobdingnag, however,
where the king criticizes the English and calls them "the most perni-
cious Race of little odious Vermin that nature ever suffered to crawl
upon the Surface of the Earth" (p. 132) that Gulliver can begin to appreciate the absurdity himself: "Undoubtedly Philosophers are in the
Right when they tell us, that nothing is great or little otherwise than by
Comparison" (*Gulliver's Travels*, p. 87).

Having shown that humans are defective in body, Swift, like Hall,
proceeds to demolish our pretensions to wisdom in Book 3, the most
dystopian of the four lands, and the one closest in spirit to the *Mundus*:
the flappers in Laputa are suggestive of the attendants in Ucalegonium
who open their master's eyes when he awakes and do all menial chores so
that he can focus his attention on food; the canal cut through the mountains (*Gulliver's Travels*, p. 177) resembles a similar project in Pazzivilla; the swine who plow the fields in Lagado (*Gulliver's Travels*, p.
180) perform the same duty in Ucalegonium. But even when we cannot
demonstrate specific borrowings, Swift is aiming at the same abuses as
Hall: in Laputa poetry is composed by machines, in Yvronia by drunkards, but it is worthless in both places; the Projectors at the Grand
Academy of Lagado and the Troverense in Variana devote themselves to
the discovery of new things, but all their inventions are useless. Hall
vents his ire mainly on alchemists and heretics, Swift on scientists and
politicians, but they are both looking backward to a better age, convinced that the old ways are more valuable than the new. Book 4 of
Gulliver's Travels again goes one step further than Hall, demonstrating

that man does not lose his reason by abusing it because he does not have it to begin with. In Swift's own words, the land of the Houyhnhnms is meant to prove "the falsity of that Definition *animal rationale*; and to show it should be only *rationis capax*. Upon this great foundation of Misanthropy . . . the whole building of my Travells is erected" (*Correspondence*, 3, 103). It is a definition with which Hall would have concurred.

THE AIMS OF *MUNDUS ALTER ET IDEM*

Mundus Alter et Idem is a work born out of Hall's disenchantment with the world and with the spirit of the Renaissance. The Renaissance— driven to discovery, enchanted with novelty, and almost drunken in celebration of its greatness—is the inevitable object of attack for a person so little convinced of the world's wisdom or goodness. As Hall viewed it, the English Renaissance was merely an excuse for scuttling all the old virtues like honesty, piety, valor, and duty. At Cambridge, as Fuller tells us in his *Worthies of England,* Hall was first noted for "his ingenuous maintaining . . . that *Mundus senescit,* The World groweth old" (p. 129). But Hall is no sophist; he really does believe no previous age has ever been as degenerate as this one. While it brags of knowledge, no other age has had "less soundness" (*Works*, 7, 499):

> That Ancient of Days, to whom all times are present, hath told us, that these last shall be worst. . . . This censure . . . is not confined to our seas; but, free and common, hath the same bounds with the earth. I joy not in this large society. Would God we were evil alone! How few are those whose carriage doth not say, that profession of any conscience is pusillanimity! . . . They are rare hands, that are free either from aspersions of blood or spots of filthiness. Let me be at once, as I use, bold and plain: wanton excess, excessive pride, close atheism, impudent profaneness, unmerciful oppression, over-merciful connivance, greedy covetousness, loose prodigality, simoniacal sacrilege, unbridled luxury, beastly drunkenness, bloody treachery, cunning fraud, slanderous detraction, envious underminings, secret idolatry, hypocritical fashionableness, have spread themselves all over the world. (*Works*, 6, 241-42)

In this letter, written before 1608, Hall cries out against many of the vices that masquerade as virtues in *Mundus Alter et Idem.* He insists one cannot merely withdraw from the world or just amend one's own sins. Instead, he calls upon everyone to correct the viciousness of the times:

> I am deceived, if in this cause God allow any man for private. Here must be all actors, no witnesses. His discreet admonitions, seasonable reproofs, and prayers never unseasonable, besides the power of honest example, are expected as his due tribute to the common health. What if we cannot turn the stream; yet we must swim against it. Even without conquest, it is glorious to have resisted. In this alone they are enemies that do nothing.
>
> Thus, as one that delights more in amendment than excuse, I have both censured and directed. (*Works*, 6, 243)

When Hall, ordained for less than five years, talks of having directed and censured men in the past, he must be referring not only to his preaching but also to his satires. We know *Virgidemiae* was intended to unmask "the vgly face of vice" (*Vd.*, 1, prologue, 20); so was *Mundus Alter et Idem*.

First of all, the *Mundus* is a prophecy of what the world will become, as Hall suggests near the end of the work when his narrator Mercurius says: "In this very valley . . . I founded a school, where I—as the omniscient soothsayer—boldly wrote the truest prophecy of this age" (p. 113). In *Holy Observations* Hall remarks that "long acquaintance . . . maketh things which are evil to seem less evil" (*Works*, 7, 537). That is exactly why most people are unaware of England's degeneracy. But by describing a society based totally on evil, Hall seizes the opportunity to reawaken men to the pervasiveness of evil in the world and the chaos to which it will lead. As Hall says in one of his Epistles written about the time of the *Mundus*, "There are good uses to be made of others' enormities; if no more, by them to correct our own: who loathes vice in another is in good forwardness to leave it in himself" (*Works*, 6, 154).

Hall's world therefore exists, according to Northrop Frye, in the realm of myth:

> There are two social conceptions which can be expressed only in terms of myth. One is the social contract, which presents an account of the origins of society. The other is the utopia, which presents an imaginative vision of the *telos* or end at which social life aims. These two myths both begin in an analysis of the present, the society that confronts the mythmaker, and they project this analysis in time

and space. The contract projects it into the past, the utopia into the future or some distant place. ("Utopias," p. 25)

The myth Hall creates is not romantic but ironic, a vision of a society that has refined all European vices to perfection: a dystopia. If the utopian myth is "comic in direction, [moving] toward the actualizing of something better" (Frye, "Utopias," p. 38), the dystopian myth is inevitably tragic. For if man's worst impulses were to triumph, society would inevitably collapse, since these impulses are exactly what society's laws and ethics have attempted to eradicate, or at least restrain. *Mundus Alter et Idem* is just such a nightmare vision of man's darker side, where gluttony, drunkenness, oppression, folly, trickery, and thievery reign. To Hall, this is what Europe is most likely to become. Hall's cities are the Renaissance equivalents of Sodom and Gomorrah, his narrator's 30 years of wandering from city to city the modern counterpart of Israel's wandering in the desert. Everywhere the narrator Mercurius Britannicus roams he finds more idolatry, not of golden calves but of bodily pleasures and material possessions. We see this unrelenting evil throughout the societies he visits, even when the narrator often does not. When a land merely astonishes Mercurius, we must step back and judge what faulty vision he has. When he laughs, he betrays his defective moral sense, for the world he surveys is no less than demonic, what Frye calls a "blasted world of repulsiveness and idiocy" (*Anatomy*, p. 239) that a man ought to flee or fight to the death.

Given its moral underpinnings, and its adherence to the standards of Menippean satire, the *Mundus* often describes types rather than real people. This technique is one Hall exploited even more fully in his *Characters of Virtues and Vices* (1608). The people Mercurius meets often totally lack individual traits, with no more verisimilitude than a character lifted from *Piers Plowman*. For example, the Duke of Courroux personifies tyranny:

> The Reader will marvel and scarcely believe my description of what this man does: what he commands and how impetuously, what he reduces his subjects to, and how he punishes them. It seems to me that that former infamous Russian tyrant was a gentle and civilized man in comparison to this one; he is the most bloodthirsty of the infamous Caesars, and, indeed, even of the Patagonians. (p. 83)

If the reader expects specific information about the Duke, he will find little except what relates to his temperament. We learn that he eats his prisoners and decrees all cities in his realm to be made of wood so they can be easily burned at his whim, that he likes Ethiopians in place of thrush and Englishmen in place of quail, but again these characterize only his moral dimensions.

Even rivers and plants assume moral qualities: the river Zornus (from the German *Zorn*, "anger") becomes rage incarnate, growing hot, even in the midst of winter, and "giving off ill-smelling vapors"; in Lavernia the trees are as covetous as the inhabitants, their limbs so viscous that "whatever birds sit in their branches stick to them and are plundered by the wayfarers."

Related to Hall's primary moral aim is a secondary one. *Mundus Alter et Idem* is meant as a serious dissuasion from travel. In a tract entitled *Quo Vadis? A Just Censure of Travel, as it is Commonly Undertaken by the Gentlemen of our Nation*, written about 1616, Hall states his views clearly. According to him, and contrary to common opinion, travel is neither broadening nor enlightening. Rather, it is dangerous for several reasons: it exposes one to popery; it encourages one to experiment with novelties and vices not common in England; it is likely to jeopardize one's health. And if a person visits some truly exotic place he may even hazard his life. Clearly, all these are dangers encountered by Mercurius in the *Mundus*. He is definitely no better for all his travels — and lucky not to be any the worse.

Mundus Alter et Idem is a burlesque of those serious but unrealistic travel tales of the Renaissance, which borrow their literary structure from romance. Because they do, their realism resides mainly in the minutely detailed descriptions they offer of generally fanciful objects and events. For example, just as Virgil's *Aeneid* was the epic of the Roman nation, Hakluyt's *Principal Navigations* are "an epic of the English nation as they told it themselves" (Blacker, *Hakluyt's Voyages*, intro., p. 1). And just as it is inconceivable for Aeneas to be defeated in his search for Rome, so too is it inconceivable that the great English nation be humiliated in its search for new colonies. The age is too vital, too self-confident to permit it. Moreover, some of Hakluyt's *Principal Navigations* are mere propaganda: "They praise England, promote colonialization, rally support for the growing naval forces, hail the achievements of the great captains. . . . A few of the pieces . . . are nothing more or less than a real-estate promoter's descriptions of lands he wants to develop. Praises are sung of the opportunities to be gained by investment. The climate is praised, the natives hailed as friends, the land described as rich and abundant" (Blacker, *Hakluyt's Voyages*, pp. 3–4).

But if we can now see those works as truth embellished, and people like Hall could see this when they were written, there were many gullible people who did not recognize that the reality of a voyage and its written description were likely to be quite dissimilar. In *Virgidemiae* Hall shows us what happens to the unsuspecting who, filled with these fanciful tales, sell their farms and ship off to find fortune and adventure (4, 6, 1 ff.). What they usually find instead are rough seas, warlike natives, and barren isles, often losing their health, perhaps even their lives, in the process. In *Mundus Alter et Idem*, by giving a description of the worst possible land one could discover, Hall appears to be acting as a counterbalance to Hakluyt and his kind.

Mundus Alter et Idem is a satire on national traits. Many books of the Renaissance—such as Jerome Turler, *De Peregrinatione* (1574), translated as *The Traueiler* in 1575, and John Florio, *His firste Fruites* (1578)—contain capsule summaries of various European countries on a variety of subjects supposedly helpful to would-be travelers. Turler, for example, claims that toward strangers "the Germans are roughe and in hospitable, the Frenchmen gentle, the Spaniardes curteous, and the Italians diligent" (*The Traueiler*, p. 41). In love, "the Germanes be ambitious, the Frenchmen inconstant, the Spaniardes impacient, the Italians jelous" (*The Traueiler*, p. 41).

Hall, on the other hand, avoids the aphoristic platitudes of the guidebooks for a sharp but hilarious mockery of national traits. The Swiss (apparently as rich then as now) are reported to have goiters not because of their mountainous climate but because of a strange disease called Argyranchen that "attracts money to [their necks] no less than a magnet attracts iron." The Sicilians, called Scioccians in the *Mundus*, are said to be so insensate that they do not know into what opening to put their food, whether "through their nose, or through their ears, or through some other, less suitable opening." Likewise, the Italian's love of graffiti, the German's love of deep metaphysical speculation, the Englishman's love of tobacco, and the Spaniard's love of titles and long names are all ridiculed in their turn.

Mundus Alter et Idem is a burlesque of the embellished travel tales of the Middle Ages such as those of Marco Polo and Mandeville. In *Virgidemiae* Hall calls such yarns as Mandeville's "whetstone leasings" (4, 6, 61), harkening back to the tradition of giving a whetstone to the biggest liar at a country fair.[25] In the *Mundus* he shows himself as

---

25. Davenport, *Poems*, note to *Virgidemiae*, 4, 6, 61 (p. 226). *Virgidemiae* cited hereafter as "*Vd.*"

capable as any of devising tall tales. We discover geese being produced from fallen leaves, lambs that grow on trees, and fish that beg to be caught. Hall's new world has its monsters as well. For example, RUC—a flying monster borrowed from Marco Polo—visits Pamphagonia once a year with "an astonishing troop of Harpies, ravens, vultures, and hawks crowding around on all sides" to partake of the banquet of elephants, rhinoceroses, camels, and more common livestock that the natives have assembled for his visit. He and his flock will grab what pleases their palates and fly away. But as always, the biggest grotesques in the *Mundus* are the people themselves, for they stuff themselves so excessively on whatever remains "that for nearly 40 days they abstain from meat, during which time they are fed with fish—but cooked in wine and spices at far greater expense— . . . so that they may both restore themselves a bit by so many varieties of food and return to meat, so long neglected, with a sharper appetite" (pp. 35-36). One cannot deny that his exaggerations have a chilling plausibility about them.

Mundus Alter et Idem is a harsh satire on the Catholic church, not at all surprising given Hall's vigorous attack on it in *Virgidemiae* (*Vd.*, 4, 7, 1 ff.). The Paradise of Moronia Felix in Book 3 is a satiric exaggeration of the cozenage done to the faithful by the Church in the pilgrimage shrines of Europe, deluding the people in their hopes, defrauding them of their money, and—worst of all—ministering to their selfish desires. The ridiculous credulity of the Moronia Pians, who believe that rocks "hear, weep, laugh, extend feet and retreat, cure diseases, sweat blood, and daily prophesy everything," is Hall's slap at the supposedly miraculous statues and relics of the saints. The Church's ludicrous rituals, such as black flyswatters to drive away flies from a dead cardinal's body, Rome's hypocrisy in living off the income of prostitutes, and the degeneracy of the papacy all come in for ridicule. Some of the strange heresies of the early Church are also exposed, but Hall is clearly most engaged by the outrageousness of a religion that preys upon human weaknesses and the stupidity of the faithful.

Finally, *Mundus Alter et Idem* is a travesty of scholarship and philology.[26] Hall constructs an elaborate series of names that he invents from Greek and Latin—as well as from Italian, French, German, and Spanish—descriptive of the people and places, usually sarcastic, and

26. Sandford M. Salyer, "Joseph Hall as a Literary Figure," p. 257. Cf. what Northrop Frye, *Anatomy of Criticism*, p. 311, says about the Menippean satirist who "shows his exuberance in intellectual ways, by piling up an enormous mass of erudition about his theme and in overwhelming his pedantic targets with an avalanche of their own jargon."

sometimes possessing double meanings. His copious marginal notes in the text and his Index of Proper Names at the end—themselves a travesty of the Renaissance love of learning turned into mere pedantry—point out these fanciful derivations to the reader. Thus our narrator speculates that Ponfinia, a city in Yvronia, is corrupted from *bon vinea*, "with a *p* instead of a *b*, and an *f* instead of a *v*, badly pronounced as is the custom of the Germans." Or the Valley of Actaeonius is glossed as coming "*from Actaeon, a great hunter, who (as is customary) was eaten up by his dogs.*" In this way Hall again and again ridicules what is Europe's degeneracy disguised by a veneer of sham learning. Likewise, his catalogue of Paracelsus's jargon functions like Jonson's language in *The Alchemist*—to discredit the intellectual pretensions of the new sciences—and his lists of heretical sects stand as an emblem of man's love of novel opinion gone mad. It is no doubt a mark of kinship that Burton's *Anatomy of Melancholy*, another mass of erudition that Frye calls the "greatest Menippean satire in English before Swift" (*Anatomy*, p. 311), should so frequently mention the *Mundus* by name.

THE SETTING OF THE *MUNDUS* AND THE CHARACTER OF ITS NARRATOR

In choosing Antarctica as the location for his dystopia, Hall displays his inventiveness, as well as his acquaintance with the travels of the period. The explorations of the English (along with those of the French, Portuguese, and Spanish) were beginning to push into the southernmost recesses of the Atlantic and Pacific oceans, bumping into large islands that they took to be the coastline of a southern continent. The tradition of a *Terra Australis Incognita* had begun to flourish as early as the thirteenth century when Marco Polo referred to the reputed existence of a great southern continent (Rainaud, *Le continent austral*, pp. 1–18). By the mid-sixteenth century, maps by Ortelius and Plancius show the southern pole circumscribed by a vast land mass, and by 1597 the Dutch historian Wytfliet describes *Terra Australis* as the most southern of all lands and gives some circumstantial particulars regarding its geographical relation to New Guinea, venturing the opinion that it would be regarded as a fifth part of the world were it thoroughly explored.[27] For Hall's purposes an unknown southern continent is perfect: it provides

27. Timothy A. Coghlin, "Australia," *Encyclopedia Britannica*, 2, 958. Cited hereafter as "*EB.*"

the distance necessary to establish an imaginary society, and given its
geographical relationship to Europe, Hall is able to present a *mundus
inversus*, a world upside down, filled with people whose actions and
ideals contradict those supposed to reign in Europe.

Hall's choice of a narrator for this tale is just as suitable. At the time
the book begins, Mercurius Britannicus, like Hall, is a student at Cambridge.[28] Though he has to be persuaded at first to hazard his life on a
journey to the South Pole, before he leaves he behaves as all good scholars should and reads some Renaissance travel books, rudimentary guides
not only setting forth the dangers and the advantages of travel but also
explaining how to spend time wisely on a journey. In particular, he
appears to have read Jerome Turler's *De Peregrinatione* (1574), or its
anonymous translation *The Traueiler* (1575), since this book is quite
specific about what a traveler must observe:

> Consider the lande what maner one it is, and consyder the people
> that dwell therein, whether they bee stronge or weake: manye or
> fewe: the Lande good or bad: what Cyties there bee: Walled or not
> Walled: the soyle fertile or barreine: wooddie or champion: So that
> there bee fiue principall poyntes too bee considered in euerie Cun-
> trey: the Fame, Figure, Bignesse, Jurisdiction, and situation. To the
> Fame belongeth howe it was called of olde, and howe at this present,
> for oftentimes the names of Regions ar changed according to varietie
> of time, and inhabitauntes. . . . By the Figure I meane the fourme
> and fashion of the Cuntry. . . . By Bignesse I vnderstande the capaci-
> tie and widenesse, which is discerned in length and bredth of a Cun-
> trey: likewise in the compasse, boundes, and buttes, wherwith it is
> enuironed in respect of the Coastes of the world, and Peoples,
> Riuers, or Hilles wherevpon it bordereth. By Jurisdiction vnder-
> stande, the rule, and maner of gouernment which is in that Lande
> which being diuerse among diuerse peoples, and belonging rather
> to euery priuate prouince or peculiar citie, then vnto whole re-
> gions. . . . The situation of a Countrey is eyther hillie or plaine, and
> the same againe either coasting, or inlande. (*The Traueiler*, pp.
> 50-52)

---

28. Although the composition of the *Mundus* apparently extended until 1605, it was
begun before 1601, while Hall was still at Cambridge.

Mercurius, obviously wishing to extract the most from his journey, seems to have swallowed Turler whole. He is forever noting the minutest detail he encounters. Thus we get catalogues of each region's cities, the land's form and variety, the inhabitants' character, the province's history, its chief crops and industries, rivers, mountains, valleys, and plains —ad nauseam. The problem is Mercurius; he has no critical eye and little critical intelligence. He cannot discriminate between the important and the unimportant; nor can he evaluate, except in the crudest manner. He is seldom shocked by what he sees, and seldom very impressed. More or less static throughout his travels, he exists as a camera eye, recording whatever comes into his range rather than evaluating it. Yet, paradoxically, this is also his strength. A better man would have fled this world at the first, and there would have been no tale to tell.

As one reads *Mundus Alter et Idem* it is important to recognize the distance Hall has placed between himself and Mercurius. Besides the vast difference in moral stance between the two, Mercurius is described in the introduction as a man well acquainted with travelers of all sorts and a person convinced that England does not "produce anything worthwhile which it could have concealed for very long from me." While Hall does know travel literature well, there is no evidence that he knew any travelers. More importantly—as he makes clear in *Quo Vadis?*—he has little tolerance for the "pusillanimity of us English, [that] we are still ready to undervalue our own and admire foreigners" (*Works*, 9, 537). Also, what draws Mercurius to this voyage is his "most ardent desire for learning." In contrast, Hall quenches his thirst for knowledge with books and considers it the height of folly to travel: "I have known some that have travelled no farther than their own closet, which could both teach and correct the greatest traveller, after all his tedious and costly pererrations" (*Works*, 9, 539).

The name Mercurius Britannicus is merely the Latin equivalent for "A British Mercury"—a reference perhaps to Mercury's function as the messenger to the gods. Indeed, our British Mercury does serve as a messenger to the English nation, bringing back news of this other continent. But the news he carries is not good. Nothing he discovers is unknown in England: it already possesses these vices itself, though not in such refined states. His voyage is therefore even less profitable than those of many explorers, since they do occasionally discover something useful that England lacks.

But it is the other characteristic of Mercury that explains why our

narrator is so well suited to his role and why he is so seldom upset by
what he sees—and when he is, why he is not roused to great anger.[29]
Mercury is the archetypal deceiver, whose skill in all things—inventions, music, speech, disguise, and thievery—makes him the perfect
narrator for this kind of voyage, unlikely to be shocked. He is clever,
knowing that Yvronia should be entered only by the cover of night,
knowing when to hide in order to see one of the Yvronians' great banquets, and knowing how to disguise himself as a woman in Viraginia to
make his escape. Elsewhere he is lucky. His British citizenship saves him
from death in Viraginia (England being such a friend to women); his
visit to Larcinia just happens to coincide with their jubilee year, which
occurs only twice a century, during which time they are at peace with all
nations; on his visit to the Shrine of Schlauchberga he just happens to
encounter a pilgrim along the way whose holy presence shields Mercury
from having to drink a flagon at the hospitality booths placed every three
miles along the road.

Likewise, the few voluntary actions Mercury takes on his journeys
show him to be true to form. In Viraginia Mercury swears an oath to be
subservient to a woman's will in exchange for his freedom. Though he
does not really agree with the oath, he freely swears to it and admits he
would have sworn to still tougher conditions—exactly what we would
expect from an inveterate liar. In Larcinia, Mercurius sets up a school of
astrology. Like alchemy, astrology is a sham science and one Hall
abhors (*Vd.*, 2, 7, 1 ff.), but again it is perfect for an arch-deceiver. So
while he can be tempted to display those vices dear to his heart, our
British Mercury is more often noncommittal about what he sees, and he
knows enough to shun those places where he fears bodily harm. In short,
he is a person just corrupt enough, lucky enough, clever enough, and
equivocal enough to be ideally suited for taking this journey and returning in one piece.

While the attributes of a classical Mercury perfectly outfit a narrator
for this difficult journey, the allegorical meaning ascribed to him by the

29. The two times Mercurius is roused to anger—toward the Catholic church and
drunken poets—I would argue that it is Hall's personality emerging. When the carousers
in Yvronia attempt to play the poet, inspired only by their wine, Hall cannot let their
transgression go unmentioned because his conception of the poet is such an exalted one.
Thus he speaks through Mercurius: "[It] aroused the greatest amount of spleen in me [to
see them] relying solely on the power of Bacchus and ecstasy" (p. 46). Hall's antipathy
toward the corruptions of the Roman church (cf. *Vd.*, 4, 7, 1–74) accounts for the other
outburst.

Christian mythographers of the Renaissance also suits the aims of the *Mundus*. Because of the role Mercury plays in the *Aeneid*, these writers often interpret him as "conscience." In the words of Boccaccio,

> [Virgil] demonstrates how we are conveyed back to virtue by bringing in Mercury, interpreter of the gods, to exhort Aeneas to glory, and away from vanity and lasciviousness. By Mercury, Virgil means either the prick of his own conscience or the reproving speech of some eloquent friend by which we—sleeping in a bed of shame—are reawakened and brought back to the straight and beautiful path that leads to honor. (*Genealogia*, 14, 13)

It is this very prick of conscience that Hall hopes Mercury's tale will give us by the end of the book.

PREFACE TO THE TRAVEL

Hall intends us to see that—just like the traveler—the reasoning behind the travel is less than perfect. The introduction begins when two friends of the narrator (Peter Beroaldus, a Frenchman, and Adrian Cornelius Drogius, a Dutchman) fall into a discussion of travel with Mercurius and try to convince him to accompany them on a trip to the South Pole. Beroaldus, the more persuasive of the two, has peculiar ideas about travel. To him, travel to a nearby country is of no profit whatsoever. A man who travels such short distances changes neither the sky nor the air nor even the soil under his feet. Even the few novelties he can find near home have been minutely described by earlier travelers, and he can just as well read about them as visit them. This is exactly Hall's argument against travel, but instead of concluding—as Hall does—that one should stay home and read, Beroaldus says that one must therefore push farther into the unknown. Only the great explorers like Columbus, Drake, and Magellan are worthy of the name of traveler; the sole criterion is to be first.

Beroaldus feels the farther the travel, the better it is for another reason: the fame received. In contrast, Hall feels the farther the travel the worse it is, because of the physical danger and the great opportunity to be infected with new vices. As for fame, Hall values it at nothing: "To be carried away with an affectation of fame is so vain and absurd, that I wonder it can be incident to any wise man; for what a molehill of earth is it to which his name can extend, when it is farthest carried by the wings of report! And how short a while doth it continue where it is once spread!" (*Works*, 7, 518).

As Beroaldus argues his beliefs he becomes more and more excited, eventually whipping himself into a frenzy. Unfortunately, he excites the same vain desires of novelty and glory in his listeners; they lose their reason as well and agree to follow him. The three set sail in a ship called "The Phantasia"—an appropriate choice of a name in two ways: it clearly signifies that this is an imaginative rather than a real voyage, and all three have abandoned their reason in deciding to seek out new lands. As Hall remarks in *Quo Vadis?*: "He therefore that travels only to please his fantasy is like some woman with child, that longs for that piece which she sees upon another's trencher, and swoons if she miss it; or some squire of dames, that doats upon every beauty, and is every day love-sick anew. These humours are fitter for controlment than observation" (*Works*, 9, 536).

When they reach Belgium Drogius is forced to disembark for Delft, and when they reach Aquitaine Beroaldus leaves for Montauban, "both of them, to be sure, most unwillingly" (p. 17); Mercurius is forced to continue alone. For two years he sails, past the Fortunate Isles, past the land of the Monomotapensi, past the Cape of Good Hope, until he finally reaches the black headland of Crapulia, where his tale begins.

PUBLICATION DATA

The early printing history of the *Mundus* has been confused. An article by the present author helps clarify matters (Wands, "Early History," pp. 1-12), so only a brief summary need be given here. The undated Frankfort edition (entered 2 June 1605 in the *Stationers' Register*) was surreptitiously printed in London and appeared in late 1605 or early 1606[30] with Frankfort misleadingly given on the title page as the place of publication. There can be no doubt that it was printed in London, and by Humphrey Lownes, since damage to the triangular lace ornament on H1v and M8v corresponds to that in other works known to be from Lownes's press. The edition printed in Hanau by Wilhelm Antonius, though dated 1607, appeared in Germany in the fall of 1606.[31] Then,

---

30. *Catalogus Universalis pro Nundinis Francofurtensibus, spring 1606*, C1r [New York Public *KSD].

31. Ibid., fall 1606, B4r.

about the fall of 1607,[32] perhaps because of damage to signatures ¶8 and
D8 of the Frankfort edition, a reissue appeared in Germany with the
Frankfort title printed on corrected Hanau preliminaries and bound
with gatherings A-O8 drawn from both editions. Most copies so far
examined with a Frankfort title page are thus mixed, and this reissue has
frequently been mistakenly accepted as the edition that appeared in late
1605 or early 1606.

One other oddity is that at some point in printing the *Mundus* the
Frankfort title page was reengraved when it began to wear. In copies
containing reengraving, crosshatching is added to the top of the oblong
pedestal below the South Pole, and to the front of the pedestal surrounding the words "FRANCOFVRTI APVD *haeredes Ascanij de Rinialme.*"
Though one would expect the later state of the engraved title page to
appear only in the reissue with corrected Hanau preliminaries, it also
appears on the majority of extant copies containing all gatherings ¶8,
A-O8 from the Frankfort edition—fairly clear evidence that ¶1r of most
preliminary gatherings was blank when the engraved title page was sent
to Germany, where the reissue of 1607 was probably assembled, and only
sometime after the appearance of this reissue—when this engraving
returned to England—were the preliminaries stored in London given a
title page and bound into books.

Each edition contains its share of misspellings, turned letters, and
so forth, the Hanau edition having slightly fewer accidentals than the
Frankfort. But the Hanau edition omits eight words present in the
Frankfort edition, demonstrating that the latter could not have been set
from the former unless the compositor had also had access to a manuscript with the correct readings. Of the 52 spelling errors in one or both
editions (28 in Frankfort; 18 in Hanau; 6 in which a variation exists
between the two editions, but neither reading seems preferable), only
two misspellings occur in both editions. Yet the signatures in Frankfort
and Hanau editions follow each other so closely—the ability of the 1607
reissue to interchange signatures demonstrates this—that one must suspect that whoever set the later edition must have had access to the earlier.
Although internal evidence is inconclusive about which edition came
first, the external evidence favors Frankfort as having appeared some six
months before Hanau, and given the superiority of the Frankfort edition
in substantive readings, I have chosen it as the copytext in preparing this
translation, collating it with the Hanau edition. The only other Latin

32. Ibid., fall 1607, C1r.

edition that appeared during Hall's lifetime was the one bound with More's *Utopia* and Campanella's *City of the Sun,* printed in Utrecht in 1643, but it has no textual authority because Hall, who had just been released from the Tower, was in Norwich attempting to fulfill his duties as a bishop while being harassed by the Puritans and could scarcely have had a hand in this edition. This text has consequently been disregarded.

EDITORIAL NOTE

My commentary, which appears after the translation of Hall's text and his Index of Proper Names, explains Hall's allusions to and borrowings from other authors, the echoes of the *Mundus* in his other works, and—occasionally—any problems in translation. The commentary relies heavily on the use of abbreviations, and readers should consult the bibliography for those and for the short titles used throughout. The introduction to the commentary explains its format.

I should explain that Hall's own marginal notes to his text—many of which are abbreviated in the original—have once or twice needed to be expanded or emended to make sense. This also occurs (and much more frequently) in the Index of Proper Names, where Hall often specifies the language from which he is constructing his place-names but not the specific word involved. I have encased these additional words in brackets to indicate that they do not appear in the original.

The attempt has been made to simulate the printing of the original text as much as possible, with chapter headings and subheadings reproduced as they appear in the Frankfort edition. The spelling of place and proper names conforms to this edition, except that in a few instances names have been regularized according to majority usage. The nearly 200 marginal notes Hall provides to his text have been printed here as they appear in the Frankfort edition, including the printer's idiosyncratic use of italic and roman characters. Italics were used for most notes, with roman normally employed for emphasizing specific words and phrases, though this rule is sometimes ignored. In particular, authors and titles are seldom distinguished from one another, both being almost exclusively set in italics. However, unlike the Frankfort edition, which places Hall's notes in the margin and indexes them to the text with letters of the alphabet, the marginal notes in this translation are placed at the bottom of the page, indexed to the line number at which they begin in the Frankfort edition, except in perhaps a dozen instances where it is clear that a note was originally misplaced, or that two separate notes have been mistakenly amalgamated into one.

A NOTE ON THE ENGLISH TRANSLATION

The only previous English translation of the *Mundus* is John Healey's, published about 1609 and called *The Discovery of a New World*. His version, though enjoyable to read, might perhaps be more accurately called an adaptation. Healey himself, writing a preface to the second issue, claims the two works are completely different:

> But as touching this present pile of *English,* it is mine, it hath no further alliance to his, then chalke hath to cheese, for as these haue no cohaerence in their nearest proprieties (which translations should neuer want) but onely in their generall kind of essence as they are both corporeall substances; no more doth this worke any way resemble his in fashion, stile, or discourse, but onely in the inuention and proiect. (2nd ed. [c. 1613-14], ¶2v)

We are left to wonder if such protestation is not excessive, aimed more than anything else at distancing the original from the translation and thereby sheltering Hall's reputation, especially considering that *The Discovery* is noticeably coarser and broader in its humor, and a young churchman could scarcely be pleased to have what was (in Latin) relatively inaccessible suddenly available to the masses. More said he would rather burn his *Utopia* than have it translated; one wonders how Hall felt.

Every translator must feel his work represents an improvement over what was previously available; after living with this book for several years I am no exception. Though I enjoy *The Discovery of a New World* for its liveliness, I am less happy with its variance in tone from the original and the changes in meaning it introduces. Almost every page contains one or more omissions, additions, or mistranslations of some sort. Sometimes the change is as minor as a marginal note incorporated into the text; elsewhere as many as two or three sentences may suddenly appear or disappear according to the whim of the translator. More than 80 of Hall's marginal notes are lost, and more than 120 new ones are added, so that fewer than half the marginal notes in *The Discovery* are Hall's, and the impression one receives is markedly different.

Healey's deletion of many of Hall's marginal notes removes one or more references to classical authors such as Apuleius, Aristophanes, Cato, Horace, Plato Comicus, Pliny, Ptolomy, Silius Italicus, Strabo, Virgil, and Varro. With the loss of these the translation appears far less learned. Replacing them are notes commenting not too subtly on Hall's text, belaboring the parallels between England and *Terra Australis*, poking us in the ribs to explain Hall's allusions, and presenting such thoughts of Healey's as: millers and tailors are thieves (*Discovery*, p. 134), Adam and Eve were fools (*Discovery*, p. 98), and bribery exists even in England (*Discovery*, p. 133).

The liberties taken with the text itself are less severe, but if there is any systematic bias on Healey's part in the translation it is to make the subtle obvious, to change Hall's irony to ridicule, to exaggerate the vices.[33] This is accomplished in several ways. First, Hall's use of litotes all but vanishes. In Hall the Chinese laugh at our belief that we are the only learned people, "not without reason" (p. 13), but in Healey's rendering, "they laugh at us for it and well may" (*Discovery*, p. 13). In Pamphagonia Mercurius is so nauseated by the people's practice of keeping cheeses until they are destroyed with worms that he says: "it is nearly impossible to speak about [it]" (p. 30). In contrast, Healey has Mercurius cry out "foh, nasty!" (*Discovery*, p. 31). On the same page Hall refers to these people as "most delicate feasters," a phrase heavily ironic; Healey uses the simple pronoun "they." These and similar changes turn Mercury into a person much more impulsive in his actions, less subtle in his use of language, and less detached from the people he observes.

While it is true that Hall creates many of his effects in the *Mundus* by adding to or extending European vices, Healey exaggerates them even further. At the shrine of the Good Goddess in Moronia Felix, Hall's description of one man praying for the death of one uncle becomes 20 men praying for the death of 20 uncles; one churchman praying for the death of another becomes 20 churchmen praying for the death of 20 more (*Discovery*, p. 113-14). Hall describes Butinia Forest in Larcinia so filled with robbers that in comparison to it the German forest of Hercynia, "surrounded by ten thousand highwaymen, looks like a narrow orchard, or even, as it were, a simple hedge" (p. 108). Healey's expanded rendering is "If *Hercynia* keepe ten thousand theeues (as lightlie it doth alwayes,) *Booty-forrest* shall keepe a thousand thousand: Baw waw!

---

33. I cannot concur with Claude Lascassagne, "La satire religeuse dans *Mundus Alter et Idem* de Joseph Hall," p. 142, that Healey's changes do not seriously tamper with the original sense, tone, or intention of the *Mundus*.

Hercynia? why 'tis a blanket for a Catte, a petty Cock-pitte, nay a very Tobacco-boxe in respect of *Booty-forrest*" (*Discovery*, p. 126). Likewise, Hall's "Italian . . . bandits" (p. 108) grow to be "damned, soule-lesse, fiend-bred, hell-borne, *Italian* theeues" (*Discovery*, p. 127), and while people who fall ill in Crapulia are compelled to be purged (p. 30), Healey's rendering adds: "[whatever] he voids at either end during this purging time is immediatly confiscate vnto the Dukes treasurie, and *strained*, . . . not strained through a colander you must thinke, but seazed vpon by those inquisitors" (*Discovery*, p. 31). These added grotesqueries are unfaithful not only to Hall's Latin but also to the tone and the conception of the original.

Healey sometimes even reverses the meaning of the text, as when he has sellers of goods in Moronia Mobilis buy back goods they have sold "if you dislike it" (*Discovery*, p. 85), when the Latin ("ubi emptori placere inaudiverint") states they buy them back "if they hear that these have pleased the buyer" (p. 75). Similarly, Healey has the women in Moronia thank the Viraginians for making the vanquished men obey their will, when in the original it is the vanquished men who thank the Viraginians,[34] "for to rule themselves up to now had seemed most troublesome and full of ill will" (p. 73). Elsewhere, national vices are transformed. Fat Italian women become fat German women, low Germans become low Dutch, and Frenchmen become eunuchs.

Finally, Healey's decision to render all the Latin place-names into English seems to me the worst alteration of all. Hall's Latin names function as did More's Greek names, making possible the erudite jokes in both works. When Hythloday becomes Nonsenso, for example, as he does in Paul Turner's otherwise admirable translation of the *Utopia*, any possible gain for the uninformed reader comes at the expense of an egregious loss in subtlety for everyone else. In *The Discovery*, where several hundred names are Anglicized (and sometimes mistranslated), the change is even less felicitous: Hall's Lavernia (from Laverna, the goddess of rogues and thieves) becomes Theeuingen; Vetulonia (from the Latin *vetula*, a contemptuous term for an old woman) becomes Old-Mumpington; the River Meionium (from the Latin *meiendo*, "making water") becomes the Piss-on, and so forth.

Given the variety of problems with Healey's text (which for some readers may extend even to comprehending Healey's Renaissance En-

---

34. "Victi pergratum id sibi futurum respondent; molestissimum enim sibi hactenus visum, & inuidiae plenum, imperare."

glish), I believe a modern translation has long been needed. In reaction to Healey I have retained all of the Latin place-names, for without this the subtle innuendos of the original are lost. I have also striven for a close translation of the Latin, preserving as carefully as possible the rhythm and tone of the original. Hall's frequent use of litotes and of convoluted sentence structure results in English sentences that are sometimes quite long and complex. Yet I believe they are justified to reflect accurately the learned and allusive prose Hall consciously adopted in this work.

ANOTHER WORLD

AND YET THE SAME

or

The Southern Continent, before

THIS ALWAYS UNKNOWN, THROUGH THE EXTENDED
TRAVELS OF A WANDERING
ACADEMIC MOST RECENTLY
SURVEYED

AUTHOR:
Mercurius Britannicus

FRANKFORT: AT THE HOUSE OF
the heirs of Ascanius de Rinialme

engraved by William Kip

TO THE MOST HONORED LORD,

Whose virtue is no less than the splendor of his *Illustrious Birth,*

to LORD HENRY,
Count of Huntingdon

MERCURIUS BRITANNICUS
HUMBLY DEDICATES
HIS WORLD

TO THE READER, GREETINGS

Contrary to expectation, dear Reader, driven neither by storms nor by the never-ending tossing of waves, without winds, without sails, you have been driven to a new world. Where, after you have accurately surveyed the breadth of the lands, the location of the regions, and the customs and temperament of the peoples, you will at last distinguish the face and deportment of the whole world. Indeed, you will recognize the shape of this old world to be such that although you see it to be another world, you will believe it to be the same. But perhaps you think that our decrepit world created this offspring absolutely similar in all respects. Indeed, experience often teaches that a child marvelously reproduces the character of its parents, as does the poet:

> The moisture which flourishes in leaves derives from the roots,
> Likewise, manners pass from a father to his sons with his seed.

That our old world is able to procreate not just to the age of 60, but even almost to the age of 6,000, how greatly that departs from all reason and from all philosophical teaching! And, above all, if the world had ever before been endowed with the same power to procreate, would it not have rather spent its more vigorous years in producing children? Even its own children, long since grown to adulthood, would have propagated this very same excellence far and wide to such an extent that their offspring would have prospered too, not to a boundless extent, but would have increased manyfold, and so many of these worlds would have existed—some young, some old—that no Alexander would have longed for worlds to conquer, but that, indeed, these worlds would have longed for Alexanders to be conquered by.

And in any event, as far as I am concerned, I believe that this new world you are about to discover is that same one the Platonists dreamed of so many generations ago; which the ancients called the *invisible world* and the *archetype of the world*. For if you will accurately observe this world's members and features, and carefully ponder them, you will say that you have gazed at the true and living ideal of the world in which we dwell and its epitome. Therefore, this distinguished sight which has lurked in Cimmerian obscurity through the entire past age, is now— thanks to the ingenuity and labor of this author—at last offered for clear contemplation. That world, once invisible, has been exposed to view through this work and laid bare for the first time by the craft of magic or optics, I know not which.

What appeared especially singular to me was that our world and this one of his were forced to suffer exactly the same fate. For each, as soon as it was born, was sentenced to darkness by its father: and each was denied light by its creator, and each was given light from another source. No Titan offered light to this world. It was discovered and then immediately hidden away: nor was light ever to be glimpsed—or even hoped for—except from this ingenious man. His illustrious work would easily have reclaimed this dark and hidden world from the mist, had it only been possible for the book to reclaim itself from a mist just as thick. That unknown world would have revealed itself to us more quickly, had this little book stepped forth more swiftly into the light.

Certainly the writer and explorer of this unknown world had long ago said good-bye to the Muses (of whom he was a noted supporter) and had devoted himself to the sacred calling of Theology. Furthermore (being wholly departed from the Muses), he despised this book and several other of his learned inventions as trivial and vain, though all most worthy of notice and praise, and could not be induced by any entreaties whatever to permit them to be printed. He excused himself, moreover, on the grounds that although he had composed certain exercises of the sort for his own training and amusement in a youthful and leisurely academic period, he had now come to scorn them as useless trifles, disown them, and deem them unworthy ever to come into the public's glance in his name.

Whence is the reason that this most truly elegant and delightful little book has been hidden away in the shadows for so long, held by the cruel bonds of obscurity, unknown to the world of the learned, till I, whom the author himself (because of his extraordinary humanity) used to consider a friend and intimate, lamenting the unfortunate and miserable lot of this most charming and fruitful offspring, endeavored with all the means and reasons I possessed to remove this creature from its prison and set it forth in liberty and light. And when I clearly saw that the author's mind was truly immovable and steadfast, so that his opinion would be swayed by no petition, or persuasion, or logic: nor, in fact, that any other hope remained for this new world to be disclosed to our world, I finally decided to violate the sacred laws of friendship, rather than forever deprive the ingenious minds of the learned everywhere of his extraordinarily sweet and delectable fruit.

Consequently, so that I might offer this same sweetness that I had tasted to all scholarly men, I decided to communicate to others what I had previously had all to myself. But before I dared to undertake this project, much time passed. Indeed, I hesitated because of my conscience: it seemed a very bold deed, and I feared an offense to that most esteemed man whose friendship to me I had always felt was most important to cultivate. At last, overcome and enraptured by the beauty of the work, since I believed that there was nothing injurious or unseemly in it which might reflect upon the author, but on the contrary that much goodwill and fame—and, in truth, much profit and enjoyment—would be bound to spread to the republic of letters, I was unable to restrain myself any longer until, all my hesitation removed, I released from my custody into the hands of the printers a copy of this work, which had been entrusted to me as a measure of our friendship.

And so, thanks to my concern (and my not insignificant labor besides), this new world, shut up and barred for so long, is at this moment opened to you, Reader. For this service I entreat and beseech this one reward from you, that if you detect anything thankworthy and agreeable in it, you will intercede zealously for me with the author (who I am afraid will take it hard) to calm his mind, so that he will not decree something more unjust against me because of the misdeed I have committed, but rather moved by just reasoning, he will comprehend my deed more kindly and retain and preserve me in his accustomed regard.

And so farewell, and what you are awaiting from this new world may you abundantly enjoy.

WILLIAM KNIGHT

INDEX OF CHAPTERS

BOOK I
[CRAPULIA]

[YVRONIA]

6

BOOK II
[VIRAGINIA]

BOOK III
[MORONIA]

BOOK IV
[LAVERNIA]

THE OCCASION OF THIS TRAVEL
AND THE
INTRODUCTION

I do not know whether it was the kinship I had developed in the past
with travelers, as the Academics of England know quite well, and the   5
books and letters of friends even now abundantly testify to, or whether
that Homeric passage impelled me to this desire,

> for all strangers and beggars come from Zeus,

or whether I might better say that it was the sweetest customs and characteristics of these strange lands, and a certain innate thirst and predispo-   10
sition that arose from my most ardent desire for learning: for our region
of the world did not produce anything worthwhile which it could have
concealed for very long from me—at that time a true Athenian seeker of
wisdom.

Of all the many other conversations I had with Peter Beroaldus, a   15
Frenchman, and Adrian Cornelius Drogius, a Dutchman, the one concerning the usefulness of travel stands out (in which, during our not
unpleasant comparison of laws, customs, languages, and cities, a certain
friendly dispute arose). "Really," said Beroaldus, "I don't know what it
means to travel. For if I were to cross the border of my native land to tread   20
on your neighboring land, or to cross some narrow strait or river (for
example the Rhine, or the Tweed), I would receive the name of 'traveler'
according to popular opinion. Yet one enjoys the same sky, the same
stars, and scarcely even notices a change of soil. I don't see what is hard or

noble in that. Right now my dear parents and all my friends from
Montauban earnestly call me back home, as though I had been a long
time absent. I, in the meantime, according to the rather obscure opinion
of Socrates, feel I have spent these two years at home. Indeed, how little
5   distant is Paris from Montauban, Calais from Paris, and Dover from
Calais? Truly, when I consider the whole earth, the distance seems to me
to extend a mere arm's breadth; on a map, the width of a finger; surely
when I contemplate the heavens, nothing at all. Nor do I see why Europe
deserves the name of 'homeland' any less than France: for in regard to the
10   variety of languages, doesn't everyone know there is as great a discrep-
ancy in sounds and in origin of the various dialects among the people in
France as in the whole circle of European provinces? As regards the customs and innate character of the people in this country, you have not just
an image of our world but indeed an image of the whole universe, since
15   each and every province mirrors the customs and habits of every neighboring people, not unlike the polypus fish, who turns the color of any
stone it comes near."

I replied, "In earnest, we envy you, Beroaldus, because you so
greatly despise the freedom of travel while we—miserable men—are
20   held fast to our small houses like tortoises; now that you have freely con-
templated the delights of the whole world, with a mind fully sated you
despise and disdain them. If I could gaze upon the snowy Alps or the
shady Pyrenees, how much would I bless the time spent and rejoice in
my leisure! where everything I saw and heard would serve as a lesson and
25   enrich this breast, eager for learning, with new ideas!"

"How much do things unseen promise a man, my friend," he
answered, "and what vain hopes dupe the inexperienced. I used to be of
the same opinion myself when lurking inside I used to enjoy the warmth
of my home. But now, having once gone abroad, I have learned traveling
30   is empty and unprofitable. For it is so easy to be glutted by such a trifling
journey, and by things never seen before. And also, since foreign sights
differ so little from native ones, whatever comes into our view for the first
time can scarcely appear brand new. What is there, I pray, in such little-
known and remote parts of the earth that a prudent person—by consult-
35   ing the maps and listening to the stories of travelers—would know less
well than by his own travels? Camden described your Britain: would
whoever has read him—being remote from the cities and villages, rivers,
and whatever antique monuments or extraordinary works of nature are
still visible in any place—not be able to judge these just as accurately as a
40   person who has individually examined each one with his own eyes? And

finally, what part of Europe is there whose renowned achievements and works of art are any less visible through someone else's eyes? In truth, if anyone desires to know the customs of the inhabitants and their common qualities, they are well enough known to him in the same way that they are known to everyone; yet, they are not so constant in all countries as to be comprehended by the eyes or the pen of one person. The French are commonly called rash; the Spanish arrogant; the Germans drunkards; the English meddling with many things; the Italians unmanly; the Swedes timid; the Bohemians inhumane; the Irish barbarous and superstitious; but is any man so dull that he supposes no prudent Frenchman to have been born, no timid Spaniard, no sober German? They are deceived, believe me, who think the makeup of a person's mind and the formation of his character to be so totally from the heavens that there remains nothing peculiar to his nature, nothing inherited from his parents, and, lastly, nothing left to the method of his rearing. Behold these very dwellings of the Muses, under whose more bountiful protection we happily enjoy this philosophic leisure. Imagine that from Italy, Spain, France, Denmark, Belgium, and Poland an excellent community of scholars has gathered here. Do you think that you could find a greater variety of natural dispositions among these than in your own country?

"Therefore turn wherever you wish, I do not see either how such a short travel, a true foot-and-a-half walk, merits the name 'journey,' or how anything useful to the traveler will finally emerge from it (except for observing the teaching of illustrious men such as Whitaker, Reynolds, and Junius). I am certain that I would have properly termed as 'travelers' only your Drake, and Cavendish, and the Portuguese Sebastian del Cano who, for example, recently measured out this whole world on their ocean voyages. Nor, in truth, will I begrudge this name to Christopher Columbus, who discovered the West Indies, or to Ferdinand Magellan who discovered the Moluccas, or to Francisco Pizarro and Almagro, who discovered the province of Peru, or lastly, to Hugh Willoughby, who first was able to reveal the Arctic continent; nor to any of those, whoever they were, who either discovered new worlds by dangerous investigation or settled such discoveries. And in truth (for I may confess to you freely), I do not know exactly what sort of heroic venture my mind impels me to attempt: one that will astonish this age and will make posterity always recall my memory with gratitude."

Here Beroaldus was silent, and blushed, as if he had let something rather audacious or secret slip out. At that Drogius, gently smiling, inquired, "So truly, Beroaldus, why won't you dare to reveal it? Or is it

perhaps your desire to twist the minds of your listeners, held in suspense
so long, a little while longer on the rack of curious and anxious questioning? Or finally, is it that you are afraid to have this modest secret,
which has thus far lurked, hidden away in your breast, divulged to so
5   many ears? Whatever it may be, we have honest faces, faithful hearts, and
ears eager to hear. Nowhere will the plan of so difficult an undertaking
be revealed more safely, nowhere more suitably."

"Truly, you interpret my silence badly, Drogius," answered Beroaldus, "mixing it with a number of conjectures. Because great undertak-
10   ings never proceed without a great apparatus and a long preamble of
ambiguous terms (like princes who are not accustomed to appear without a crowd of attendants), I seem to have thrust before you naked, all of a
sudden, and without any warning, a plan of the greatest length—the
offspring of one year. Indeed, the very plan I now communicate to you I
15   had previously wanted to explain to you from its inception, gradually,
not without some appropriate preparation of your minds, without
which even those new designs that are most prudent may appear unpleasant and foolish. Now, truly, I see it is necessary for me to rush headlong into an inopportune speech about the whole matter (lest you suspect
20   my friendship). Therefore I will do it, by Hercules, somewhat earlier
than I had expected but surely no less willingly. Only imagine that a
long introduction, which I had in mind, had come first in regular order,
so that you miss nothing from my complicated plan.

"It has always disturbed me to meet constantly with *Terra Australis*
25   *Incognita* on geographical maps, and indeed, is there anyone who is not
completely senseless who would read this without some silent indignation? For if they know it to be a *continent,* and a *southern* one, how can
they then call it *unknown?* And if it be unknown, why have all the geographers described the form and the location to me? They are idle men
30   who can say it to be thus and still claim not to know it themselves! And
finally, who will not be vexed to remain ignorant of that which it is
profitable for us to know?

            Certainly, if no one ever
            . . . had trusted a fragile bark
35   To the angry sea

there would not be lacking to us any arguments by which we could
excuse this everlasting inertia (which we—good men—by no means

_____

33 Horace, book 1, ode 3.

conceal). And truly now, since the earth is exposed to the sea on all sides, there is scarcely a novice sailor who does not know the winds, straits, sea banks, and harbors of the whole world. Away with the excessive indolence of our times, the fear certainly unworthy even of women, and the vain suspicion which deprives us, not reluctantly, of another world.   5 Besides, why should we spread forth the cover of this ignorance? What do we hesitate for? What do we fear? Shadows? Ourselves?

"There is heaven, there is earth, and without a doubt there are men, perhaps no less cultured than we. Who would have expected such acuteness and skill among the Chinese? Why so many arts and such complex   10 scientific achievement? While we believe that all Muses have been limited to our occidental hovel, the Chinese laugh—not without reason —at the thought that there are other learned people besides themselves, for they contend that they are the only real seers. Europeans, they claim, are one eyed; all other mortals are blind men, no matter how many there   15 are. Or, if there be no men there, it is shameful for wise men to complain about solitude or to fear it. These candid thoughts have frequently inflamed my heart (and I grieve because I see this adventure neglected by all the rest), and from this has arisen a desire, more high minded than is common, for boldness."   20

"It is a great thing you embark upon, Beroaldus," said I, "and one scarcely of human capacity. Therefore, whatever of this plan may be accomplished, I congratulate you for your judgment, so worthy of you. But it is necessary to remember that great deeds, which ought not to be mentioned (in your judgment) without the preliminaries of many words   25 so that they may be favorably accepted, need an even greater preparation of thoughts. Have you considered all the dangers of so great an enterprise, the costs, the difficulty, the expectation, the conclusion, and everything else pertinent, and weighed them properly in your judgment? There is heaven, you say, but perhaps you can scarcely see it through the   30 continuous darkness. There is earth, which you won't dare to tread upon perhaps, because of the multitude of beasts and serpents. There are men, but you would prefer to do without their company. What if some Patagonian Polyphemus were to tear you to pieces and then straightaway devour the throbbing and still-living parts? Where would our rash in-   35 vestigator of the earth be then? It's certainly safe to contemplate those things, but not—if you're in your right mind—to try to experience them."

"But don't you know," Beroaldus retorted, "don't you know, my

14 *Chinese proverb.*

friend, that opposite my unknown land lies the Cape of Good Hope? We
must certainly dare, and we must certainly hope. Those apparitions of
danger may frighten weak minds, but they serve to excite bolder spirits:
for if fears were taken into account, no one would know any part of a
country, or of a city, or even of a house except his own. It was for this one
reason that that American continent was so long hidden, and moreover I
believe it would still be hidden today had God himself not lately sent us a
dove from heaven, who, plucking an olive branch from this land, taught
us that there still remains some land left that is insufficiently concealed
by the waves; ought not his name inherit perpetual fame and holiness
from the thanks of his successors? Indeed, as long as there is an earth,
likenesses of him will be circulated, which we will gaze upon, not without a certain reverence and astonishment. Nor, truthfully, does it sound
to me any less honorific to be called *Discoverer of the New World* than to
be called *conqueror*. Why shouldn't we win the same success and the
same glory? Moreover, the famous and often repeated prophecy of the
tragedian Seneca does not a little excite my mind, a prophecy which now
rests to be fulfilled by us:

> . . . Time will come
> After a long span of years, when the Ocean
> Will relax the bonds of circumstances
> And reveal a great continent.

What could more clearly or happily declare the outcome of my planned
voyage?"

    Here Drogius interrupted and said, "Be careful, Beroaldus, when
you erect so lofty a structure on so poor and slender a foundation. That
Columbus of yours has fulfilled a long time ago whatever your tragic
poet prophesied under divine inspiration. These are the 'long span of
years.' It is obviously the great American continent that has emerged at
this very time. What other age are you dreaming of, what other land?"

    "I know that this may be the feeling of the common people, but I
doubt it is true," Beroaldus replied, "and, if I'm not mistaken, I shall
prove my case so that either you will grant the complete falsity of that
feeling or deny that that was the prediction in question. Since every
prophecy refers to some future time, what if I can prove that the West
Indies were known in earlier times, so that consequently Seneca might
seem not so much to foretell a thing to come, as to relate what had been
done by others before him? Nothing is more convincing to me than that
some part of this western land was that golden Ophir which they say was

once explored by the sailing fleet of Solomon and Hiram in a three-year voyage. And truly, five conflicting opinions appear among the authors: the first, of Hrabanus Maurus and Nicolas de Lyra, places the land of Ophir in eastern India; the second, of Raphael of Volaterra, and even of Abraham Ortelius, fixes it on the island of Sofala in the Ethiopian Ocean, based upon the doubtful account of some unknown Ludovico of Venice; the third, of Gaspar Barreiros, proclaims that it was located somewhere in the lands of Pegu, Malacca, and Sumatra; the fourth, of Francisco Vatablus, relying on the testimony of Peter Martyr, supports Columbus, who believes that it was the island of Hispaniola; the fifth, and last, of Postellus, Goropius Becanus, and Benito Arias Montano, confidently states this region was in Peru. Of these, the last two, by far the most truthful of all the others, will do for us. Whichever of these two finally prevails, for my purposes I will have won either way—as I desire. And, indeed, concerning the first two theories, Gaspar Barreiros has so plainly refuted these that to add anything more would be superfluous. In respect to the third, all that remains is for me to move through these places one after the other and demonstrate that Sumatra, Malacca, and the golden Chersonesus have been incorrectly confused with the region of Ophir. It is sufficient, indeed, that the sacred pages teach that this Jewish fleet from Tyre took up an entire three years on its voyage. And those who sail from the Red Sea to Sumatra and back accomplish the whole trip in ten months or, at most, one full year. How do the times agree in this matter? What semblance of equality? What can Barreiros say for himself here? Perhaps the art of navigation was then not as well known as it is now, owing to the earnest labor of the Portuguese. And, exposed on all sides to the elements because of this imprecision and uncertainty, perhaps the unskilled sailors navigated the journey incorrectly. And from where then, my friend, does Solomon know of this most remote land? I believe you say, 'from the heavens.' And in truth I believe it is from heaven, as it is in all other matters. Very well, then, who would inform him there was a golden land, and even advise him to go there, and not constantly show him the way? Besides, it is certain that the duration of the journey is always fixed: never does the loaded fleet return sooner; never does it delay longer. And what seems to indicate the very great remoteness of the place is not the uncertain wanderings of the sailors but the fact that the name itself speaks plainly to us even now: transpose one letter and the sound itself can become ambiguous. You will seem com-

---

37 Ophir, Peru.

pletely incredulous and obstinate to me unless you confess that this land
of Indians was well explored long before the time of Seneca."

I answered, "It is plain that you're the victor, Beroaldus, and may
now fittingly enjoy your triumph. It is reasonable that this golden land
5   was rescued from an earlier obscurity by the efforts of Solomon, the
wisest king, and then opened by his fleet, but do you expect this whole
region to have been equally well known from this time onward? Certainly, given the excessive remoteness of those peoples—with whom
none but the Jews ever had commerce—or the great difficulty of trade,
10   couldn't memory of them have vanished before the time of the Romans?
In truth, if you will concede that fact, the discovery of this land has
occurred according to your opinion and according to Seneca's prophecy,
too."

"But I will not succumb so easily, my friend," Beroaldus responded,
15   "and I yield not at all to these empty shadows of reason. On the contrary,
what strengthens my foothold even more are exactly your so opportune
doubts. For the histories—witnesses of truth—are not entirely silent but
convey knowledge of this land of Ophir to the Romans and all the way to
their posterity. You know that between the time of Solomon and the
20   beginning of Carthage, 150 years, more or less, elapsed: and, in truth, the
Carthaginians—as Aristotle avows (which I cannot believe happened
when the city was still in its infancy)—after a lengthy voyage, found this
island (which cannot be any other) located beyond Gades in the Atlantic
Ocean. And they enacted a law (which is the reason why this most rich
25   and wealthy island was not occupied by Phoenician farmers and was not
known broadly to the rest of the world) that no one of their people
should emigrate there in the future, fearing, indeed, that the loveliness
and wealth of the place would allure citizens, and they might decide to
establish a second Carthage there, abandoning the seat of their home-
30   land. Since this was a report that the Greeks received from the Phoenicians, who would doubt that the Romans learned it by way of these two
peoples? Now, my friends, believe—if you wish—and affirm so clear a
truth with me, or—if you prefer—stick to your doubts. Certainly, to me
this would be the most persuasive argument that the huge land of Seneca
35   has been hidden until now and still awaits us, the most fortunate of
travelers, provided we are industrious and courageous.

"Behold, my world, I am coming to you now, after so many vows,
after so many delays. I am coming, I repeat, full of hope and confidence,
and in my boldness either to share you with the world or to share my
40   body with you. By all means, friends, rouse yourselves. If any spark of

ancient courage or any ambition to earn a glorious name still remains, dare to execute this deed! Be comrades with me in my voyage and sharers of my fortune. Away with those cold hearts, which have no taste for anything, except for something that involves no danger and no glory, hearts which no grave pleases that is not covered by their native soil. 'We shall hunger; we shall thirst; we shall sicken; we shall die.' Spiritless words, unworthy of philosophers, unworthy of travelers searching for other worlds and scorning this one! Nothing, indeed, is lacking except spirit. If you be men, submit yourself to this and take courage: persevere in this assault against weak imagination; gird yourselves for this journey, perhaps delightful, certainly distinguished, leading through many tortuous paths straight to immortal glory. But if not, sit at home, inactive and inglorious. I shall find other men who will favor and share my plan, whom you, perhaps—after the completion of this most prosperous enterprise—will envy too late."

So he said and, gazing at us with a countenance a trifle agitated, Beroaldus was silent. Nor did such a vehement oration from this impetuous young man leave us unmoved to thirst for both novelty and glory (from whose speech of a thousand paragraphs I have here cited barely its closing lines). Why should I belabor the matter? There is no need to recount separately what this man questioned, what that man said, what a third man did, or what we all prepared. We appointed the day; we embarked on the ship named The Phantasia; we set sail from port, not, however, without this voluntary and reciprocal courtesy: everyone hailed his loved ones along the way, and with their blessings took his leave.

Now after three days we reached the Belgian shore, and after the seventh day the shore of Aquitaine; there Drogius was snatched away from me to the village of Delft, and here Beroaldus to Montauban—both of them, to be sure, most unwillingly. However, they cajoled me either to press miserably on, a solitary traveler, against innumerable and unknown perils or be exposed to the derisive laughter of my friends after so great an expectation.

However, my own unexpected solitude did not terrify me. I continued on lightheartedly: and after two years, having left behind the Fortunate Isles, the coast of Africa, the land of the Monomotapensi, and the Cape of Good Hope, I greeted the Black Cape of Crapulia.

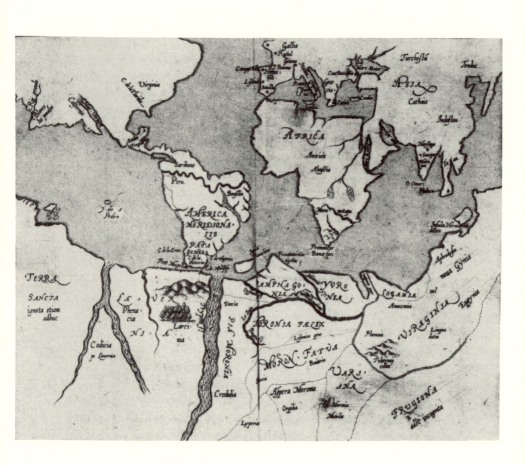

THE WORLD

BOOK ONE

CRAPULIA

CHAPTER 1
The Location of the Region

Crapulia is a large and splendid region—bounded on the north by the   5
Ethiopian Ocean, on the east by Loçania and Viraginia, on the south by
Moronia Felix, and on the west by the Tryphonian Swamp—customarily depicted by modern geographers in the same part of the world
where the prodigious monster RUC snatches a whole elephant in his
claws and devours it at one gulp.   10

The soil is very fruitful, enjoying an extremely favorable climate,
and I, not without some silent envy, often lamented that it did not have
more worthy inhabitants. Its longitude extends to 74 degrees, while its
latitude, to be sure, extends to 60 degrees. Eleven degrees distant from the
Cape of Good Hope, it lies almost directly opposite Africa. It is com   15
monly divided into two provinces, Pamphagonia and Yvronia: the
former with the same longitude and latitude, by and large, as our beloved
Great Britain (something which should not seem a bad sign to anyone);
the latter, however, with the same longitude and latitude as the two
Germanies. Both are under the same ruler and the same laws; nor are the   20
people's customs, or their disposition, or their appearance at all dissimilar.

---

5 *Crapula indicates a vice, from which the name of this region derives, and it is also
appropriate for excess drinking: because* κραιπάλη *in Greek means either* καπήνου πάλη,
"afflicted in the head," or ἀπὸ τοῦ τὸ κάρηνον πάλλεσθαι, *"shaking the head," since the
top of the head shakes from wine, especially from seasoned wine, Pliny, book 21, chapter 2,
or from* ἀπο τοῦ πηλοῦ, *"clay," which, as Phocion says, signifies wine in the language of
the poets, but those who gorge themselves either with food or wine are called* crapulari.
Hence we have divided this land into two provinces: Pamphagonia, *a well-known word, it
embraces the most voracious gluttons;* Yvronia, *from the French word* Yvre [ivre] *or*
Yvrongne [ivrogne], *which means intoxicated,* soft-headed drunkards.   6 *In Spanish*
Loçania *signifies* luxury; *it is placed next to Crapulia since those who indulge too much
because of their fondness for good living are more inclined to sensual pleasure:* "Without
Ceres & Bacchus," *etc.*   7 *Next to it lies* Moronia, *since, if the poet is correct,* "A fat
stomach begets a thin mind."   7 *Seek the reason for its name and location in the
description of* Lavernia.   9 *Who is considered the local deity because of his incredible
voraciousness.*

CRAPULIA

Chapter 2
Pamphagonia. *Land of Gluttons*

Pamphagonia is almost triangular, in the shape of the Greek letter Δ, not unlike ancient Egypt: encircled with mountains and hills protruding skyward. The soil is so extremely rich that the birds which usually   5
flock together here—thanks to its food—if they remain here for three months, because of their crammed weight, are unable to cross the mountains and unable to escape the hands of pursuers. Nor are they any less fat, after such a time, than the Italian Ortolani and Beccafici. Moreover, we know what occurs even in Scotland, that from fallen leaves geese are   10
produced; and—according to the testimony of a most honorable old ambassador from our country—it is extremely probable that in the world of the Euroboreali a lamb is generated and thrust out of the earth joined to a stalk and eats the adjacent grass. Who would not easily allow himself to be persuaded that this actually happens? But the fish as well,   15
which are most abundant along this coast, are so extremely ravenous (either because of the nature of the place and the custom of the people or because, like Nero's turbot, they perceive beforehand the honor of so magnificent a burial) that as soon as a fishhook is cast into the water they immediately flock to it, not unlike the miserable little souls who crowd   20
about Charon's boat, according to Lucian. And those who are not snagged by the hook cling together (like coal and iron miners, who normally yell for a rope to be lowered when the dimming of the lamp foretells deadly vapors) and plead to be drawn up.

In addition, the harbors are most convenient to this people (if not to   25
anyone else), serving no other purpose except the transporting and importing of edibles, for which the people normally exchange excess sheep pelts. Nor can any inhabitant export anything that might seem to pertain—even indirectly—to the palate. I saw no trees there except those

---

3 *In like manner the Nile shapes the central region of that country, which once bore the name Egypt, whence the ancient inhabitants bore the name Egyptians. These same people revered the ibis very highly because an image of their land appeared in the imprint of his foot.* 10 Barnacles; *however, others prefer the explanation that worms are created from waterlogged wood which has rotted for a long time, and the geese arise from these worms.* 13 *If what nature produces astounds, that can't be helped: the softest fleece of that animal, handsome nearly beyond measure, is reserved for the Duke of Muscovy and is called a* Samarcandean pelt: *it grows in the Horda Zavolhensus, a Scythian land. Julius Scaliger writes about this lamb in exercise 59 to Cardan, as does Baron von Herberstein, and Libavius in his treatise on the vegetable lamb.* 18 *Juvenal, satire 4, "and consume a turbot reserved for your reign. It wanted to be caught, etc."*

bearing fruit. They detest mountain ash, oak, willows, and similar types
of sterile and unprofitable plants since they don't impart anything besides shade, which is barren and useless. All the hedges there (which can
also be seen scattered throughout Yvronia) are entwined with the vines
5   of hops: a custom the Welsh and the Lombards have learned from this
region.

Frugiona, a land somewhat more remote, claims this region for
itself, according to the ancestral right of its forefathers, because they say
that in Saturn's age, the Frugionan princes had jurisdiction over this
10 entire area, and they occupied it as their own. At that time, because their
more simple ancestors were fed by beech trees [*fagus*], the whole region
was named Fagonia. But now, customs having advanced and changed,
and the yoke of earlier authority having been dispensed with, the natives
desired something that would approximate the ancient name and thus
15 called the place Pamphagonia.

Chapter 3
The First Province of Pamphagonia

The province of Frivianda—to begin with the closest, lest I seem arbi-
trary to some local wit—is too warm to produce real gourmands since
20 the farthest point of land, which other geographers name the Promontory of the Southern Continent, is about the same latitude as the southernmost part of Castile and 42 degrees distant from the Equator. The
inhabitants are swarthy skinned, with frizzy hair, and they seek neither
quantity nor numbers of edibles as much as they seek delicacy. In this
25 same promontory, which we will call Black (because the region is full of

5 *The inhabitants of Shropshire and Worcestershire; where* "every hedge is frequently
loaded with Crustumian and Syrian pears and heavy warden-pears" Virgil, Georgics,
2.   7 Moronia *interposes itself between Crapulia and Frugiona: although, strictly
speaking, this word pertains to clothing,* Varro, De Lingua Latina, book 4, I have used it in
an extended sense, deriving it from Frugi, "worthy," which the French, most expressively,
term Homme de bien.   18 *The French call more delicate cuisine* viandes friandes; *aptly
combining them, we have made one word from two. We have situated this province,
moreover, at the threshold of this region, for since the inhabitants possess a more delicate
and queasy palate than their countrymen, it could not have been located in too much heat.
Those farther south we have, in truth, conceived as more gluttonous because of their
innate coldness.*   25 *In imitation of Pliny, in whom the* White Cape *occurs twice:
the one in Africa, preface to book 3; the other in Phoenicia, not far from Tyre, book 5,
chapter 19.*

smoke, partly due to the very thick vapors of the place, partly due to the proximity of Tierra del Fuego, which, according to the agreement of all geographers, lies quite near it on the East), is the city of Cucina, with very high buildings, though poorly constructed and ill smelling. Perhaps the people who settled Cacuchina at one time named their colony after this place.

Here is a famous temple of the divine Omasius, in volume a most vast edifice indeed, furnished with a thousand altars and an equal number of fireplaces, which burn perpetually (if you except the celebrations for RUC). In the middle of this city rises a pyramid which excels everything else that could be constructed by a man's hand, in height only a little inferior to those structures of Memphis, called the Cheminea Tower. Since it is visible from far away it gives the signal for war to the adjacent region, but while our countrymen, having filled a tar barrel, set it afire on the highest mountain as a beacon to warn our people of the danger from the advancing enemy, they, on the contrary, prepare for war when the smoke *stops*: because once the perpetual smoke has ceased giving off its black circles, then it is an indication that the enemy is approaching; it is the Hambrians in particular, who, above all others (to use Apuleius's testimony), are the greatest terror to these people.

Most of the villages are under the Friviandans' control and recognize the rule of this capital city. Charbona is the largest village, and—something you will never see anywhere else—it is located under the earth. Above its sterile soil is built Favillia, a little less imposing. This omits Tenaille, the most narrow hamlet, and the most spacious, Batillum, equal to prominent towns. On the west Assadora, Marmitta, and Culliera are subservient to it, all of them splendid because of the number of visitors. Of these towns, Marmitta is brushed by the River Livenza, a burning torrent which boils up twice every 24 hours, just like that English fountain named the Peak.

---

3 *Cucina is Italian for* kitchen, *whence the English word, influenced by the Italian pronunciation.*   7 *To see who he was, look in chapter 11 of this book.*   9 *Immediately after the religious festival which is held yearly for the local deity; these celebrations undoubtedly correspond to ours before* Lent.   12 Caminus, *French for* chimney, *perhaps from* chemin, *"a road," since it furnishes a path for the smoke to escape.*   14 *In English,* Beacons.   19 Hambre *is Spanish for* hunger; *however, for a description of this island of hunger see chapter 12 of this book. Let us not overload the margin excessively with the meanings of proper names. An index at the end of the book will explain them: the reader is referred there.*

CHAPTER 4
The Second Province of Pamphagonia

Next comes the most pleasant part of Pamphagonia, the Golosinius
Tract, overloaded with grapes, almonds, figs, olives, red apples, citrons,
5   and finally aromatic nuts, through which serenely flows the pellucid
River Oglium. Here lies Marza-pane, a beautiful city with towers tall
and gilded, but too exposed to its enemies. Next to it overhang the
Zuckerius Hills, from whose bowels a certain substance sweet, white,
and hard is mined, something scarcely known in prior ages, which the
10 ancients sought from the reeds of Arabia and India. Here you will see
very few adults who are not toothless and do not have a most detestable
breath.

Close by is Seplasium, a small city, admitting no citizens except
those who make medicine boxes or deal in spices. The city is very well
15 known to the Viraginians, with whom they daily transact a huge business, and especially because of the Loçanians, who exchange crystal
mirrors for their lozenges and ointments. The location of the place, as
well as the generosity of the heavens, favors their profession, for periodi-
cally this whole region is thoroughly covered with little aromatic lozenges
20 that fall abundantly, just like large hailstones, which I consider the same
exhalation as that honeydew, which we often see—particularly in the
springtime—wet the oak trees in our country. Only it differs in con-
sistency, for whereas our honey is spattered in drops, these droplets grow
larger in the cold of the middle atmosphere, and when they hit the
25 ground they rebound.

CHAPTER 5
The Third Province of Pamphagonia

At the fifty-fifth parallel we come upon the Lecanican Plain, the very
bowels of Pamphagonia, where the first city, Cibinium, appears to us,
30 washed by the somewhat acidic waters of the Assagion River, in whose
forum you can see a tomb which—as I conjectured from the remains of

---

3 *Spanish for* "The coast of sweet-meates." 8 Zucker, *German for* sugar. 9 *Scarcely
known in Galen's time.* 10 *Pliny, book 12, chapter 8.* 28 Λεκάνη *is Greek for*
plate; *this is therefore the* Plate Plain. 29 Cibinium *is a city in the Danube region, now
under Turkish jurisdiction; we were thinking of its meaning, not its location.*

the inscription—was of that Roman Apicius, a tomb certainly not elegant but ancient, sculptured in the form of a sea crab. And, it could very well be (no matter how much the testimony of Seneca hinders us) that this famous gourmand, after having vainly ventured to Africa seeking crabs larger than those provided by France, receiving a rumor of this shore, finally turned his ship hither and eventually perished here from intoxication. The Critics will understand.

Following advice I purposely pass over the most fertile fields of Offulia and Lardana; the most elegant of all the cities, Mortadella, whose site would have been most pleasing to me had it not rather often tasted more of sea salt than of water; the most fetid village of the entire district, Fourmagium; and—at the very borders of Yvronia—the most marshy city, Manteca.

I hasten to the metropolis of the whole region, which by itself, whether one considers the form of its buildings, or the customs of its people, or its patterns of life, or its laws, will be of the utmost value to the sagacious reader.

Chapter 6
The Metropolis of Pamphagonia and the Customs of the People

Here the villages, more than anywhere else, are extremely scarce, so that the traveler may justly conclude that all the villages have been devoured by the cities. The cities are not as numerous as they are exceedingly populous and huge: of which one readily hears that Artocreopolis is the mother city predominant. The tradition is that in the past there had been two most famous cities, Artopolis and Creatium, that for a long time had strongly contended with each other for first place (as is the custom with important people and places, so much so that the two most learned academies in the whole world are constraining themselves from that same most disgraceful dispute with difficulty—both of them my mother, and one of them even my wet nurse, true sisters).

Artopolis prized itself first because of its antiquity, and in truth, during Saturn's age it had no equal, nay even a rival. Creatium boasted of its splendor, loveliness, and power. At last a council was called, and by a vote of all the nobles, Creatium prevailed. I know it is the injustice of

---

1 *Volaterra, Anthropologia, book 13.*

the times that, although the head has been white with the snow of age for
quite some time, the judgment is that nothing should be granted to
simple antiquity in comparison to haughty and precocious novelty. The
other city, now utterly neglected, grew decrepit, so that today you can
discern no broken stones or vestiges of so magnificent a city; neither does
the Verolamium of our poet more justifiably find fault with the injustice
of the times and of men. Now, usurping honor for itself with a new name
by making a compound word reflecting both, Creatium called itself
Artocreopolis.

The city is not as elegant as it is large, and it is well fortified by a
moat, broad and deep, always filled with water, flowing through nearly
all the streets of the city, in which one can discern a thousand evenly
divided varieties of fish; on its surface swim swans, ducks, gulls, herons,
teals, and whatever other winged species water nourishes. Augsburg
wisely copied its canals from this place. This moat is called Gruessa: its
double walls were generously provided from a butcher's stall, from the
bones of cattle which are slaughtered here every day, erected in such a
manner that the larger support the whole pile like pillars. The smaller
ones are then placed on top, and the smallest, finally, fill in the cracks,
and the whole is joined together with cement made of egg whites—an
artificial wonder.

Their dwellings are neither beautiful nor, in comparison to other
cities, too loftily erected: so there is no need for any Augustus to issue an
interdict that "the height of the building should be less than 70 feet,"
which we read happened in Rome. Nor could there be any opportunity
for a Seneca or a Juvenal to complain about the construction of the
stairs. The citizens do not care for construction with beams and stair-
cases; they don't tolerate it, partly because of the weariness induced by
ascending, partly (and most importantly, since they are accustomed to
drink heavily) because of the danger of descending. Instead of tiles, these
buildings are skillfully roofed with the rather broad shoulder blades of
animals.

The cities admit none to citizenship except those who look after the
table in some way. Farmers, carpenters, millers, and butchers live in the
town as free men. However, those who grow their paunch to a certain
size are promoted to be full citizens, a position to which no one is admitted from the beginning except cooks, bakers, innkeepers, and the

---

6 *Spenser, Ruins of Time.*   24 *Strabo, Geography, book 5.*   26 *Controversiae, book
3.*   26 *Satire 3.*

most eminent senators of the city, who are chosen at a solemn yearly
ritual, not—as elsewhere—because of prudence, or riches, or the abundance of their beards, but because of the size of their stomachs; and the
more one gains, the more highly he is promoted. Thus I saw some from
the basest and most obscure villages in the city come to be, by their own   5
merit, awarded citizenship and finally grow to the most famous honor of
the city, the rank of Senator. However, if their figures should waste away
to leanness because of either illness (which often happens) or age, they
lose all their previous honors along with their flesh.

I was completely amazed that the streets in such an indifferent city   10
were paved with marble. Then I guessed that they were paved because it
was a little less laborious and because it would be dangerous for the citizens to raise their feet too high on account of the uneven height of
cobblestones. Also, it was so that the sedan chairs of the senators could be
drawn more easily; nor, indeed, do they ever go to the forum or to public   15
banquets on foot, on horseback, or even in litters, due to their weight.
They are conveyed to and fro only in huge coach chairs, running on four
wheels, particularly since in this manner they can be conducted back
home safely confined in their seats, shaking and covered with foam.

At the four gates in each quarter of this round city, four senators sit   20
every day. Called *Buscadores,* their purpose is to examine carefully those
who come in and go out: those who go out, in case they dare to leave
fasting, which the senators can easily guess from the distention of their
bellies. When this is confirmed they make the accused eat two dinners.
Those returning, on the other hand, are examined to see whether they   25
carry something with them as they return: for it is unlawful for anyone
either to leave without a full stomach or to return without full hands.

Every month in that land there is a day appointed by law—certainly
with no protest—when prescribed feasts occur, during which all the
senators of the city must be present. Immediately after the dinner is   30
finished (because nobody is allowed to vote without having eaten first),
they discuss public affairs. Pythonos-come is the name of the magnificent
building. Everyone knows his own seat, and he has a pot stored in a box
reserved for him. There, after they have prepared themselves with the
hottest wine and the most pungent spices, everyone reclines at the table   35
according to his rank. Rare delicacies are always served at the first course;

---

21 *Spanish for* Inquisitores.   32 *A place in Asia, where the storks fly as soon as they
enter the country and whichever one arrives last they tear to pieces. Pliny, book 10, chapter
23. The same in Solinus. Others incorrectly read* Phririonis cumen *from Strabo.*

indeed, they believe it is silly not to devour the best courses with the greatest appetite. Nor is it permitted—as is most customary with us— for them to serve boar, sheep, goat, and lamb cut up in parts. Instead (which was perhaps taught them by the old Romans) the sweating
5   servants bring in the whole animal on big serving carts, like those I remember having read about in Petronius. No one stands up before six hours without giving offense, because they eat and drink little by little for a long time, obviously for the same reason that that daring and most notorious glutton, once upon a time, is said to have wished he had the
10 neck of a crane.

They measure the time for departing from this banquet with a door in the palace large enough to accommodate the men's empty stomachs; through which narrow bounds the arriving guests enter, and having finished with the banquet, everyone tries to leave through these same
15 limits. Whoever sticks fasts is let out another way. But if he can go out just as easily as when he came in, fasting, the Magistrate of Manners makes him wait and, receiving him a second time, makes him eat against his will until he is unable to exit. I would think Wilfred's Needle—a fine examination of holiness—is certainly a comparable example, well known
20 to modern Catholics.

They have gardens of untold acres there, but all unsightly; every one is inferior to those of Adonis and Alcinous, and truthfully even to that of Langius. If you were to expect the splendor and order of garden beds, or the most beautifully colored flowers, you would be disappointed. In-
25 stead, all you can discern here are radishes, garlic, cabbage, and musk- melons, which even richer Italy seeks from this place. So much sump- tuous food could entertain a hundred Pythagoreans at a table:

There one could see cabbages with noble heads,
And both kinds of scallions, and dwarf lettuce,
30   And beets helpful to a slow stomach.

There is also a public poorhouse in which as many as have contracted dropsy, or gout, or asthma from gluttony and drunkenness are sustained by the state. But those who have become toothless, either from age or from accident and incautious chewing, are sent off to the Island of
35 Sorbonia.

---

9 *Philoxenus, according to Aristotle in the Ethics.*   18 *Once upon a time in our country in* Bever Castle.   28 *Martial, book 3, epigram 47.*

You will see, indeed, that everyone of the richer folk employs many working as slaves, tending the fields and gardens and taking care of the most menial kinds of jobs: when they reach the right size, however, they are given their freedom. If any of these aristocrats of the kingdom should perish from drinking too much, he is then handed over to the slaves for consumption at one of these solemn feasts (since his entire body is a combination of the most select kinds of food), for it is unlawful that such a delicacy should be allowed to perish lying in the grave.

Men with fat and heavy bodies are objects of admiration, and no one is worthy to be kissed whose chin does not reach all the way to the middle of his chest and whose belly does not protrude and hang down to the lowest part of his knees. Nor is the case otherwise for women (whose form Italian women imitate to some degree, but which Barbarian women imitate almost perfectly); maidens are not permitted to marry until a public examination has been made and the men have decided that their hanging chins have reached their breasts.

All walk about nearly naked; nor do they care for clothes. Only the Magistrates, and those of higher ranks, are allowed to wear togas, made from the skin of whatever animal that person can devour at one sitting. However, each individual carries a knife and a very broad spoon fastened to his right hand. In front, on their chests, approximating what Virgil said, "they wear smooth-shorn napkins" with which, so that nothing might be wasted, they are able to catch little crumbs falling down and also wipe their mouths. In truth, the napkins are so excessively used that even the most eagle-eyed spectator would hardly be able to judge whether these napkins were once white or black.

They are extremely slow in thinking and most inept in all sciences; however, they are expert in every art that they trouble themselves with. The only schools in that place are those established by gourmandizers in which all children must be instructed immediately from tender youth in the arts of eating, drinking, and carving. At the time when I visited a certain Archisilenius, a most outstanding glutton, was the head and lectured upon, in place of Grammar, some fragments of a certain Apicius. In place of a library there is a public repository of tankards in which all the cups are arranged in graduated order within certain classes. Goblets and dishes are their books: for new recruits, the smaller; for adults, those somewhat larger. For this one, a small cup; for that one, a cup four

---

13 *Barbarian women, eager to grow fat, eat puppies.*   33–34 *According to the testimony of Suidas, this man has written books on gluttony.*

times larger; for a third, a pint. To this one a hen, to that a goose, to a
third a lamb or a leg of pork. Nor are they ever given permission to break
off their studies until everyone has completed his daily tasks, because if
they have progressed too little in gluttony in seven years they are banished
to the Famelica Islands; nor is it lawful to stay in school beyond that
time. And, indeed, doctors and anyone else who has prescribed a diet to
anyone are dispatched there. Whoever is ill (no matter how much Asclepiades objects) eats a radish, as Celsus commands, drinks a little hot
water, vomits, and is purged on the spot. Whatever one needs to recover
is provided by the public treasury.

There venison is counted among the greatest of delights, even though
they are quite unable to acquire it by hunting. Only deer coming to them
by their own accord are they able to entangle in their nets and snares. Yet
they consider swine the best and most useful of all animals, either because of the similarity of their natures, since they know it was solely
made for the table, or because, although it is not stuffed with the richest
of food, it nourishes and fattens the most swiftly of all animals.

Finally, who would believe that with such a profusion of food,
parsimony would persist? Indeed (I admit it should be least expected
here), I have seen the greatest saving of the tiniest morsels, such as
crumbs, bones, and bits of food. For the same reason they maintain no
dogs, or cats, or hawks, or anything else carnivorous. On the contrary,
when someone takes the trouble to cook a pigeon or a capon for himself,
he must first remove the raw corn buried for a long time in the deepest
recesses of its little stomach and set it in front of the others, a custom
which today's Venetians have opportunely learned from these people.

Furthermore, if anyone keeps even a trifle of food until it rots, he is
immediately bound to the stake, except that venison may be laid aside
until it is enveloped by a certain wooly mold, and (though it is nearly
impossible to speak about because it nauseates me) they generally keep
their cheese until the whole is destroyed by worms. Then these most
delicate feasters avidly devour the living vermin themselves and the very
same rotten, disgusting food—with a little sugar sprinkled over. I certainly wonder why the lower Germans borrowed that most wretched
custom from this land. The region abounds with rivers that flow uncer-
tainly, shifting back and forth because of the infinite quantity of sewage.
But always at the beginning of January, and at the end of February, they
overflow their banks and threaten the neighboring pastures.

14 *Plato Comicus, according to Clement of Alexandria, Stromateis, 7.*

CHAPTER 7
The Wars of the Pamphagonians

The Pamphagonians wage an implacable war against two enemies: the Famelica Islanders, or the Hambrians, and the Frugionans. The first are located not far away to the west in the Ethiopian Ocean, as we shall mention in the appropriate place; the second are somewhat more remote, separated by the largest part of Moronia and a section of Viraginia.

The histories relate that in the beginning the Hambrians, confederated with the Larcinians, rather often invaded this land and one time even conquered it. At that time the inhabitants fled to the woods and to some subterranean caves where they hid themselves desperately until their deities, finally moved by their prayers and vows, caused this new race to die by their own throats: because after such an unexpected change of locale they gorged themselves so full that, having contracted disorders from their gluttony, within three years they perished—every single one—by their own hands. Also, many times the ancient inhabitants, the Frugionans, have vainly tried to set foot in their land, but since Fortune favors the inferior side in most cases, the Frugionans have suffered defeat because of the Pamphagonians' too fortunate success in repelling them.

They proceed to battle, especially the front lines (since this vanguard cannot escape by flight), covered with ox hides, sheepskins, swine pelts, and goatskins: so that to you, observing from afar, they appear as some cattle being led to water. They are nearly all armed with barbecue spits and kitchen utensils, though there are those who carry missile launchers and bows fashioned from the ribs of the largest oxen. But the Yvronians, more belligerent by nature, aid them when necessary, without whose opportune support the Pamphagonians would doubtless have succumbed long ago.

CHAPTER 8
Ucalegonium, a Free City

Not yet mentioned, but not to be passed over in silence, is Ucalegonium,

---

32 *City of idleness. That Ucalegon in Virgil, formed from* οὐκ ἀλέγων, *having few cares, as our Professor Downes once taught us in his lectures.*

a free city, possessing the greatest power and located at the very border of
the Lecanican Plain, toward Moronia. No place in Pamphagonia exalts
itself either for greater antiquity or for greater splendor: whose citizens
(so they say) lead an existence more fortunate than any Monk's. What-
5 ever could help them to enjoy life they possess in abundance.

In the first place, the city is superlatively fortified by its location and
completely impregnable, so it is justifiably able to mock the vain plotting
and invasions of the enemy. It is situated on a rock of the greatest height
and maximum steepness that extends for ten German miles above a
10 hollow valley through which the Oysivium (a river or a swamp, I don't
know which) creeps along at the most sluggish pace. There is only one
means available to the inhabitants for ascending, an unusual path. Nor
is it some winding road, as might be expected, but by a lowered rope and
a wicker basket (which is the custom for air shafts).

15 The birds peculiar to this place supply nourishment for these people,
but they are not to be found anywhere else. The inhabitants call them
Gutiges, birds not unlike coots and similar to them in three ways: for
besides supplying eggs along with their flesh, they supply such an over-
abundance of fish to feed their offspring, while they build their nests day
20 by day, that they nearly bury the people, and the twigs collected for these
bird nests serve to feed the Ucalegonians' fires throughout the year. What
more could you want? In addition, the citizens stuff their beds with these
birds' down and softest plumes.

An interior region produces the most abundant grape vines and the
25 richest wheat fields; nor is there anything else that the Ucalegonians care
for that they do not have. Therefore, here the people possess a most indifferent disposition or, according to Apuleius's meaning, are truly un-
concerned: they dine, they sleep, they rise, they breakfast, they lie down.
Here by Sybarite law live in exile not only all Frenchmen but also every
30 kind of artisan because the swine alone serve as farmers, as was the case
with the ancient Egyptians; there is no need for any other workers. However, there are servants for the richer: one to open the master's eyes gently
when he awakes; another to cool him with a small fan while he eats; a
third to put morsels in his mouth; a fourth to draw out his urine; a fifth
35 to tighten and loosen his belt. It is enough for the master to chew the
food placed in his mouth, to digest, and to evacuate. Other cities such as

---

13 *This can be observed in almost all respects in a certain castle in Scotland.*   27 *Instead of fat, he called it a* heedless sheep.

Lirona and Roncara shelter themselves under the protection of the Ucalegonians and enjoy the same privileges, except that the inhabitants are
always sleeping and—as Pliny says about bears—are overwhelmed by
such a deep slumber that they cannot be awakened even when beaten,
and from this idleness they grow miraculously fat.   5

CHAPTER 9
The Laws of the Kingdom

The magnificent building of Pythonos-come, most handsomely constructed and opened on all sides by windows, displays the inscription,
"To leisure and to order," on its facade, written in gold letters. In the   10
middle of the columns hang sacred tablets of laws, bearing approximately these regulations:

1. Eating only once a day shall be a crime.
2. He that carelessly overturns a full dish or a goblet shall, while
standing upright, devour with the tiniest spoon a dish of broth   15
placed at his ankles.
3. No one shall eat alone, lest by eating privately he violate the laws
of the table with impunity; citizens are to eat in the streets or in
front of windows opened on all sides.
4. Whoever shall omit a meal by sleeping a whole four hours and   20
thus defraud the deity shall be obliged to eat twice.
5. If one's mouth be full, it shall be satisfactory to answer with
one's forefinger.
6. A party guilty of treason shall perish by starvation; the punishment for a party guilty of a lighter transgression shall be the loss of a   25
tooth.
7. Whatever cook shall prepare food in such a manner that it cannot
be eaten shall be bound at the public stake, near which shall be
hung the half-raw or half-burned meat until some miserable and
starving onlooker shall eat it all up.   30

1 Liron *means* dormouse *in Spanish.*   1 Roncar, *Spanish deriving from the Latin, the
Latin in turn deriving from the Greek* ρευχειν, to snore.   3 *Pliny, book 8, 36.*   10 *Part
of a saying of Synesius:* "The god walks leisurely and at the same time orderly." *Under this
was a verse in the Pamphagonian language:* "This is a place of joy; depart far from here all
sorrowful ones." *This inscription is in Bologna at the entrance to the estate of* Casaltutula.

8. To belch in any manner shall not only be lawful (as some rulers decreed) but honored as well; whoever shall have belched most manfully, clearly, and powerfully shall be assigned as the leader of the next feast.

9. Whoever holds his breath while his girth is being measured shall automatically be considered unmanageable and be condemned to a day in prison without a meal, put behind bars in such a way that he might gaze upon the rest of the noblemen eating (for some this punishment has been deadly).

10. How much anyone consumes shall be measured weekly at the magistrate's, so that if he eats less than what is prescribed, the penalty that fits his crime shall be imposed.

Those who sin the least seriously are confined for a whole day to jail, which they call the Temple of Famine, in contrast to the House of Bread of our countrymen. This prison is placed outside the city, as Asclepius's temple was in Rome, not for the sake of health, as Plutarch said in reference to it, but so that the very damned might not even be fed by the aroma of cooking. Its walls are painted very realistically with the lively representations of all dishes (to stimulate the appetite of the prisoners in vain), from which one should search for the Chambers of Meditation of present-day Jesuits.

These people do not employ money, nor, indeed, do they consider such dead and unsavory metals of much value. Rather, they buy and sell goods only by barter, which Aristotle teaches was done in antiquity. Thus, two sparrows customarily sell for a starling; two starlings for a thrush; two thrushes for a hen; two hens for a goose; two geese for a lamb; two lambs for a calf; two calves for a goat; and two goats for a cow. The same holds true for vegetables and fish—by a set of values established long ago. To be sure, the magistrates oversee this so that nothing bad or too high priced is forced upon the purchaser.

Chapter 10
The Religion of the People

They abhor Jove because when he thunders he sours the wine, and be-

---

1 *Suetonius, Claudius.*   5 *See the following chapter for the reason behind this law.*
24 *Politics.*

cause he drowns the produce of the fields with unseasonable rainstorms.
I saw there an elegantly built temple in honor of the God of Time, the
most devouring of all things, in which Saturn is sculptured with astonishing skill on the tomb of his children. The day before Ash Wednesday
they make a sacrifice to the deity of the place—for they acknowledge   5
almost no other divinity—who appears once a year in the shape of an
extremely large and voracious bird (the inhabitants call him RUC)
expecting their votive offerings. They offer whole hecatombs of raw
meat to him in the following manner.

There is a vast Plain of Lecanica, ringed on the south by mountains.   10
On the appointed day all the inhabitants make their way here, leading
an innumerable flock of all sorts of livestock, cattle, and poultry: elephants, rhinoceroses, and camels, which they fatten just for this day (nor
is it their custom to keep or fatten so useless an animal for any other
reason), as well as oxen of the largest size, boars, sheep, goats, and every   15
kind of bird, shorn and defeathered, and confined, as it were, in this
gigantic enclosure. The people, orderly arranged on the sides of the
mountain, as though in the seats of some theater, await their deity's
arrival on bended knees.

Finally, with an enormous clamor, and the most disconcerting   20
rumbling and belching, you will glimpse this sacred bird from afar, with
a hooked beak, curved talons, gleaming eyes—and with an astonishing
troop of Harpies, ravens, vultures, and hawks crowding around on all
sides. With a horrendous hissing they fly closer, and, owing to their
number, they blot out the sun and the sky with the shade of their wings,   25
like a dense cloud which covers the valley. Three times they circle the
plain, while the inhabitants shout, pray, tremble, and rejoice. The
leader of the birds chooses prey for himself, selecting from the whole
multitude whatever arouses his palate the most. One time he snatches
two oxen, the next time he grabs an elephant. Then immediately the rest   30
of the birds land on the remaining flock, each according to its own habits
and appetite. You will observe this one loaded down with a calf, that one
with a lamb, another with a boar, still another with a goose or a swan.
After this is completed, all of them—eager to escape the eyes of the spectators—fly away, not without the harmonious applause of all the people.   35
Whatever remains (which, of course, must necessarily be very much) is
consumed—as their piety requires—that very same day by the people in
attendance. With this food they stuff themselves so excessively that for

35 *Into the forests of Larcinia, and there they live: see book 4, chapter 4.*

nearly 40 days they abstain from meat, during which time they are fed
with fish—but cooked in wine and spices at far greater expense—and
with Golosinian specialties, so that they may both restore themselves a
bit by so many varieties of food and return to meat, so long neglected,
5   with a sharper appetite. I would guess the 40-day religious fast in the
regions of the Papacy may have come into practice from here.

CHAPTER 11
The Election of the Grand Duke

I hasten to the palace of the Grand Duke, to which my spirit opportunely
10   led me on that very day when the new prince was being elected, according to the custom of the country. Situated exactly in the middle of an
isthmus between the two provinces is a most splendid and expansive
citadel, which they say, once upon a time, a certain giant named Omasius
had constructed, no mate of the one whose effigy—cut out of the nearby
15   hills—our Academics gaze upon and marvel at but rather a monster of a
man whose two molars, scarcely smaller than a human head, I believe I
saw dug out of a certain well in Cambridge. That tooth found on the
shore of Utica, written about by Sigebertus, is clearly inferior. Indeed, in
comparison to this man, that famous Orestes of Pliny, or that Orion of
20   Plutarch, was a dwarf. Rather, imagine an Antaeus of 60 cubits, or
imagine that man mentioned by Boccaccio of 200 cubits—as could be
conjectured by the hipbone—whose body was dug up not far from
Drepanum. I would believe him to be his twin brother.
    It is clear that he first subjugated that land, previously under the
25   jurisdiction of the Frugionans, ejected the prior inhabitants, and brought
new people and new laws. They believe his soul adopted the form of an
extremely monstrous bird, according to the delusion of Pythagoras, and
every year on the appointed day they venerate him, under this assumed
name, as we have related. He is revered by the miserable rabble no dif-
30   ferently than Mohammed is everywhere worshiped by his Turks. Here,
in the spacious hall of the palace, you may see a monument sacred to his
memory, a statue of considerable height, only a bit higher than the
ancient bronze Colossus of Lysippus, and next to it the tomb, on which I

---

19 *Seven cubits, Pliny, book 7, chapter 16.*   19 *Sixteen cubits, which, however, was*
believed to be the height of Otus.   33 *Or the statue of Chares, a pupil of this Lysippus,*
70 cubits in height.

saw certain inscriptions, but so corroded by hostile time that it was difficult to discern the words or their sense, just as Ovid has said:

> . . . but long existence has destroyed it,
> And prolonged age injures even stone.

So stood the remains of the inscription: 5

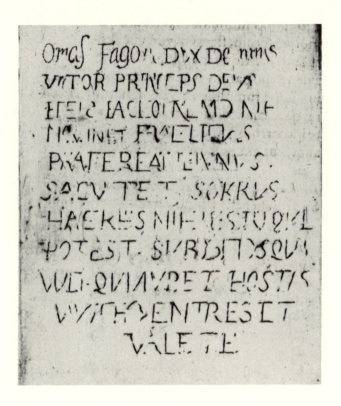

I propose the following reconstruction; let the Reader judge:

> I, Omasius, the leader, lord, victor, prince, and god of Fagonia lie
> here: let no one mention my name fasting, or pass by hungry, or
> salute me sober: Let him who can be my heir; let him who wishes be
> my subject; let him who dares be my enemy. Live ye gluttons and   10
> farewell.

This palace belongs to the Duke, an office which that first ruler

wanted to be enjoyed by no one dynasty—as elsewhere—but to be always
unsettled and ever changing. Thus it is permissible for any one of the
most honorable families of the kingdom, whose number is great—Mentones, Buccones, Ventricones, Palatini—to be a candidate for the Duke's
5   office and, according to merit, claim it. The Duke is elected in this
manner: every year a solemn contest is organized, which is, of course,
executed not with lances, or chariots, or oars but with teeth. He who
prevails in that contest, besides the honor of a crown of vines, is hailed
from that moment as the next steward to the Duke. At the end of the
10   contest everyone rises, and the victor—his hands touching the sacred
tomb of Omasius—invokes Bacchus and Saturn, and the departed spirits
of Omasius, that he will execute this following contest without fraud or
deceit. Next, each contender enters the theater in his turn, hoping that
on this day the competition will not be too keenly carried out.
15   At last, the new steward steps forth carrying a golden girdle, ap-
propriately studded with huge gems and indeed of immense length. The
natives call it the Sacred Belt of State, on which I noticed the saying
woven: "Nothing if not in excess." First of all, last year's ruler dons the
belt and marks the size of his stomach; following him the rest of the
20   nobles step forward, each according to his rank: whoever is actually able
to force this belt without distending his belly or holding his breath, so
that another hole is deemed necessary, is saluted as the new Duke of
Crapulia with the greatest applause and acclamation of the people.
Immediately, on bended knees the royal cupbearer presents a huge
25   amphora to him and bids that he drink a health to his people. Having
snatched up the vessel and uncovered it he delivers a speech to his
people: a suitable one, if he is able; if not, at least a bland and flattering
one. I applied my ear and my mind trying to catch his address, but owing
to their guttural speech I shuddered at the sound and did not compre-
30   hend the sense. Consequently, an interpreter gave me a summary of the
entire oration:
        After he had given great thanks to Bacchus, the goddess Carnea, and
however many black deities there are, and especially to the bounty of the
Imperial Stomach that had today elected him as the highest leader, he
35   displayed his joy in his gleaming eyes, which had seen him elected to the
highest office before they were too old to see. Then he turned to the
people and, in a most ingratiating speech, solemnly swore by Omasius
that he would defend our liberties, promote our businesses, put our
enemies to flight, follow our counsel, advance our studies, carry out our
40   wishes, extend our palates, increase our measures; finally he would pre-

serve the quality of our life and make us the kind of people we desired to be. Next, he professed himself the worst enemy to Hunger, Abstinence, Diet, Bad Beer, and Leanness; and swore anew that during his administration no one would fast with impunity, no one would imitate the Greeks unwillingly: "Therefore," he said, "act in the name of holy satiety, be always of good cheer, and to the extent you are able, be friendly, and let this beautiful little goblet delightfully enter and safely leave your mouth." Having said this, he slowly drank the wine to the dregs and, turning the goblet over, put his fingers to his lips, as is customary, and said, "I hope that like me you are always drunken, satiated, and fortunate."

With a delightful cry the people filled the heavens and repeated, "Cagastrius (such, indeed, was his name), the most splendid ruler of Crapulia; let him live, reign, and prosper!" The insignia of the kingdom were immediately handed to him, an ostrich devouring a sword, with the words "Digest and Conquer"; and finally, instead of fasces, a sword, or a scepter, the governor took a small knife and a little golden flask in his hand and solemnly said, "Use and enjoy."

With pleasure I pass over the feast which I saw later that night, piles of dishes, torrents of wine. One thing I cannot pass by: on this night all the crossroads were strewn with as many drunken bodies as are usually found in the camp of a conquered enemy after a huge massacre. There is almost nothing extraordinary that the rest of the cities contain: Devoracum, Porcestria, Sarcoboscum, Verulanium, Lingastrum; the Reader will readily surmise their laws and customs from the one already mentioned.

CHAPTER 12

Famelica Island, or the Land of Hambria

We had forgotten to mention Famelica Island. This island (lest anything be unknown to the reader) has a longitude of 330 degrees and a latitude of 54 degrees, directly opposite from Cabo Blanco on the north and from the Tryphonian Swamp on the south.

The land is rocky, mountainous, infertile, barren, and sandy; there are a few trees here, but leafless and without bark, bearing neither fruit

---

13 Cagastrum *is a Paracelsian word, the opposite of* Iliastrum, *and we derive it from* κακῇ γαστρί, "bad stomach."

nor blossoms. Indeed, none of the sort of flowers or grasses that elsewhere flourish spontaneously grows anywhere in this place. The succession of spring and winter is unknown to the soil, which is dry and absolutely dead, either because the voracious natives pluck any herbs or leaves as
5   soon as they issue forth and devour them or because of the curses of an angry Ceres who they say (while roaming through land and sea solicitously inquiring for her recently lost daughter) accidentally ran into this island and suffered a shipwreck on the reefy seashore. Accordingly, she cursed this land and ordered nothing to grow in this place thereafter.
10   None of the inhabitants lives here voluntarily but is an exile banished from his native land. They are all tawny and unsightly: their skin hard, shrunken, and wrinkled like an elephant's. They are the thinnest people the sun ever gazes on, so that anyone unacquainted with this land of cadavers would call each inhabitant a skeleton covered with new skin
15   or the shadow of a man. You will see some here setting traps for flies, other for worms. In fact, there are those who shave the surface of the earth with penknives as they search for the tiny, hidden roots of herbs. In addition, whenever possible one man sets traps against another for the sake of prey. Indeed, they defend doing this according to the prudently
20   made rule of Aristotle: namely, with the number of sojourners increasing, the scarcity of everything must increase too, and only his strength or his leanness can save a new arrival.

For the most part they are all blacksmiths, even though the Pamphagonians banish all their philosophers and doctors here, and the
25   Spaniards banish all types of free men. A horribly shaped beast, headless, roams throughout this desert island. They call it Nuchtermagen, who fills the heavens with its horrendous barking. He who does not hear it once every twelve hours will have become deaf, and truly, he who hears it three times and does not throw it any prey before twelve hours are past,
30   dies. I saw no other animals here, except wolves and Cercopitheci with their tails a little bit shortened.

---

26 *Composed of two German words:* nuchter, *hungry, and* Magen, *stomach; hence the*
English word maw, *the* g *altered to a* w.   30 *The Cercopitheci eat their own tails, unable to endure their hunger.*

YVRONIA, THE SECOND PROVINCE OF CRAPULIA

CHAPTER 1
The Character of the People

I enter Yvronia,[1] of which no one should expect an accurate description   5
from me, for I did not dare to visit their cities until it was already dark
and the citizens were drowned in wine and sleep. You ask me what I
feared; I will not hesitate at this, Reader: I feared the generosity of the
Burgomasters, who habitually receive whatever strangers that arrive
with I know not how many measures of wine and who congratulate their   10
arrival so magnificently in the name of the state and at public expense. It
is required that these newcomers must drink these measures themselves,
unless they want to be considered ungrateful and (what is worse) an
enemy of the state. I was apprehensive of this dangerous honor for
myself.   15

The region is somewhat larger than Pamphagonia, and, as it is
richer, it is that much more intemperate. In width it is either equal to the
two Germanies or even a little wider. There is no region either more
plentifully provided with grapes or more fortunate; this is true to such a
degree that the same grapes native to the European nations individually   20
all grow here abundantly: those of Germany, whiter and most delicate;
those of France, ruddy and somewhat stronger; and those of Spain,
midway between them in color and most excellent in quality.

The temperature of their bodies differs somewhat from that of the
Pamphagonians: those latter delight more in heat and dryness; the   25
Yvronians in heat and humidity. The Pamphagonians spend their time
in the kitchen and in the dark; the Yvronians spend their time in the
cellars and are jokingly called the Red Crapulians by their neighbors.
Nor are the Yvronians less intelligent, especially because they are much
more eloquent, inasmuch as they are more immodest. Indeed, when they   30
are young they are, for the most part, all quite ingenious, but once
advanced in age—and especially when they become decrepit—they
become so absentminded that scarcely a single one remembers his own
name.

---

1 Land of drunkenness.

41

CHAPTER 2
Yvronia Divided into Its Parts

This province is generally divided into three parts by its inhabitants: Oenotria, or Ponfinia; Pyraenia, or Zythaenia; and Lupulania, which is called Houbelonia by others.

    As regards Ponfinia (a word I supposed is corrupted, with a *p* instead of a *b*, and an *f* instead of a *v*, badly pronounced as is the custom of the Germans), the salty River Meionium divides this region from Pamphagonia on the west and encircles the palace of the ruler. However, the inhabitants believe its waters are not derived from the sea but that they swirl together from a certain aerial flux. This region contains many outstanding cities. First to come to my mind is Pampinola, or Ampelona, a five-sided little hamlet which sprawls beautifully through the Olmius Hills and extends all the way to the small town of Traubena, walled with red brickwork.

    In the bottom of the valley which is called Torcolia is the natural bed of the most elegant River Licoris, along whose most gorgeous banks, thanks to the foresighted choice of their founders, I glimpsed towns scattered here, there, and everywhere: Beachera, Krugtopolis, Chytraea, and Cadilla, surrounded by wooden walls. Truly, the rest of the world, no matter where, has no river to compare to this one: the Danube, the Thames, the Volga, the Tiber, the Seine, or that Raleana of Guiana seem paltry compared to it. For, in addition to its exceptional transparency and the silent flow of its wanton meandering, the water is so sweetly flavored that it need not yield in distinction to the best possible wine or to a draught of Turkish mead.

    A certain extraordinary variety of fish, a rather small whale, which the inhabitants name the Sprukwall, claims to be the oldest inhabitant of the ocean, whose custom it is to spew out the greatest abundance of musty liquor from his spout, which the neighboring people eagerly collect in skiffs and store at home. Here, as the Licoris flows downstream, it

---

3 *Drinkers are intoxicated by three kinds of liquor: wine, beer, and distilled waters hotter than wine, whence the three divisions of Yvronia:* 1. Oenotria, *from* οἴνῳ, *from which comes the Latin* vinum, *"wine";* 2. Pyraenia, *from* πῦρ, *"fire," and* οἶνος, *"wine";* 3. Houbelonia, *French for* hop, *hence the English name.*   28 *Gesner gives this name to this fish; we call it the* Whirlpool.

visits Faessera, truly a remarkable city when viewed from the side, and finally alters its course through the wide plain of Vinicella, toward the metropolis of this province, Zouffenberga.

Chapter 3
The Description of Zouffenberga, the Metropolis of
Yvronia; and, in This Chapter, the Condition and
Customs of the Yvronians
5

Zouffenberga, a name unknown to me, except that it seems almost German in sound, is built on the top of a hill, shaped like a two-handled tankard when viewed from any direction whatsoever. The city is exceed- 10 ingly famous, and its market, owing to the favorable location, is one of the most convenient. On the east it is strongly girded with ramparts made of barrels, the staves of which even form the roofs of all the houses. Placed right in the vestibule of the city's gate from morning to evening, as prescribed by an inviolable law, is a colossal pitcher, the "Hospitality 15 Cup" as the citizens name it in their language, whose handle is inscribed from an earlier time: ἤ πίθι ἤ ἄπιθι, "Either drink or be gone." Whoever enters either drinks all of it or is brought before a magistrate to explain the reason for his intransigence. Above the gate I saw the arms of the city carved: a leech sticking fast to a naked foot, with the saying placed 20 nearby, "Being full, I rest." Here, just as I was about to enter the city, I quite opportunely met another traveler, a man from Loçania who called himself "Cinciglio" in his own language. Toward evening he led me in secretly and taught me many things I would never have discovered myself. 25

The structure and the material of their buildings are not unlike the Pamphagonians', except that the fronts of their houses are so completely hidden by vines that if there weren't signs of shops hanging out everywhere you would surely think you were walking in the midst of a vineyard. It was, by Hercules, not an unpleasant sight. In the public forum, 30 suspended by bronze chains, are the standards for every single measure, stamped on the upper edge with the seals of the kingdom, and next to them the tables of the sacred laws which we will faithfully mention a little further on.

---

23 *An Italian word coming from the sound made by wine being distilled.*

The inhabitants stroll about naked, except that everyone's temples are shaded with garlands of grape leaves. Their skin, however, is marvelously painted, in the manner of the ancient Britons: on this one is depicted Centaurs; on that one Tragelaphs; on a third doves, the most

5   drunken of all birds. And you might see another on whom the shape of a drinking mug has been painted so that with his arms curved at his side you would swear he was a living amphora. I also saw one who resembled a whale so beautifully that when he vomited no one would doubt that he was a whale and that he was spewing up the ocean.

10   My mind burned with the desire to observe—hidden from the citizens—the conduct of their public feasts. At last my guide assented to that, though not without many and indeed serious warnings of danger and examples of proper behavior. Once properly instructed, I was conducted by my faithful guide to the imperial hall where the feasts are

15   carried on after dark. They assemble and take their places in quite the same manner as the Pamphagonians, as I mentioned earlier, except that here I saw more drinking and less eating. Two pots accompany everyone, one on each side: a chamberpot where urine and a basin where vomit are to be collected. In the beginning, at least, they drink to Bacchus,

20   their traditional deity, not the way the old Romans used to, pouring a little wine upon the ground, but far more ceremoniously. Placed at the head of the table a statue of Bacchus rises, holding a gigantic vessel in his right hand; though, because of its excessive weight (as Virgil once expressed it), the left hand sometimes aids its weary sister. Into this without

25   stopping a priest pours a cask of wine (nor, indeed, does it hold any less) as an offering in the name of the participants at the banquet, which is conducted through certain tubes, just like veins, all the way to his mouth and to the juncture of his thighs, where it bursts forth, making it look as though he were vomiting and passing water simultaneously. This is

30   their water clock, governing the feast; because once it stops pouring out it is a sacrilege to keep pouring in.

Next, many varieties of salted foods are served: salt biscuits, pickled fish, cooked and salted red herring, many Westphalian hams, forest artichoke roots, and anchovies—all things that produce thirst. Then,

35   immediately full goblets fly about, which echo when empty, so that after a while you can scarcely decide if they were filled to be emptied or emptied to be filled: and (as that character in Plautus said) they drink from the reservoir of the water clock, from tankards, and from goblets.

When they carouse together one challenges another to a solemn drinking song: with right hands tightly joined and violently shaken and the drinking vessel of one raised to the lips of the other, the business is attacked. And after many fetchings of breath in between, and much diminishing of the liquor, and much flattering conversation, the handle   5
of the goblet is not relinquished until every bit is swallowed up. The other responds in the same way.

The second course of the meal is not as large or as sumptuously prepared, but it is customarily tempered, once again, with a new round of drinking. At length comes the third course, most rarely prepared with   10
fruit and richly served; when this is nearly finished, and the tablecloth is already rolled up, the Master of Ceremonies cries out "Gesundheits" three times in a loud voice. When I heard this, I, in my ignorance, thought he was dismissing the assembly and moved my foot, intending to leave. Then my guide, pulling me gently by the sleeve, asked, "Where   15
to so fast, my sleepy spectator, when the feast is scarcely begun? Notice that the statue of Bacchus isn't running with a weak stream; stay awhile and patiently await the climax of this scene." I obeyed and remained.

Then one of the revelers removes his wreath and on bended knees— as if to say his prayers—snatches a pint and says, "Health to Cagastrius,   20
the most powerful archduke of Crapulia." He delivers his speech, drinks, inhales, exhales, and belches. Finally, after a certain interval, having swallowed as many pints as the letters in his name, he inverts his goblet. Having accomplished this he plays dice and, as Horace said, "stains the pavement with splendid wine." Everyone follows his example to the   25
letter and, with the same goblet, deed, and gesture of faith, proves himself a friendly citizen and, as each one desires, a vigorous drinker.

Immediately another rises and says, "Cheers to you, cheers to us, cheers to the most renowned and majestic Zouffenberga," and meanwhile loudly belching, on bended knees he drinks and drains the cup;   30
nor does anyone dare not follow. A third proposes a toast to Yvronia and the nobles; one by one each proposes another toast to entice the rest to renewed drinking.

Finally, after everyone had drunk the same amount in the same

---

1 *After that he cries out that famous Greek phrase, used in the symposia of the ancient Romans*, "drink five, and beyond that, drink another three, but not four," *Plutarch, Symposiacis, decade 3; Athenaeus, book 10; Plautus in Stichus.*

manner, then every single one played the poet (which aroused the greatest amount of spleen in me) without the consent of the Muses, relying solely on the power of Bacchus and ecstasy, probably emulating the ancient custom which Plutarch recounts in his *Symposiacis* where everyone sings his silly song. For a lyre each had a knife resounding on a cup and played on it quite harmoniously, to be sure. One praised his mistress; another extolled the power of Dionysus; another divulged those things that had occurred at home with his wife, so that suddenly that ancient verse of Laberius came to my mind: "Drunkards possess a humorous disposition."

Another abused one absent with an invective, a song (so it seemed to me) obviously composed of Anacreontian verses: a fitting cover for such a small dish. Meanwhile, as these things were going on, one could discern as many dispositions as there were faces, all different. This one, out of pure love, was weeping on his companion; that one was kissing the nearest carouser; another was dissolved in uncontrollable laughter; another, out of devotion, was prostrating himself to Bacchus; another, to whom the goblet was not brought sooner, was out of humor and cursing a hundred thousand devils; another was swaying and foaming at the mouth at the same time.

However, from the beginning of the feast, seeing that most are so slippery of memory that they are forgetful of their duty, a public notary, called an Auffzeichner, sits slightly above the crowd and registers in his book what each person drinks, as a public record. He carefully notes what each has drunk and to whom, and at the end of the dinner he recites it, assuming that anyone can pay attention:

> Trinkenius to Bibulus: 21 pints.
> Bibulus to Oesophagius: 10 1/2 gallons.
> Dipsius to Leinius: 2 pints.
> Drollius to Biberius: The same.
> Zaufenius to Saturio: 18 quarts.

If anyone is discovered by the official to have failed in his manner of

---

3 *Horace spoke truly of such people,* "Either the man is insane or he is making verses." *From this custom, without a doubt, comes the Greek saying,* "You make dithyrambs, you're crazy," *so says Aristophanes in The Birds.*   9 Nonius.   18 "Having been made drunk by the bounteous service of the wine," *according to that writer on elephants.*

drinking, he must give satisfaction immediately; if not, he is obligated to repay his debt, not without great interest, at the beginning of the next banquet. The list having been read through and the hourglass having run out, I inquired, "I have a small question; how are these people to be easily taken home?" "That's simple," my guide replied. "Do you see   5
these ropes which are bound here in the forum to an equal number of iron rings? The more heedful attendants (whom it is customary to honor with a drink before the end of the dinner) attach them to their masters' doors, since they, to be sure, scarcely dare to trust themselves, and, Ariadnes following a new thread, each attendant returns straight to his   10
own home with his cargo, no matter how great a quantity he consumed that night." "But what if someone has switched the rope in the meantime?" He smiled. "And do you think that at this time of night anyone is on watch?" he asked. "However, we know this sometimes happens. And then he goes to a home and a wife that is not his own. However, she,   15
perhaps just as intoxicated, does not realize it before noon the next day; then, what they have done unwittingly, they wittingly laugh at. For certainly, with them it is an established rule that 'anyone who is drunk cannot offend, since it is not he but Bacchus who does it.'" However, that saying of Lucian occurred to me, "It is not Dionysus that does it, but   20
excessive drinking."

CHAPTER 4
The Knights of the Golden Barrel, and the Laws of the Place

And in the town hall of Zouffenberga I saw that golden barrel which gives its name to the order of knights: because he who drains that barrel   25
three times and remains sober is declared a knight by the Duke and given an extraordinary chain for his distinction. Nor are the privileges of these knights unimportant: for they have absolute command of both tables and taverns wherever they are; they are allowed to appropriate wine of any sort for free; and they regulate the manner of everyone's drinking.   30
    At every solemn feast they fight with a number of goblets, just as the Roman gladiators once fought with swords, and whoever has drained the larger number while still sober emerges as the victor and—in truth— makes a triumphal procession. However, the judgment of sobriety is

---

20 *Lucian, Dialogues.*   32 *Or according to the custom of the Spartans with the Helots.*

normally made in this way: he who is able to place his outstretched
finger just into the flame of a burning lamp without wavering is considered sober no matter what he says or vomits forth.

Now, dear Reader, here are the laws of both Zouffenberga and all
Yvronia. Hold your laughter, if you are able:

> Any agreement made in the afternoon shall be null and void.
>
> No one is to have his own cups.
>
> Anyone who drops anything except mere foam in a drinking game
> shall be made to bend over and lick up the spilled liquor.
>
> Everyone shall respond to a pledge with the same cup and in the
> same manner that he was challenged; he who behaves differently
> shall thirst for two days.
>
> The cups must always be either empty or full: whatever waiter shall
> serve up halves, or whatever reveler shall accept them, shall be guilty
> of an offense against society.
>
> A sober man who strikes a drunken one shall be disabled from
> ever being a witness by reason of misconduct; whoever drunken
> strikes a sober man shall be acquitted.
>
> Whoever sober shall rob him who is drunk shall be forbidden
> wine forever; whoever kills shall perish from thirst.
>
> Whoever proposes a toast to the Duke of Crapulia with an empty
> goblet shall be condemned of high treason.
>
> Whoever abstains from drinking because of nature or disease shall
> be banished.
>
> Whoever leaves a banquet without staggering shall be considered
> a scoundrel.
>
> Whoever remains three days in the city shall offer a sacrifice to Bac-
> chus.
>
> Whoever calls a citizen an adulterer or a thief shall be unpun-
> ished; whoever calls him a teetotaler shall be indicted.
>
> Whoever mixes water with wine shall be sent to eat with the dogs.
>
> Whoever swears by Bacchus and breaks his oath shall be barred
> from being a witness and from making a will.
>
> Whoever attacks another in anger with a goblet and either spills
> any wine or breaks the goblet itself must keep his hands and lips
> away from any goblet for the next day.

In the vestibule of the hall I found the inscription:

This house is always filled with cheer and good fellowship.
Here peace, here rest, here pleasure is always honored.

written by Stilliard.

Chapter 5
The Arts and the Technique of War of the Yvronians 5

Almost all the Yvronians are bleary eyed and paralytic, and are marked
by their well-known tumors—the kind that the inhabitants of the Alps
and the Pyrenees take pride in. Their painters are by far the best when
drunken age makes their hands tremble, so that here you would justly
reflect on that saying of Lucian: "What a great man he would be when   10
sober, if being drunk he can do all these marvelous things!"
    The Yvronians also have a great number of poets, whom their Duke
does not crown with laurel (since, according to their religion, the plant
is too hostile to the grape vine for them to tolerate it); instead, he bestows
ivy. They are the most sordid of people and the lowest dregs of the   15
common mob; I was no less indignant at them for bearing that sacred
name than Apuleius writes Antigenides was because the mere horn
blowers who played at the tombs were being called musicians. Clearly,
they are unschooled runts: illiterate and scarcely able to chant rhymes in
their mother's tongue. These parasites live on others: with new Epitha-   20
lamia, Elegies, and Epitaphs they flood the taverns; they describe tri-
umphs; they produce masques; and have the same control over plays and
choral productions that their knights have over drinking bouts. This age
has produced, so they say, only one true poet, who I heard was starved to
death for speaking the truth, unseemly behavior.   25
    They very often go to battle, sharing the common wars, but they are
always unarmed, without even a woman's shift, the armed apparel of the
Irish. As lances they use elm tree stakes, which normally support the
vine, pointed and hardened slightly by fire. Neither can I tell you, nor
can you believe, how strenuously these people have fought and how   30
many times they have defeated the enemy. Of course, they do take the
precaution that no one meet the enemy sober: accordingly, wine brings
boldness, and boldness frequently brings good fortune.

---

17 *Apuleius, The Golden Ass.*

CHAPTER 6
The Funeral of a Burgomaster. The Sacrifice to Bacchus

On the same night that we witnessed the feast, a certain Burgomaster,
whose house was situated on a rather high hill, fell out of a window
5   which he, in poor control of himself and not feeling carefully, mistook
for the door; and since he broke his neck, he immediately expired. I saw
his funeral celebrated with much pomp and lamentation. Everyone dyed
himself black and, in place of garlands of grape leaves, draped himself
with cypress. The body was not laid on a bier or a pyre but was placed in
10   a huge, half-full wine cask and then in a well filled with wine—not so
much buried as submerged, I reckon. For whereas the Roman custom
was to throw on top of the funeral pyre pieces of frankincense (to speak
according to Lucretius) and every kind of aromatic fragrance, here everyone poured a small tankard of wine into the grave and bade farewell to
15   the dead man. A statue was erected to him in the middle of the court of
Bacchus, inscribed in their language with these verses:

> The doors were closed, but a certain window stood open in the night,
> It was the gateway of death; it will be the gateway of honor for you.

I had stayed there undisturbed for two days when my guide came to
20   me saying, "Alas, until now you lay hidden very well, but if you spend a
third day here it will be necessary to sacrifice to Bacchus. Now that is my
concern because I don't want to prove false to my oath or to our friendship."
     I asked him, "And what is that custom, please, that I must submit
25   to? Once I know it, I will either do it and stay longer or leave this place
tomorrow and free you from that anxiety and danger."
     He replied, "Yesterday you saw the statue of Bacchus in the forum
and the crater into which they pour the wine to be drunk, which, once
filled, empties by two spouts. You must place your mouth at either of
30   these two openings, and from there drink more than enough to satisfy

---

17 *And* to that another: "Wine has slain [our brother], pour wine on his tomb; for the
darkness of death has not ended his thirst," *Siena, in the Church of St. Dominico. And to
that a third:* "Wine gave me life; wine brought me death; sober I could not see the dawn. My
naked bones are thirsty; pour some wine on my grave, and quaff a small cup, dear traveler,
and be gone. FAREWELL DRINKERS." *Written in Siena in the Church of the Holy Spirit.*

you, until you fall flat on the ground; then finally, lying in the same
place, you must submit to the dripping shower of wine, until it stops
flowing."

"But, pray, tell me seriously," I said, "were there ever any travelers
who did this?" "Every one to the man," he replied, "some quite willingly;   5
others, however, most reluctantly."

"Indeed, I shall be going," said I. "If you please, help me by telling
me which part of the rest of Yvronia you consider second in importance."
He praised Zythaenia to me, which others call Pyraenia, under the rule
of Tricongius, who is descended from the most noble family of the   10
Cantharidi. And he immediately showed me the way, easy enough, and
bade me farewell.

CHAPTER 7
Pyraenia, or Zythaenia, and the Pilgrimage to the Sacred Womb

I proceeded alone to the northern region and, having left the white River   15
Schaum behind, went on to Kotzunga, the most repulsive and rankest of
all the places I ever saw. And now ending up at the boundaries of
Ponfinia itself, I greeted Vale-dolium, quite clean and neat; where, however, I observed neither fountain nor stream, so that, I heard, no wine
could be adulterated by the nymphs.   20

The only thing I lament (which I want to warn the Reader of) is that
as I journeyed about I was molested by full goblets (just as travelers in a
hurry are by Italian and Spanish crosses) which are distributed at every
third mile under a sacred arch, and it is unlawful for travelers to pass by
without stopping to drink from them. At last, I joined a traveler clothed   25
in a very cheap, shaggy cloak, bareheaded and barefoot. I immediately
questioned where he was heading so rapidly. He said to me, "I have
undertaken a long pilgrimage to the sacred womb of Schlauchberga."

Marveling at the strange name of the city and at the extraordinary
journey, I questioned him at length about the location of the region and   30
the city, about the reason for his decision to go there, and finally about
the virtue of that shrine, to which he responded: "Schlauchberga is a city
on the very border between Pyraenia and Loçania, most frequented by
both regions, in which, besides other quite marvelous religious monuments, there is the temple of Bacchus Pyrodes, called Ardens Chapel,   35
where Bacchus is chiseled out of solid rock: not, as in other places, adult

and bearded but childlike, in the same embryonic form as when he was
snatched from Semele's burning womb once upon a time by his father,
playing the office of midwife. From the roof of this grotto, magnificently
ornamented with little bronze and gold flames, there distill into the
5   womb below in a constant stream, like waterfalls in some Indian sea,
drops of a warm and constantly fuming liquor which is endowed with
such a celestial virtue that whoever will conscientiously and devoutly
quaff a large draft from it will never afterward be capable of being thirsty
before midnight or being drunk before noon. In truth, both aids may
10 accomplish much in my dealing with people: for I am able neither to
sleep to midnight without being interrupted by excessive thirst nor to
wake up in the morning without being overwhelmed into a stupor by
drink before noon. Therefore, I have drunk nothing in this country
except a little water today from an undefiled fountain; for these three
15 days I have marched along thirsty so that I might merit much more from
this fiery deity, nor does anyone dare to force a drink on me or on anyone
accompanying me when I am clothed thus."

I eagerly accepted so opportunely offered a favor and followed him
and quite resolutely requested his company and protection. At last,
20 when we had gone not a little way, chattering all the while, I, observing a
change of soil, asked him what region we were now in. He replied,
"From that wide swamp that we crossed, named Lake Methius, the area
is called Uscebatius, a region rather close to Pyraenia, not so well cultivated but much more productive than our Oenotria, either because of the
25 excellence of the land or because of the temperateness of the climate." As
soon as I first heard the name, I perceived the origin and meaning of the
word: for they are accustomed to drink even to the bottom (usque
Bathos), or from the handle of the goblet called Bath (οὖς τοῦ σκεύεος
βατίου): which is truly what those who are better acquainted with
30 the southern languages think.

In fact, the people are exceedingly sordid and barbarous, nor, except
when drunk, do they ever not seem disagreeable and fierce: but (since
they are exceedingly superstitious) they were friendly enough to me on
account of my most pious companion. Indeed, we spent the first night
35 quietly enough in the public inn of a certain obscure little town, for we
found the inhabitants all drunk and in the deepest sleep of the half dead
both when we arrived and when we left. The rest, in which I observed
nothing worthy of being noted down, I pass over willingly.

We arrived, at last, through many pathless forests and vast swamps, at the most celebrated and frequented little village, Port Aqua Fortis. I, who had promised myself a rest a long time ago, asked, "Where are we going now? Or is this your hope, that best beloved Schlauchberga?"

"It isn't," he answered, "but, to refresh you a bit, not an arm's length more land is left to be traversed on foot. We will go the remaining   5
way by boat. After we have happily passed through this strait lying before us, and by the quiet shores of Pyraenia (for this region, in the manner of Denmark, is cut by the ocean and split in two), we will come to the most agreeable port."

We boarded the ship, left port, and at once we were tossed about in   10
the midst of the waves. But here even now my heart turns cold with fright when I remember how we escaped such a great danger on this occasion. For behold, every sailor, to the man, was completely drunk, with no control over himself. One sleeps here in the stern; another suffers Pali-nurus's fate and falls headlong into the deep and sinks, while now one   15
and now another who vainly try to offer him aid fall overboard them-selves and are themselves duly rescued by our hands. A third goes crazy and pitches an oar at a fourth sailor nearby because he did not offer to aid his lost friend: to which he, provoked by these repeated blows, responds in the same manner; the rest join one side or the other. Now converted   20
into clubs, menacing oars fly this way and that way, and they beat not the water but the wind. They are quickly laid out on the deck, those on whom Bacchus had earlier cast a harder blow. Two sailors remained victors (no more than that survived) and too late disgusted by so much violence, looking fiercely at us, attacked. For they claimed that we were   25
the cause of all that had happened. But we, considering it a disgrace to be overcome by two drunkards and equipped with some weapons belonging to the men who were laid out, easily subdued that impotent pair of adversaries and, having stripped them of their weapons, bound them up. Then we played sailors ourselves, but the very ship, as if no less intoxi-   30
cated, tacked this way and that, so that if a drier wind had not been opportunely sent by Aeolus to push the clearly unwilling ship on a straight course, we wretched oarsmen would have ignominiously buried all hope along with our bodies, and my religious companion would never have gazed at the womb of his Bacchus.   35

In the midst of our navigation, which I don't want to pass over in silence, far off on the left and a bit to the north I saw a certain island,

---

14 *Virgil, Aeneid.*

mountainous and snow covered. When I asked about its name and climate, my companion replied: "That is called Glacialis Island, to which Bacchus, still beardless, fleeing the rage of his angry stepmother, was exiled by his father, but when the inhabitants treated him so in-

5   humanely and finally drove him away by armed force, his angry father commanded the land to be covered by perpetual snow and darkness."

   "But what is the origin of that smoke that we see from afar erupting from the peak of that snow-covered mountain?"

   "That is the sacred mountain of Dionysus, in whose fiery bowels

10   they say those souls who tried to live too soberly or temperately or those who laid violent hands on him are made to atone. Here the miserable shades are punished, tortured unceasingly until one of their remaining friends will visit Ardens Chapel and set his soul free by pouring that fire water onto his grave." I smiled. Now I saw for certain the origin of that

15   most highly praised Purgatory. How wrong was that Abbot Odilo and the monks of Cluny who, 600 years ago, thought that this place of atone-ment of the souls was fixed in Mount Aetna. Finally we landed and found the city, undoubtedly elegant enough but roofed and paved every-where with leather-covered bottles. Nor do I remember seeing any artisan

20   here except leather wineskin makers, so that I well understood what was done with the hides of the Pamphagonians. The reason for such shops is that the inhabitants use no unadulterated wine like the rest of the Yvronians but lap up a certain liquor distilled from the strongest wine, which is so powerful that this fragile glass cannot contain it alone, on

25   which account they make a kind of envelope strengthened with pitch and resin.

   The citizens are almost all ruddy faced, bleary eyed, irritable, envi-ous, suspicious, trembling of hand, staggering in gait, and, what terrified me the most, they drink and breathe pure flames. In fact, they pour in as

30   much of the hottest liquors as we drink water or the lightest beer, so that whenever I saw any of them I couldn't help but remember Francis Drake's fire. I, therefore, who had just been imperiled by water, was now even more afraid of being burned. Consequently, I left my companion praying to his Bacchus, considering it far better to preserve my own

35   body, and withdrew myself the very next morning from this city of Vulcan and the Cyclops, rather than of the father of Bacchus.

   And just as I was considering returning along the extreme borders of Loçania, in order to visit Houbelonia, the third region of Yvronia,

---

16 *In the year* 1000.

behold, an armed force of Viraginians appeared, surrounded me, arrested me, and carried me, a most miserable voyager, off on an immense journey to the capital of the region, Gynaecopolis. However, I don't want the Reader to be annoyed that the remaining part of Yvronia will remain untouched, owing to this accident; for, as my recent companion 5 told me, this is the basest part of all and differs little from the rest, except that Houbelonia is less dignified and more beastly in its drunkenness.

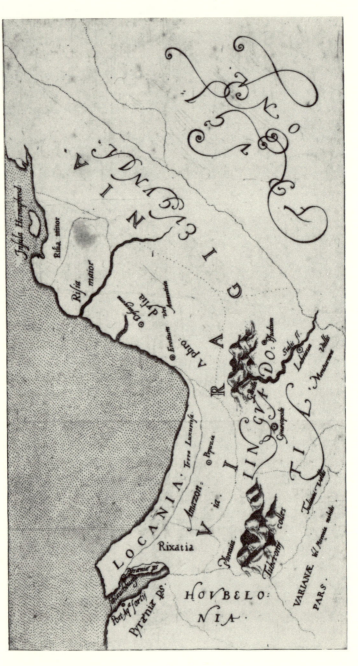

VIRAGINIA

BOOK TWO

VIRAGINIA, OR NEW GYNIA

CHAPTER 1
The Location of Viraginia and Its Regions
A Land of Women   5

New Gynia, which others incorrectly call Guinea, I correctly call Viraginia, located where European geographers depict the Land of Parrots.
On the north, Loçania touches these most unfriendly people; on the
south, Frugiona; on the east, Moronia Mobilis and Moronia Felix. The
land is perfectly fertile but badly husbanded.   10

It contains within itself many large regions, each quite different
from one another in character and custom. The principal parts are
Linguadocia, Rixatia, Ploravia, Risia major and Risia minor, Aphrodysia, Amazonia, and Eugynia; Hermaphroditica Island is not far distant
from them. I passed through certain of these regions quite unwillingly. 15

Linguadocia far surpasses the rest, in which there are very many
very famous cities: Garilla, Psudium, and Labriana, through which an
enormous river flows. The neighbors call it the Sialon, which often overflows, scarcely able to be contained even in such a vast channel, and
indeed, the more low-lying part of the region—which they call the   20
Menturnea Valley—would be daily threatened by it had not the rather
clever inhabitants carefully walled up the banks with bones. But claiming and maintaining first place among the cities of Linguadocia and all
of Viraginia is Gynaecopolis, where I sojourned longer than I wished.
Therefore I will first tell you what was done to me, and thereafter I will 25
describe in order what can be disclosed about this new race.

CHAPTER 2
What Was Done to Me by the Gynaecopolitans

The instant these hardy conqueresses, who had seized me at the border of
Loçania, brought me to their forum they rang a little bell; to which, as   30

---

6 New Gynia *is ordinarily described as the extreme eastern portion of the unknown
southern continent, very near the kingdom of* Maletur and Beach, *and here we have located*
Guinea *too.*

soon as they heard it, the citizens immediately rushed together ready for
battle and curiously gazed at me while one of my abductors, who at that
time appeared to be the leader, after giving a signal for silence (of which
there was need), addressed the others. She did not know who I might be
5   or from what country, only that I had been arrested within the borders of
such a depraved region, and she admonished them that they should
think carefully about revenge for the numerous, severe injuries inflicted
by the Loçanians and bring me to judgment.

I disclosed my nationality and my reason for traveling with gestures
10   and whatever words I could manage, said that I was totally ignorant of
the Loçanians' deeds, that I was one of those who had always wished her,
and her people, and her sex well, and that it was unworthy of her gentle-
ness and of the fame of her most just regime for an innocent traveler who
deserved nothing ill from her sex to be condemned without a hearing. So
15   humble an oration, and one with the appearance of truth not too greatly
embellished, moved those women not a little; and therefore the opinion
of the majority prevailed at last: to imprison the fettered one, namely me,
in the jail—called the Gynaecium—and to hold me there until the
senate could establish my fatherland and the reason for my journey.
20   Here I endured a long and miserable servitude; nor, had the name of my
country (which is justly esteemed throughout the world as the "Paradise
of Women") not saved me, I would not have been able finally to escape
from this place alive.

Indeed, whatever Loçanians they apprehend they generally either
25   hang or assign the most vile duties in this infamous prison. It is no
wonder that the Viraginians punish the daily injuries of the Loçanians
in such a fashion; for even though these men are so lecherous and so
much inclined to sex that their lust burns with desire for boys, for
whores, and perhaps even for mules and cattle, they either neglect their
30   wives entirely or else hold them prisoners out of jealousy and suspicious
zeal. How many noble captives taken from ships did I glimpse here
growing old doing such Herculean labors as gathering wool and spinning thread!

At last, the sacred name of my country and ruler, once upon a time
35   well deserved, liberated me—not absolutely unfettered and unsworn,

---

21 *French proverb:* "England is the paradise of women, the purgatory of servants, and the
hell of horses."

however. I had to go and touch Juno's altar, of course, and publicly give
my oath to observe absolutely the following laws:

> That I never contrive anything against this most noble sex either
> by word or by deed.
> That I never interrupt a woman speaking with my chatter.   5
> That I yield to the woman the rule of the house wherever I might be.
> That I never return to Loçania (for it is a common saying of
> theirs: "Many go there as good men to return as wicked husbands").
> That I never seek to have the love of more than one woman simul-
> taneously.   10
> That I not betray any of her secrets.
> That I never deny my wife anything that pertains to her ornamenta-
> tion or attire.
> That I should voluntarily praise women's intelligence, beauty, and
> eloquence and defend them from all malicious detractors.   15

I acknowledged all this willingly. Nor, certainly, in my eagerness to
get away would I have refused even harsher conditions. Thus the Reader
sees that even now as I write some restraints are placed upon my pen;
after swearing that oath it is not possible for me to speak out on all
points. I shall be allowed to write about whatever is not bad; I cannot   20
write about evil things as though I had not sworn.

CHAPTER 3
The Form of Government and Elections

Their political condition seemed democratic to me, insofar as everybody
studies how to govern, but none studies how to be governed. Nor do they   25
allow themselves to be coerced by laws; all matters are decided simply by
a public vote. The way this is done seemed astonishing to me, a traveling
man: for they all talk at once with a clamor. No one remains silent and
listens to the others.

They hold an almost continual parliament in which the most   30
important business is handled: so that our Desiderius, if he were alive

---

31 *Erasmus, Colloquia.*

today, would not believe that women could introduce so many petitions. Actually, an ongoing parliament is necessary because of the uncertainty of the laws. It is permissible, even the next day, to retract any law with a plebiscite; it is not allowed the same day, lest they might seem too
5   inconstant.

The votes of the citizens are universally equal; however, their status is not. Indeed, a certain number of Stateswomen, whom they call "Hundred Women," render decisions in matters of great importance because of their high office in the city. Nor, in truth, are these women born mis-
10   tresses of such matters but are elected, so that it appears a woman can gain prominence merely by Beauty and Eloquence (for those are the only two qualities considered in every election).

Once upon a time the general public had the power to elect and be elected, until eventually everyone advanced herself for the ballot; the
15   confusion bred about who was the most praiseworthy forced this system of election to be suspended. Then it was decreed that only those might sit as judges in such an envious dispute who publicly declared themselves neither beautiful nor eloquent. When this was done and the people had gathered together many times, not a single one was found in so numer-
20   ous and crowded a multitude who would assume the place of electrix, for the elder reckoned themselves no less well spoken than the young affirmed themselves fine featured.

Finally, it was agreed to confer this honor upon twelve of the eldest matrons from the village of Vetulonio, to which honor they wisely added
25   an even more prestigious title so that it might be more gladly sought. And besides, it is impossible for them to refuse the title because old women, rich in all other things, esteem titles very greatly. To be sure, these old women fly everywhere just like Lauriotian owls, and through bribes the ambitious young women struggle—at an enormous cost—
30   and indeed capture the favor of the judges (which is up for sale), so that I could not imagine a marketplace itself more corrupt or more wealthy.

Instead of scepters or fasces or battle-axes, they prefer huge plumes and mirrors. Even when they stroll through the village they never cease to gaze at themselves and to adjust their hair, their faces, and their gait
35   according to the advice of their mirrors.

---

24 Vetulonia, *Ptolemy's city of Hetruria. Thus, Silius Italicus, book 8.*   28 *Aristo-phanes.*

CHAPTER 4
The Origin of the Viraginians

Very few Viraginians were born here, but they flock here from every other
place in the world, either driven here because their husbands are extremely ferocious or exiled here voluntarily because their husbands were   5
extremely cruel and jealous. All those who are ejected from their homeland along with their husbands—because they have unjustly ruled their
marriage—and are driven to the frontiers of this kingdom, especially to
that part which is called Gynandria or Amazonia, inhabit fortified cities
and work as garrison soldiers.   10

  In truth, the voluntary exiles, who are commonly less warlike and
more pleasant in disposition, dwell in peace and beauty in the center of
the kingdom. Nor may you flatter yourself that a Republic of so dubious
an origin is about to collapse at any time from a lack of citizens. In fact,
so many voluntarily arrive here daily—particularly my fellow country-   15
women—that it ought instead to be feared that there soon might not be
any room remaining for new citizens. And certainly I am very much
afraid that our women might come to know where this place is from my
writings, and pretty soon there will scarcely be a woman left at home to
preserve the hope of future generations with her fertility.   20

CHAPTER 5
Aphrodysia

Armed therefore with a passport from the capital of the region, I next
continued on from here to the southern part of Viraginia that faces
Loçania: Aphrodysia, an exceedingly prosperous land, to be sure. I   25
know not how many miles distant I was from Erotium (or Amantina),
the nearest town of the region, when vapors of the most delightful sort
filled my nostrils, as if the most precious, aromatic druggists' boxes
stood nearby. Here every dealer reeks with ointments and with Golosinian delights. The rest I pass over in silence.   30

  The women I saw here were slender, gracefully adorned, and (had
rouge not removed the loveliness of their complexions) extremely beautiful. All strolled about with an exposed face and breasts. The rest is

---

22 *Lascivious land.*

covered, but with a material of the most extreme lightness and the most splendid colors. Yet their naked parts appear so obviously painted with white lead, according to the custom of the Moscovites, that you would swear you saw a mask, a statue, or a plastered wall, not a human skin.

5   The women of Desuergona (the first city of Aphrodysia takes pleasure in that name) dwell in glass houses transparent on all sides. Seek none of them at home (lest you be frustrated), except when she is dressing or painting to go out. But you will find them if you search in the forum or the theater (for here they waste the day), either laughing, or singing,

10   or dancing.

A spider was never more intent on catching flies than these women are on catching travelers from Loçania, despite the fact that these people are their deadly enemies, though most of these men submit to the wantonness of these women voluntarily or for profit. First the women

15   lure these men to themselves with lascivious gestures; next they entreat them more rudely; then they assail them with money; and finally, if none of these works, they compel the men to serve their most unseemly lusts by force. And after the men have once made love, they are kept in a rather secluded stable, no differently than stallions are kept at stud for mares, to

20   be feasted with I know not what Indian roots and the most potent love potions.

I hated those women and departed quickly; nor did I consider myself safe despite my immense learning. Obviously I would never have dared to trust them with my good name and my hope for salvation, had I not

25   been aware long ago of my own lack of beauty. Therefore, it was once helpful to have been ugly: so that even such things on whose account we commonly accuse nature the most may on occasion be the most useful, even when we least expect it. (Thus nature exercises its supreme wisdom for us.)

30   CHAPTER 6
                                    Hermaphroditica Island

Not far from Guinea, the last island of the Moluccas, between Cape Hermosa and Beach Promontory, I saw Hermaphroditica Island, not unlike our Isle of Man in either form or size, where nature has standard-

35   ized, as it were, the forms of everything indigenous into just one form: I observed no one without a double nature. Absolutely no tree exists that is

not loaded with various kinds of fruit or designated by a mixture of names; they are called pear-apples, plum-cherries, and date-almonds. And even the form of their clothing is composed from the characteristics of both sexes, for those who have more masculine qualities look like men from their heels to their hips, while the rest of their body looks like a woman's, and the opposite is true for those predominantly feminine. And they zealously pay attention to this in proper names (lest they disguise part of their nature). For example, there are Phillippomaria, Petrobrigida, Amarichardo, and Thomalicia.

Adolescents and whoever cannot both generate and give birth serve the rest. If they discover anyone of our people of a single nature among them they display the person as a great monstrosity and show exactly the same astonishment as we do when we see offspring with two heads, or mutilated, or lacking their private parts. They boast that they are the perfect offspring of nature. Since she has provided a complete body with two ears, two nostrils, two hands, two eyes, and two feet, why, they ask, should she desire the most preeminent animal to be provided with less than two sexes? And indeed, if one will study the young women of an earlier age who tended the shrines of Cybele herself (completely free from impure rites), or the most infamous sodomites of old—and, indeed, of new—Rome, he will learn that those people coveted through evil means what is naturally given to us.

With these and with other abominable argments these quite clever people are accustomed to defend themselves, in whose reasoning you will note a man's sagacity allied with a woman's craftiness, because their body is a mixture of both. There are no cattle here except mules, nor any wild beasts except hares. Almost all the people dine on fish, and especially on shellfish.

CHAPTER 7
Amazonia, or Gynandria

Returning through the remotest part of Aphrodysia, the westernmost corner, I came (or rather, the roadside gods led me) to Amazonia, or Gynandria, the sole defense of so peaceful a nation against the rage and incursions of their neighbors. The Amazonians truly believe themselves

---

32 *In English,* Land of Shrewes.

threatened by no adjoining nation except the Loçanians (because Frugiona, a peaceful race, does not wish to provoke them, and Moronia
cannot, no matter how much it might want to); consequently, they erect
garrisons in the cities of Amazonia which are located in the eastern
5   frontier near Loçania.

I cannot here remain silent about how much my expectations were
disappointed, for I saw some in manly dress and my mind was cheered
not a little, nothing yonder suggesting itself except that I had escaped
those most offensive lands of Viraginia. But an accident taught me how
10 illusory was the appearance of the inhabitants, for here the women wear
the breeches and sport long beards, and it is the men who wear petticoats
and are beardless, who remain at home strenuously spinning and weav-
ing while the women attend to military matters and farming.

Here lies Pepuzia, a large and ancient city, whence came the Pepu-
15 zians, long ago condemned for heresy, who proposed women rulers and
priests. The Barbarians never treated their women, either in Aristotle's
time, or even now, as imperiously as the women here treat their men.
Such slavery certainly pained me. None of these good men dares to dress,
or conduct any business, or even speak up without his wife's permission:
20 or to go anywhere, or to attend to the necessities of nature, or even to look
at or speak to anyone, unless he first humbly asks permission. I learned
that this custom is more carefully observed today than in the past. They
cite the following incident as the reason for this: some wiser men, too
late disgusted with such cowardly and shameful servitude, devised a
25 plan for secretly assaulting the women on a certain night and shaking
off this most oppressive yoke by a silent massacre. Indeed, that plot
would have very nearly succeeded had not a certain timid little man, who
was threatened with a lashing by his enraged spouse because of some
slight neglect, exposed the whole plot in the evening to avoid punish-
30 ment.

While the men work, the women sit; while the men arise, they sleep;
while the men weep, they quarrel and scold. That day is a lucky day
when the men can say good-night having saved their skins from a
beating. It would have appeared to me that I was walking among some
35 Turkish slaves, had not the dress that distinguishes them showed me it
was an even baser kind of slavery. Oh, what a sight a distaff or a spindle
was in the hand of a man, and a dagger and a scepter in the hand of a

---

14 Augustine, book of heresies.   16 Aristotle, Politics 1, chapter 1.

woman! However, I concealed my disgust as well as I could, zealously
applying my mind so that I might observe everything and suffer nothing.

If a woman of milder disposition displays more forbearance with
her man, or is more gentle, immediately (as there are all sorts of infor-
mers here) she is brought to the senate and accused of treason. Her   5
neighbors direct the charge against the accused, not without greatly
aroused passion and labored speech. For if her behavior becomes known,
even by the most trivial evidence, the accused is ordinarily punished in
this manner: she must exchange clothes with her husband and dressed
like this, head shaved, be brought to the forum to stand there an entire   10
day in the pillory, exposed to the reproach and derisive laughter of all
onlookers. Nor does the man himself get away without punishment for
his audacity, since he did not modestly refuse the slight favor offered him
by his wife. When that woman finally returns home stained with mud,
urine, and all sorts of abuse, she does not take off her dress until she   15
exhibits the blood-stained staff that she has broken on her husband's
head.

Any man who outlives his wife must either yoke himself in marriage
to some servant, having first shown proof of his respect to his former
wife, or bind himself in service to the mother of the nearest family: for no   20
man whatsoever is judged capable of superintending his own domestic
affairs. When a woman sets out on a journey, either for war, or for business, or finally for pleasure, she entrusts the house keys to her maid or her
daughter—and with the keys the command. If he once dares to complain, she punishes him on her return, unless, with many presents and   25
all sorts of other entreaties, he wins the deputy governess's favor and her
silence.

Rarely are the men allowed to share the same bed, except, to be sure,
when it is for the little woman's pleasure; naturally (so these women
indeed believe) this practice smacks of too much familiarity. However, if   30
he does not arise from his antechamber every night before his wife grows
warm in her bed, and ascend the stairs barefoot, and gently knock three
times on her door, and with a submissive voice offer his ready services,
the next day he will be whipped.

Contrary to the fashion of our countrywomen, these women clip   35
their hair and let their nails grow. Among them are some women who
practice gymnastics and teach where and how teeth, nails, and heels can
be employed in the most warlike manner: finally, how to strip the skin
off a man's face skillfully, how to rip out his eyes, how to bite his arms,

how to dig through his ears, how to pull out his beard—and they instruct both by precepts and by examples.

You will scarcely believe how all their homes glisten, which the men wash, sweep, cook, and put into order all by themselves. Thus it is clear from this fact that men reject domestic work not because they are unable to handle it but because they consider it ill becomes them. I saw nothing dirty there except the men's clothes, which are obviously filthy beyond measure, so that they do not neglect themselves any less than they are neglected by the women. However, outdoors you will see that the fields and the houses, under the care of the women, are most poorly tended: the very wall of the city is half destroyed, and where it stands in one piece it is so unskillfully constructed that it seems to desire a man's tutelage and to detest the work and care of women. Now I don't doubt you wonder, dear Reader, about my safety, curious how I, a poor traveler, would finally be able to escape from so dangerous and corrupt a place in one piece. I can tell you candidly that my dress, my age, and my intelligence preserved me. Because I was walking in man's attire and was in the first phase of an adolescent beard, I was able to conceal my sex easily, and what happened to me, I conveniently chanced upon many of my countrymen (something that would seem odd in so remote a place), at once recognizable to me by their appearance. With their protection, their advice, and their warnings, like that which the Trojan horsemen once received from friendly Sibyl, I made my way through the valley of the Ploravian Swamp and the Tuberonian Mountains—not without many hardships, troubles, and dangers—and finally, a happy traveler, I came to the land of Moronia.

But you will ask, meanwhile, what about honorable women, and you will be completely astonished, perhaps. I would reckon myself an unfortunate traveler who never met those women anywhere, or an ungrateful one who silently passed over their way of life and their character. I will tell you seriously, my friend, that these women are, indeed, very numerous, but inhabit Eugynia, a part I confess I did not see, but one I know beyond all doubt by reputation. Also, there are good women living in the parts of Viraginia mentioned previously, not scarce in number, but they live an anchoritic and monastic life and accordingly inhabit the rugged and inaccessible mountains. To be sure (so they say), the most chaste, devout, and beautiful women voluntarily withdraw there. Any-

---

22 Aeneid, 6.

one who will ascend and zealously search for them will be certain to encounter not a few of their kind. I met one or two myself, whose appearance, manner, and virtue I was astonished at. But our young men (if they were, by chance, to travel to this place) would shun all the labor of finding them and reject all the pain of love. Thus it happens that they unjustly cite the scarcity of good women as an excuse.

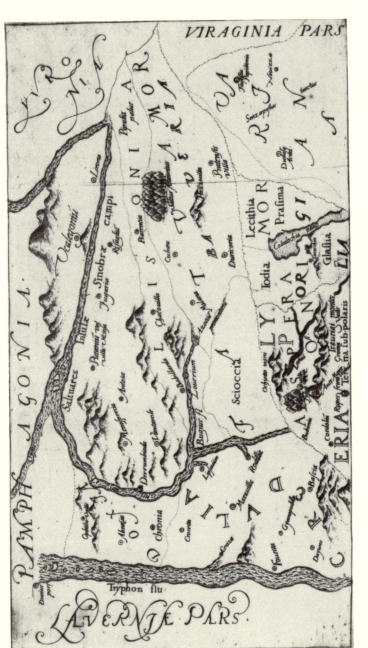

MORONIA

BOOK THREE

MORONIA

CHAPTER 1
Moronia's Rank and Its Location

Moronia is the largest, the most uncultivated, and the most populous   5
region of all I saw. In truth, if anyone were to wander about in the finan-
cial district of any of the more frequented marketplaces he would judge,
as one used to say about Paris, that the whole world came together here. I
am not ignorant of what the historians have written about the population of Europe; whatever size it is, I freely agree with it. Italy contains   10
9,000,000, more or less; Spain, somewhat less; England, 3,000,000; and
Belgium the same; the two Germanies, 15,000,000; France, an equal
number; Sicily, 130,000. And we know what is said about the Chinese
(since those who discuss large groups speak in larger numbers), of whom
70,000,000 are normally counted during this bold census of the world.   15
That place is, indeed, nothing but a desert if one were to compare its
population to the extremely dense population of Moronia.

The land is situated under the Antarctic Pole itself, exactly like the
land of the Pygmies under the Arctic Pole. And, truthfully, now I detect
that from one and the same cause, from the most intense and excessive   20
cold of both regions, has been advanced both the stupidity of the Moronians and the puniness of the Pygmies. Indeed, in some fashion, Nature
maintains an excellent balance, for whereas bodily defects are produced
in one region of the world from the excessive remoteness of the sun, in
another region mental defects stem from it. And that makes it under-   25
standable why those who live in the temperate middle zones of the earth
are accustomed to be strong both in mind and in body. But that is doubtless the concern of the philosophers. On the south it is bounded by
Crapulia; on the east by Viraginia and the extreme corner of Frugiona;
and, finally, on the west by Lavernia.   30

CHAPTER 2
The Parts of Moronia, and the Customs Common to the Entire Populace

Moronia is indeed diverse and multiform. On the east is situated Vari-

---

5 Land of fools.

ana, or Moronia Mobilis; under the pole itself Moronia Aspera; to the south Moronia Felix; between the two Moronia Fatua; and finally, to the west Moronia Pia.

Almost all the inhabitants are tall and fat (owing to the fierceness of
5   the cold), with very light hair, pointed heads, prominent lips, and very thick ears. But all do not possess the same character, the same customs, or the same life-style. I will note a few characteristics which, it seemed to me, are generally common to all. They entertain whoever arrives without exception (if you exclude Moronia Aspera) with all the riches of their
10 city, their house, and their table. Visit any of them, greet him submissively, address him, not without inflated titles and just like the Spanish, praise his beauty, or his dress, or his slaves, or his house, and agree with whatever he says: you will obtain hospitality for however long you wish, during which nothing that can be anywhere procured will be lacking.
15 Here everything comes from good words and flattering promises.

From the most ingratiating merchants they purchase plumes, or garlands of flowers, or little bells, or tambourines at hugely inflated prices. In the middle of winter they walk along bare chested and with the rest of their body lightly clothed so that the heat may enter more easily
20 and the cold exit. In the summer, however, they don heavy coats and toss a mantle over that, with whatever other clothes they own, so that the heat might not enter by chance. Other wiser ones, however, contemptuous of intemperate winter, go out nearly naked, their reasoning being that since other animals are content with their own feathers or skin, it would
25 be shameful for man, the king of them all, to need more protection.

None of them is ever alone, for each one speaks to himself and responds in turn. He banters with himself, not without great contention, and sometimes even with a quarrel. And each moves himself to copious laughter or tears.

30 Religious clergy wander through all parts of Moronia, certain men named Morosophers, a pious and witty sort of men, belonging to several distinct orders, who have the same influence in this place that the Bonzi have with the Chinese. The names of their orders escape me for the most part; yet the names sound alike, or at least they are not much dissimilar.
35 Among them, if I have not remembered incorrectly, are the Morelloscura; others are the Cluniachi and the Lateranensi; still others are the Licetani,

---

5 *As Homer says about Thersites,* "his skull went up to a point."   32 *These Bonzi, the false priests of China, cultivate their* Pagodas *(what they call their idols) with the utmost devotion and are themselves highly esteemed.*   35 Morelloscuro *is Italian for the color of the monks from the Umbrian valley.*   36 *According to the Lateran and Cluniac rules.*

Zoccolanti, Cercosimii, Matteobassi, Scelestini, Della mercede, and Della vita commune. These people generously spend all they have for others; for themselves they beg. They walk to the farthest boundaries of Moronia barefoot, and when they gaze upon a carved stone they speak to it and kiss it. Finally, they throw themselves down in supplication in front of this little stone, bestow offerings, and flood it with their prayers. They change gold for lead and a little parchment. They light candles in the middle of the day. Eating meat is a religious scruple for them, though eating fish to overflowing is permitted. Touching gold or silver with a bare hand is a sin for them. They scarcely salute any human being, nobody who is not a stone or a cross. With whips they mercilessly scourge themselves to such an extent that they revive in a crueler version the old whipping customs of the Spartans, either because no men but they will lend their backs for that improvement, or because they once received the notion that the blood from offerings was pleasing to God. They shave their heads, either to remind themselves they were born bald, or to moderate the heat of their brain, or so that no growing hair might create an impediment between heaven and their brain, lest their free celestial reflection be threatened. I judge that they are to be esteemed too witty in two matters: they cheat the credulous people so beautifully that they themselves live excellently, expensively, and idly on others; and, unwilling to create a torment in their own home, they enjoy the wives of others (ingeniously, according to Scaliger), and the little babies they themselves produce they prefer to deposit secretly in other birds' nests to be reared.

If any of them should fall ill, everyone weeps copiously until he either dies or recovers. They steadfastly shun all medicine, so much so that the dying are smeared with oil by their fellow Morosophers. They measure knowledge not by silence (surely even inanimate objects do that on their own) but by their choice of words, their number, and their polished delivery. That person is truly wise, not who says little but who says a lot that is not inconsistent.

They never ride or sail anywhere; they consider it foolish to entrust

---

1 *Certosini.*   1 *Matteo Basso, an Italian, was the founder of the Capuchins.*   1 *Celestini.*   9 *There is the well-known story about the Franciscan and the Dominican.* 18 *Hugh of St. Victor, De Sacramentis, book 2, part 3, chapter 1; Hrabanus Maurus, De Institutione Clericorum, book 1, chapter 3; Robert Bellarmine, De Monachis, book 2, chapter 40, who writes these words:* "in order that the crown may remain," *that is, a mind free and open to divine contemplation and illumination.*   23 *In the manuscript book of* Janus Dousa.

their safety either to a worn-out horse or to a tossing and floundering
shell. All the way to puberty these Morosophers hang from their mothers'
teats. They are not accustomed to burying their dead: they believe that it
is inhuman to cover with earth anyone's parent, or wife, or friend simply
5   because the person has been abandoned by the soul. Nor, in the event
that a person who has just died is survived by someone whom he has
loved or honored, is it possible for that person to cast him aside supine
and deliver his naked body to the worms. Therefore they suspend the
body on an exceedingly high wooden platform under the stars, attired
10   with the most elegant clothes he possesses, and every year they visit and
venerate him. The monuments—not few in number—especially of
Moronia Pia, instruct us quite well that this rite derived from the
ancients.

And they recognize the rule of women, but it is a rather gentle rule
15   because their wives do not know how to command. I located the origin of
this custom from this source: once the Amazons of Viraginia, almost
adjoining the very border, subdued all of Moronia by force; however,
they did not want to occupy it themselves because of the scarcity of husbandmen. They allowed the inhabitants to retain the pretense of ruling
20   as long as every year they sent an ass to their Amazon conquerors for
tribute, fittingly loaded with gold; and that was indeed done for many
years on the appointed day. But at last the Moronians refused and sent a
message: they certainly did not care so much for the gold itself as long as
the Amazonians deigned to claim what belonged to them at the ap-
25   pointed time, but that they should beat a friendly animal—longing to
remain with them—with sticks and compel it unwillingly to bear off
their hoard seemed rather harsh and unjust to them. And, besides, the
matter was very ambiguous and debatable, for, since one ass might be
stronger than another, if one year they sent one that carried more or less
30   than the year before, the Amazons could justifiably complain that they
did not receive the correct cargo—especially since they themselves had
often observed that a poor little animal, which had appeared capable of
carrying the load at the outset, had collapsed under the burden before the
completion of the long journey. Quite stirred by this response, the Ama-
35   zons declared war, invaded the land, and, since no one resisted, proceeded
finally with an armed force to the capital of the region, Pazzivilla. Upon
hearing this all the citizens grouped together in companies, but without
any order or any arms. In military fashion the Amazons' army immediately deployed itself there for battle, shouting, hurling javelins, and
40   pressing forward. The Pazzavillani, when they observed one or another

of their people hit and lying on the ground, fell to their knees in supplication, crying out, beseeching, and expostulating: "What cruelty is this,
O Amazons, to afflict so many men with so violent a death for one ass?
One live ass would be more valuable to you than the bodies of a thousand
slaughtered men. Let each of you have your ass and your gold. We prefer   5
to live without those rather than die for them. Only spare us and depart."
Finally, defeated by the Moronians' entreaties and their peace offering,
the conqueresses ceased their attack, but to these terms they added one
more condition: that thereafter all the men of Moronia would voluntarily obey their wives in domestic matters. The vanquished answered   10
that that would be most agreeable, for to rule themselves up to now had
seemed most troublesome and full of ill will.

CHAPTER 3
Variana, or Moronia Mobilis

Variana is the easternmost part of Moronia, nearest Viraginia. Don't ask   15
me for anything certain about this place, dear Reader. In what condition
I found that province, and in what condition I left it, I am indeed quite
certain, and it will be equally certain to you, but if you happen to go
there, traveler, and find things are now in a different condition, do not
assail my credibility for what I told you, because everything is fashioned   20
anew from day to day so that it would be easier for you to pinpoint the
true form of Proteus, the color of a chameleon, or the face of tomorrow's
sky.
   Whatever the Portuguese may boast for themselves in the area of
exploration and prolonged travels, I believe the old Frenchmen best   25
deserve to claim this special praise for themselves, since we certainly find
vestiges of the French here, whether you consider the names of places,
the remains of laws, or the marks on coins. The shape of the land is
manifold and uncertain, for what luxuriant pasture you see sacred to
Flora this year, expect to see as tilled fields dedicated to Ceres the next;   30
whatever mountains projected to the heavens ages ago now fill an exca-
vated valley and offer themselves to the insolent trampling of travelers.
Rivers are often astonished to find themselves in new channels, the
former having been closed off. It is, indeed, a place where "the cows draw
the plow in the place where a ship was driven by oars." In the meantime,   35

---

15 *Land of inconstant fools.*   34 *Virgil.*

the waves—making deafening roars for being shut out by the dikes of the inhabitants—are somewhere else exacting compensation for their lost inheritance.

The cities here are numerous and large, but their names and shapes
5   alter daily. The foremost city by far when I arrived there was called Farfellia; before I left, by an actual edict of the senate, it was renamed Papilionia. The city is on wheels so that it can be wheeled about here and there like a chariot, according to the whim of its citizens. They say that place has changed its location a hundred times, and thirty times has
10 altered its entire shape. When I was a visitor there it was located next to the River Sans-eau. Then, straightaway, it ascended to the top of Mount Anylos. And every river is so frozen over with ice, nearly uninterrupted, that it offers a convenient path for the moving town. Every month the city's appearance changes anew; for the buildings are constructed so that
15 they can be separated from one another without danger. Therefore, at the first moment that someone begins to dislike the people or the neighborhood, he seeks a new location in a new street. Once upon a time the shield of the city was a tortoise carrying his shell, with the inscription of the Wise Greek: "I carry everything with me." Now it is actually a butter-
20 fly on a field of many varieties of flowers with the excellently chosen word "Ubilibet" added: "Wherever I please."

Section 2. The Attire and the Customs of the People

The inhabitants are dressed in colored feathers, in the manner of Indians, which they perceive is sufficient to protect little birds against the bitter
25 cold: with these they claim themselves much better protected, considering how greatly they excel those so weak and tender little creatures. However, they frequently alter the arrangement of their feathers, in order to pretend they have new attire: so that those feathers which shade their head in the morning trail from their heels before evening. Those
30 that clothed their knees a moment ago are now hiked up on their chests.

They take wives, whom they even love extravagantly for a while, and each responds faithfully to his wife's benevolence and guards her truly until either she no longer pleases him or he glimpses another one more beautiful. Then, at last, the marriage is ended, not unwillingly, by
35 Hercules, for even more quickly had she begun to loathe the conjugal

---

11 *"Sans-eau," French for* without water: *thus More in his* Utopia *mentions the river* Anydrus.

bed. Today they treat a stranger they have never seen before with the greatest familiarity, as if they were about to enter into a permanent friendship. The next day, however, they pass him by as if he were unknown.

They scarcely say anything voluntarily that they do not retract with   5
their next breath, sooner than they promised it in earnest. They promise nothing that they do not afterward forswear before they fulfill it. In short, they execute nothing which is not carried out with regret, albeit too late. They sell for nothing today things which, if they hear that these have pleased the buyer, they will buy back tomorrow at great expense.   10
Every year they fashion new laws, for they do not think it is worthwhile that, since the conditions of life always change, the rules of living should always remain the same. In addition, since second thoughts are wiser in most cases, it is an extreme sign of slavery that having once decided on something they should never recall it if they are later dissatisfied.   15

Section 3. The Tomb of Vortunius. Ancient Coins

Here, in the field of Muerius, near the road, the small tomb of a certain Vortunius, not very old, and less elegant, is found with this inscription:

PASSERBY
Stay, Read, Walk. Here lies   20
Andrew Vortunius, neither a slave nor a soldier, nor a doctor, nor a fencer, nor a shoemaker, nor a thief, nor a lawyer, nor a money-lender, but all these. Who lived his life not in the city, not in the country, not at home, not abroad, not on the sea, not on the land, not here, not anywhere, but everywhere. Who died not from hunger,   25
nor from poison, nor from the sword, nor from the noose, nor from sickness, but from all. I, H. I., of that man not a debtor, nor an heir, nor a kinsman, nor a neighbor, nor a friend, but all of these, erected this, not a monument, not a stone, not a tomb, not a castle of sorrow, but all of them; wishing not ill, not good, but both, not to you, not   30
to him, not to me, but all to everyone.

Four miles from the city of Novizza I saw many antique coins dug up from a certain well. It will not be irksome for me to describe them, in courtesy to the reader. One was a square coin with two-faced Janus on

---

21 *This is similar to the monument of Aelia Laelia Crispis at St. Peter's in Bologna.*

one side; on the other side a small round stone appeared to be engraved, as it were, upon a smooth tablet with the nearly obliterated letters ERR. VAR. DUC.

Another was round, of which one side represented someone in a toga, nearly middle aged. His right hand rested on the head of a very attractive little dog; his left hand held a half-open book. The other side displayed a chameleon in all its various colors, and above was the inscription CONST. LIP., "Constant Lipsius."

The third was larger—so that it appeared more valuable—and oval. On the front side was a thin, large-nosed face, crowned with a garland of leaves; on the other was a polypus fish lying under a rock, and placed next to it, likewise fittingly engraved, was the inscription *Pour Bon,* "For Good." I neither know nor seek the author; nor do I understand well enough what this pretender to knowledge desired for himself: any Reader a little better versed in antiquity would with ease understand completely.

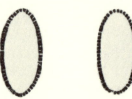

Section 4. The Academy of Variana

In the region of the Senzapesian Valley, where I anticipated no such thing, I found something resembling an Academy. They call it Dudosa, where I encountered some shades of philosophers. Anyone who searches

---

18 *"Senza peso," Italian for "without weight," "trivial."*

there for endowed chairs, lecture halls, scholars of the arts, rectors, teachers, regulations, or books will be disappointed. Everyone alternates as teacher and as pupil.

However, there are two colleges here: one of skeptics who give no credence either to their eyes or to their ears; nor do they dare to assert that they do not dare to assert anything. Steal some money from one of them, or some food, or some clothing (as one of them stole from a certain Lacydes); immediately he debates whether he ever had any such thing. Strike him a blow (as hard as you please with your fist); he doubts if he even received the blow or whether he now feels it. Speak to him, stand in front of him, touch him. He hears, he sees, he feels; however, in the meantime he is uncertain whether his senses do not deceive him.

The other college is composed of innovators, the Troverense, perhaps named from the art of inventing, for all devote themselves to discovering new things, and they carefully arrange the making of new cities, new clothes, new sports, new manners, and new forms of government. Anyone who has devised some more pleasant type of sport, or some unheard-of type of clothing will be promoted by the Duke according to the worthiness of the thing. He who first blew bubbles composed of soap and spit from a walnut shell and a hollow reed is no less celebrated here than either the inventor of gunpowder or that founder of printing from Mainz is among the Europeans. These men are in great demand as courtiers, and even as artists, especially in Moronia Felix, whose citizens arrange all their clothing and adjust their posture according to their advice. Indeed, these men have devised a new language for themselves, which their teachers call the Supermonical language; up to the present it is known only by the more learned.

For the sake of those who travel, a selection of their words added to my work will be of some value. Invented quite recently, it is now used by them for the most ordinary daily needs. Lest he seem completely stupid and Cedurinus, their language should be known by the traveler, for otherwise he will be unable to comprehend them when they speak.

Earth itself		
The soul	is called	Silo
Whatever is within the skin		Adek
		Cohos

5

10

15

20

25

30

35

---

7 *Diogenes Laertius.* 26 *The mystical language of Paracelsus, named thus by his disciples.* 31 *"Cedurinus," Paracelsian for stupid.* 33 *A catalogue of some Paracelsian words.*

The interior of the abdomen		Coostrum
An innate quality		Relloleum
Anything natural		Cherionium
Salt		Hal and Malek
5 An exhalation from the earth		Leffas
The moving of water		Lorindt
Forest honey		Tereniabin
Evil fumes of the elements		Realgar
A beginning		Ilech
10 Something supernatural	is called	Iesadach
An ointment		Oppodeltoch
A purging of the stars		Nostoch
Jupiter		Cydar
Successive generation		Dardo
15 An uncertain prophecy		Erodinium
A certain prophecy		Essodinium
Pustules		Bothor
Bad blood		Cassatum
A maimed or mutilated one		Artetiscus
20 A hunchback		Nasda

But even more astonishing to me seemed the names of minerals and vapors:

Sulphur		Chibur or Alcubrith
Quicksilver		Azoth, Sibar, Unqua-si, or Missadan
25 Unrefined tin		Wismadt
Precipitated mercury		Diatessadelton
A metal similar to iron		Robolt
The matter of a metal finally liquified	is called	Blackmal
30 Iron		Edir
Mercury		Missadar, Zaibar
Mineral gold		Chifir, Fido
Copper		Melibaeum
Vitriol		Colcothar
35 A mixture of coral and sea crab		Dubelcolep

And know even the names of spirits which are the most familiar to these people:

A good demon	is called	Evestrum	
Good spirits, revealing secrets		Zeninephidei	
Spirits of fire		Trifertes	5
Spirits of the air		Nenufareni	
Ghosts	are called	Caballi	
Activities of specters		Trarames	
Mineral spirits		Operimethiolim	
Impressed images		Gamohaea	10

The prefect of the College was Bustius Hohenheimius, principal architect of the new language. However, I have no idea at all whether this new language prevails right to the present or if another, perhaps a more recent version, will have taken its place. Whatever the case, I have acquitted my duty in warning you beforehand.   15

CHAPTER 4
Moronia Aspera

Under the pole itself, at the extreme southern tip of the Australian continent, is Moronia Aspera, a mean place: a region mountainous, rocky, and perpetually bound in ice; indeed, it enjoys a dry and extremely cold   20
climate. The rocks here are iron, corresponding in every respect to the magnets that lie under the other pole, which is the reason, unknown by sailors and geographers, why in nautical tables, once you have passed over the Equator, the magnet turns instead toward the South Pole. It contains two duchies, more spacious than productive to be sure: Lyperia,   25
which others call Maninconica, and Orgilia.

Section 2. The Duke of Lyperia, the People

The Duke of Lyperia, known as "Le Grand Chagrin" by his people, is a morose and gloomy man, and rules over a people resembling him no less than they differ from the rest of the Moronians. That ruler has an enor-   30

---

11 *That is the name Paracelsus was born with.*   19 *Land of melancholy fools.*

mous palace called Cordolium, magnificently constructed out of jet, in whose vestibule is the saying, set down in red letters:

This is a place of sorrow; depart far from here all joyful ones.

Most of the inhabitants are hairy, thin, savage, swarthy, black
5   haired, with skin tough and uneven, stern in countenance, carelessly dressed, sorrowful in mien, their eyes fixed with a certain stupor (nor can they easily rouse themselves), sunken inward as though they had been long entombed in the hollow recesses of their cheeks. No one looks for a city or a village here. The inhabitants always live alone, according to the
10 custom of hares, and live a completely hermetic life: partly because their disposition is so suspicious and fearful that they do not tolerate neighbors, partly because the edict of the Duke decrees that no one live within the sight of or place the foundation of his dwelling within a certain number of miles of another's home.
15   To be sure, they go out most rarely: either because of the impenetrable darkness, which is nearly perpetual here; or because of the Duke's decree; or rather because of their own inclination, for they prefer to amuse themselves in domestic solitude. When they do meet someone, however, they rarely greet him or speak with him, for they themselves
20 have a rule to observe: "Except in the case of necessity, no one is to go out, or salute anyone along the way, except on Thursday." Go to any of their houses and knock on the door; after a long wait your host answers in a rage. Surely they are most annoyed by the sight of a new guest.
        You ask, What do they do, or how, finally, do they spend their lives?
25 In truth, in imagining and conceiving what was never done and never will be done, in believing what they imagine and in pursuing what they believe—which is the reason why they so abhor company and do not wish to be disturbed.
        One believes himself long dead and stretches out on the pavement as
30 if he were a cold cadaver. If any member of his family approaches this man and questions him intensively, he flies up in his face, reckoning him a necromancer who has recalled his previously released soul from

---

3 *Ranzovian verses in a certain chapel, not far from Segeberg.*   20 *This rule is diligently observed today by the Carthusian monks. For persons similar to these, look in the Hospital of Melancholy Fools written by Garzoni.*   32 *The same thing happened to a certain Pisander, in Caelius Rhodiginus, book 9, 26.*

the underworld through the power of his mysterious incantation, and now he wanders about like a shade, flattering himself that he cannot be perceived by human senses. Anyone of his countrymen who approaches him, grabs him, and (if need be) subdues him with chains, he reckons to be one of the Furies sent by Pluto to reclaim his dear soul that just recently escaped from him. And his house, which he once supposed was his grave, he now reckons to be Hell and abhors it even more.

Another, imagining himself a mole, lives in a subterranean den hunting for worms and bravely digging through the earth with a well-shod nose. However, if anyone follows him or pricks him with a pin, immediately reckoning that he has been run through by a mole catcher (for that is exactly what he seems to himself to be, blind like a mole so that he can distinguish neither a man nor a sword), he cries out miserably and prepares himself for the execution.

Another man imagines himself Atlas, with the heavy burden of the universe imposed on him. Accordingly, he stands immobile, sighing frequently, now lifting this shoulder, now lowering it, and after sweating a little while under this supposed burden, if any of his friends should transfer the vast support of the sky to himself and disturb his place, he falls flat on his face crying, impatiently awaiting the collapse of the world and loudly upbraiding these most imprudent little men, so wasteful of their own welfare and that of the whole world.

Another thinks herself Megaera, or one of the Furies, and terrifies strangers with her savage gestures. She shakes her hair just like so many snakes, hisses, and extends her clawlike nails to strangers. Encountering, indeed, a puppy or a shrewmouse she will torture it as mercilessly as she can, certain that she is tormenting the soul of a sinner (just as the insane Ajax is said to have done, once upon a time, to the rams), and is herself overwhelmed with joy by the punishment and by the plaintive cries of the miserable animal.

Another, imagining his nose to have grown beyond bounds, stitches thongs together which, in the manner of Merlino's Cingar, he fastens to his back for support. Another conceives himself all made of clay or glass. Therefore he goes out of his way to avoid everyone nearby, afraid that if, by chance, he had a violent crash with someone he might be shattered on the spot. Thus there is not a single one of these people who does not elaborately contrive to be something other than what he is.

---

32 *Merlino Coccaio in Macaronicon.*

Section 3

From Mount Ochietto, the salty River Larmium originates and irrigates
the greatest part of this province. However, the Traurigian Mountains,
like the Italian Apennines, cut through this entire region and produce
5   nothing but horror and a certain dreadful solitude. For you will discern
nothing here except bears' caves and witches' huts. Both kinds of evil
beasts abound here: the bear, a truly melancholic animal who hibernates
the entire winter in its most well-hidden cave and lives by sucking its
paws; witches, decrepit and impotent old women, eyes filled with rheum
10   and teeth worn away (just as Caecilius once described), who think themselves capable of doing everything and murmur about such trifles as
stirring up storms, halting rivers, healing the sick, and raising the dead.
However, in the meantime these women die from mere hunger.
        Covering the shady side of these mountains is the Forest of Bubonia,
15   perpetually infested with ghosts (so the neighbors assert) and impenetrable by mortals. You will see werewolves running about everywhere
through this forest, and unless you are acquainted with their habits and
their deceitful voices beforehand, you will be more than a little terrified
when you hear them shrieking. But in Gramia Valley, lying at the foot of
20   these mountains, many men roam about, whom the head witch Melaena
is said to have transformed into lions and asses, although she left them
with human voices and faces.

Section 4

Not to be omitted among the remaining sights of the region is the most
25   famous. On the side of one snowy mountain, the highest and most
remote of the Traurigians, is the Cave of Maninconicus, known by
others as the Cave del Pianto. The entrance is indeed narrow and is
covered with sky-blue ice, but within, as may be conjectured from the
echo, it becomes an exceedingly spacious chamber. From the roof dangle
30   huge icicles which seem to have solidified like so many teeth in the most
frightful jaws of the cave.
        Rumor has it that here the disturbed souls of melancholic people
are tortured by the most intense cold. Whoever approaches the entrance
to gaze in—whoever does so is scarcely wise—is struck to the ground
35   dead, and there his ghostly corpse awaits the return of his most gravely

---

21 *Melancholy is asslike or lionlike.*

tormented soul. But he who will hold his ear to the ground or stand a
little farther back from the entrance, oh, what sighing (either the clang
of chains or the crash of icicles) will he seem to hear? Or he who will
sleep on any part of this mountain (for I, somewhat audaciously, tried it
myself), good God, what Chimaeras, Tragelaphs, Centaurs, and a thousand astonishing forms of monsters will he behold, not without a certain
horror!

CHAPTER 5
Orgilia, the Second Province of Moronia Aspera

The region next to Maninconica is Orgilia: a land arid, sandy, and
barren, which produces a people irritable, frenzied, and savage. In stature
they are smaller than Moronia's other inhabitants, with pallid faces, red
hair, glowing eyes, trembling lips, and an uncertain but quite rapid gait.
Here presides the Duke of Courroux, the chief and exemplar of all
tyrants. The Reader will marvel and scarcely believe my description of
what this man does: what he commands and how impetuously, what he
reduces his subjects to, and how he punishes them. It seems to me that
that former infamous Russian tyrant was a gentle and civilized man in
comparison to this one; he is the most bloodthirsty of the infamous
Caesars and, indeed, even of the Patagonians.

Perhaps even the explorer of lands, an investigator of incredible
events, will hesitate and not allow himself to be persuaded (since the
ways of the inhabitants are accustomed to conform to the nature of the
climate) that this polar region could ever have been the source of so very
hot and choleric a race, given its location in the most intense cold. But
we philosophers correctly understand that where the climate is more
frigid, this phenomenon may be accomplished by the reaction of opposites; nor will anyone scoff at this who knows that Africa, a most torrid
region, produces the coldest serpents and that flies are commonly generated in the furnaces of Cyprus, who extinguish fire with their coldness.
From the middle stratum of the atmosphere lightning and thunder are
hurled out; and finally this mass of earth is set in motion by subterranean
fire, hatched indeed from the coldness of her moving body and tossed to
and fro. Now, therefore, supported by philosophy, I hope for and claim
your faith in me.

---

10 *Land of choleric fools.*   29 *Mercurialis, Variae Lectiones.*

The province has four principal parts: Lecithia, Prasinia, Iodia, and Glastia. The color and attire of the inhabitants of each region are singular: the Lecithians are pale and march about in ashen-colored attire; the Prasinians are colored and clothed in green; the Glastians in
5   dark bluish-green; and the Iodians in red.

None of these men ventures anywhere except when loaded down with weapons, so that even he who may have few clothes will, nevertheless, not be without all sorts of arms. That man, no less than if he had been hired as Mars's porter, carries a musket on his right arm, a cudgel
10   on his left, a sword on one side, a dagger on the other, and a bow and a quiver on his back wherever he travels. Anyone who meets him going along the road, unless he yield the road a long way off, must prepare himself for battle, or death is inevitable. It is a rare trip without a wound or even a murder; and once someone kills a person he tears him to pieces
15   most ravenously, for the citizens always feed on raw flesh, usually human, which they reckon among the most splendid of feasts, and they intoxicate themselves with the drained-off blood. There are no laws there: by force and by arms are all things decided. An injury suffered is either revenged or endured. Only this one rule governs, obtained from
20   ancient law: "Conquer and enjoy."

Dueling is permitted either to seek revenge, or to recover what is yours, or to seize what is someone else's. But if more than two assemble and join in the struggle, whoever remains alive is bound over into the Duke's custody. It is evident that this is an astute decree from the Duke,
25   since it opportunely guards against the seeds of conspiracies, and under this pretext he procures better food for his table. The Duke's seat is called Tarochium, a vast city but completely made of wood, for the tyrant would permit it to be constructed from no other material, lest it be impossible to have it burned at his whim when the citizens have offended.
30   No one lives here, except blacksmiths, executioners, and butchers — in whose shops hang the legs of men, no differently than the legs of swine or cattle hang with us. To this city flows the torrential River Zornus, which they say runs even in the middle of winter, emanating heat like a mineral spring and giving off ill-smelling vapors.
35   Next to it is the palace of the Duke, a palace extremely lofty and difficult to reach, erected on a towering mountain which they call Calaver-

---

1 *Georg Agricola, De Subterraneis,* "*Unnatural bile is of four kinds: yolk-colored, leek-green, violet-colored, and watery, which resembles the color of woad.*"   27 *Garzoni, Discourse 13.* Furious fools *he calls* Da Tarocco, *hence this name.*

nius, and they say it has finally attained its present height from human skulls heaped together. The palace is surrounded by a high wall built of bricks, for that Duke lives always in doubt of his citizens' fidelity and would rather trust his iron gates than their love and regard.

They say he is attended by 10,000 executioners who all minister to his anger and his palate. If any traveler, ignorant of the state of affairs, should arrive here by chance, he is immediately seized and his head is presented to the Duke for dinner, which that man is no less enticed by than we are by a rare bird or a fish; nor does he pursue this prey from the efforts of the executioners any less assiduously than Vitellius, once upon a time, searched for the tongues of flamingoes and the intestines of lamprey. He enjoys Ethiopians in place of thrush, and Englishmen, in truth, in place of quail. However, he behaves more mercifully to those who are condemned to be killed only at his whim or for his palate, and not because of any crime committed. For no differently than Olympias is said to have treated Eurydice, he gives them the option to choose whatever type of death they prefer: whether they wish to die by beheading or by hanging.

In his palace nothing is as famous as the Inquisition Chapel, known as Saint Carniceria, a temple sacred to the Furies and the infernal gods, where horrible, sculptured figures of all of them, fashioned out of jet and coral, are seen and worshiped. Here you will see all types of tortures and deaths: a hundred gibbets, no fewer of Ixion's wheels, axes, swords, yokes, ropes, clubs, and muskets half eaten from rust—so that it is quite evident that before it was known either to the Europeans or the Chinese, the use of this lethal machine was known to them. Here a thousand altars smoke with perpetual fire, on which daily sacrifices are offered to the Devil and to the Duke. They try to satisfy the Furies with the souls and, in turn, the gluttony of the tyrant with a daily hecatomb of bodies; the blood that remains, thinned by a certain art of theirs so it does not congeal for a long time, is preserved in special jars in the manner of Massic and Falernian wine, to be served to the Duke after many years. A bloody stream, the Di-Marza, runs through the middle of the Inquisition Chapel and washes a floor defiled by blood.

The inhabitants almost always run to and fro along the street, always panting and sweating. There are two things here you will marvel at, Reader. You will see no one who is not either lame or mutilated; among them, the person whose face is most covered with scars wins the

---

10 *Suetonius, Vitellius.*   15 *Diodorus Siculus.*

award for beauty. Second, you will see no old men here, for it scarcely ever happens that any of them survives all the way to middle age.

Just about in the middle of the region is the Coledochian Swamp, surely no smaller than the Meotis or less famous, whose water is golden-yellow in color and most bitter in taste. It often overflows, but at uncertain times, and, breaching its banks, rages through a large part of Orgilia; and whatever soil the flow of the waves (whose composition is sulfurous) merely touches, it burns no differently than did Phaethon's wide-ranging chariot. Then the inhabitants fill up jugs for themselves, believing this liquor, if frequently drunk, will arouse their spirits and incite their hearts to attempt anything.

But take heed, Reader, lest you be deceived. I learned these things only by hearsay, not daring to observe them in my own person. I remember what that Frenchman some time ago impressed on me, borrowed from the most excellent and ingenious Bacon: "Il faut menager la vie." "It is necessary to husband one's life." This Moronia Aspera was much too rough for it to entertain me as a visitor. I remained at Pazzivilla, safe and taking good care of my skin, resolved that it was better in this circumstance for me to believe rather than experience.

CHAPTER 6
Moronia Fatua

No part of Moronia is as populous or as ancient as this place, which is commonly called Fatua, whose residents offer themselves as the aboriginal Moronians. Therefore one perceives that Moronia Fatua is no less the mother of all countries than Pazzivilla is the mother of all cities, and accordingly, it is located in the middle—the navel, as it were, of so fine a body. It is encircled on all sides: on the south by Moronia Aspera, on the east by Moronia Mobilis, on the west by Moronia Pia, and on the north by Moronia Felix. The more southern part, Scioccia, is more slothful and phlegmatic, while that part which lies more northerly is much more expert and industrious in doing things.

Had I not been an eyewitness of the customs and actions of this most stupid race of people, by Hercules, I might not have believed nature to have granted to such brutish forms of life the divine gift of reason. For everyone in that part of Moronia that borders Maninconica walks about

---

3 *This is the name of the gallbladder.*

bent over in the manner of quadrupeds; nor (in their marvelous sim-
plicity) do they know any other way of moving.

You will not discern so much as a little hut here: partly, because
they do not know how to construct buildings themselves; partly, in
truth, because they dare not enter buildings made by others, lest they be   5
crushed by the heavy roof falling down. Here every year many die from
mere starvation and from the cold, inasmuch as they have not learned to
cook food, or produce clothes, or make a bed; yes, indeed, they do not
know how to speak out plainly. No one knows his parent, or his son, or
his wife; no one knows how to return the same way he went earlier. No   10
one can distinguish a bear from a sheep, a lion from a puppy. Indeed,
there are those who do not know by which way to introduce prepared
food into their stomach: through their nose, or through their ears, or
through some other, less suitable opening. Finally, for it is not agreeable
to linger here, imagine to yourself an Arcadian beast given human form,   15
and you have the spitting image of a native Scioccian.

Section 2. Baveria

The remaining part of Moronia Fatua, Baveria, is more witty, and more
worthy of the feet of travelers and of the eyes of the fastidious Reader. For
the people value themselves as most wise and search more deeply into the   20
causes of all things; nor are they content until they ferret out the underlying processes. From childhood all are one eyed, since immediately at
birth the other eye, as though it were superfluous, is ripped out, for
always when one eyelid is shut we see more distinctly and intently. Part
of the nation goes naked, so that they spare both the labor and the time of   25
dressing and undressing. Another part prepares shelters for itself, but
without walls or partitions, so that the houses may be more open to the
air and therefore more healthy. Finally, a third part builds the most
towering nests, in the manner of small birds, so that they might be closer
to the heavens.   30

All eagerly pursue a certain marvelous singularity in their work and
in their speculation. A few of them, in order to capture the ear of the
people, exert themselves to such an extent that it may scarcely be believed.
For you will see some marching about on their head and hands; others,
with wings built of wax and feathers joined together, are presumptu-   35
ously flying, imitating the birds in the manner of Daedalus, so that you

---

17 *Land of silly asses.*

would think Calais and Zetes, allies of the Argonauts, had risen from the
dead. Others, like certain Thessalian Venetians, ostentatiously display
prodigies of nature and art, or the stupendous effects of an ointment, a
potion, or some machine to the gaping mobs. Finally, still others, with
5   an art gloriously lucrative, to be sure, draw forth gold from the basest of
metals. You will laugh, indeed, at their painstaking folly; for as many
times as hope eludes them, it recruits them once again.

I hear that in earlier times some of these Baverians once went to an
oracle to learn about the uncertain outcome of some most difficult sub-
10   limation: to whom the oracle immediately said, "Travaillez." Having
taken counsel, they go away with an eager mind, and now they pride
themselves that the god had looked favorably on them. And again they
squander their labor, a second and a third time, and with their labor
their riches; nor do they perceive themselves as having been admonished
15   by divine authority, that they should scorn this Vulcan's fraud and
sweat instead with a hoe and a mattock.

Section 3. The Cities of Moronia Fatua, particularly of Baveria:
The Metropolis Pazzivilla

The first city of all those I came upon here was Duricoria, a city not to be
20   contemned, which has nothing, however, that may detain the traveler.
Next to it is the Villa Pratensis, known for the intelligence of its Senators, who, not so long ago, when the sky was cloudy and threatening
rain, entered into a deliberation concerning the stopping of the rain
shower. One advised ringing the bells of the entire city; another, that
25   they burn foul-smelling manure in the open air, as the Italian women
are wont to do to avert a threatening storm. Finally, the most eminent of
this order of Senators arose and urged that whatever water the clouds
contained they should permit to sprinkle down, and he did not doubt
that by this scheme the rain might at length stop voluntarily.

30   But Pazzivilla is the queen of all the cities. Indeed, its site lies partly
on a damp and swampy plain, partly, in truth, on the side of a rather
lofty mountain. Both parts of this town are joined together by a descending path in the north and are, consequently, far from any forest or river.
The mountainous part supplies snow to the valley; the valley returns its

---

2 *Mountebanks.*   9 *Libavius recites this judgment from the common folk in sing-song*
rhythm: "Alchemy is art without art; / Which is understood part by part; / Its middle stage
is the art of deceiving; / Its final stage is to go begging."   21 *The town and its history are*
well known to the Italians.   24 *Moresinus, The Origin of the Papal Religion.*

water to the mountain, water that has been kept for a long while in cisterns and swamps. It contains sixteen gates, which they say were erected by the founding fathers so that it might be a city four times richer than any other.

The shape of Pazzivilla is not round or oval, like other cities. Rather, it is a cross between a cylinder and an inverted pyramid, plainly composed as a copy of the human body. No one should be amazed by this form who knows Belgium imitating the form of a lion, Peloponnesia the leaf of the plane tree, Italy the shinbone of a dead man, Spain an oxhide, both peninsulas of the Atlantic region fish lungs, and Asia the skin of a crocodile. And so, as soon as you see these, from a distance you will seem to glimpse the human lineaments of some Colossus, or some Prometheus chained to the Caucasus Mountains.

At the top of these same mountains a marketplace is set up, surely because it is the head of the city and administers sense and life to the rest. What a great feat of labor do the porters expend while they push any goods whatsoever, chiefly great barrels full of wine or beer, against the slope of the hill up to the summit; think of it, Reader, and laugh! You will seem to see a hundred Sisyphuses vainly rolling stones along, who, perchance, when they have ascended to the middle of the mountain with great effort, panting and sweating, are shoved back down the hill, not without great danger, by the crash of another barrel careening down from above.

Here at the head live the most grave and honored Senators, who have a lookout to gaze most conveniently upon the whole city from this place. The neck connected to this town is a village short and narrow, the seat of magistrates and beadles. In the likeness of shoulder blades, arms, and hands are two villages, one on either side. Those artisans that inhabit these places are few indeed, and not very skillful.

The trunk of this city's body is a street a little broader and more distinguished, the object of visitors, which extends all the way to the loins. Even the very part where we sit seems to be beautifully suggested by the gradual juncture of the more concave portion of the mountain with the plain. Here dwell pimps, prostitutes, and all those who maintain the public sewers in the city. Day laborers and travelers draw lots for the two legs and feet projecting into the middle of the valley.

The buildings, to a one, all lack foundations, inasmuch as they say they prefer to dig up stones rather than bury them. The Senators build themselves the most lofty dwellings so that the closer they come to the heavens, the warmer they may be, and the farther away from the inferior

and inclement air of the earth. You will see no home that is not painted
everywhere and inscribed with the names, especially of all their ancestors but even of their friends.

Section 4. *The Senators of Pazzivilla*

5   While I was there the Senators held a parliament where they debated
how an improvement could best be made to either the dignity, or the
loveliness, or, finally, the security of the city. Everyone offered advice,
according to his ability and prudence. First, for example, one proposed
bringing the sea many miles through the middle of the mountains with
10   the labor of the citizens, for he noticed other cities wonderfully enriched
by the sea's proximity.

Another arises and wrinkles his brow. He says that trust should not
be placed in so fierce and ravenous an element whose treacherous waves
have devoured many splendid states. Therefore a third urges building
15   remarkable aqueducts to fetch water from the lowest valley through
some pipes, which he doesn't doubt can easily be accomplished, since he
has often seen water bubble from the ground spontaneously and, because
it could not be contained in a narrow place, diffuse itself throughout the
plain. And on the contrary, since when rainwater runs down from the
20   summit of a mountain one wave propels and hastens the next, the same
might undoubtedly be done to make it ascend the mountain.

Another prefers to surround the city with a somewhat higher new
mountain to be raised from the adjoining valley by the hands of the citizens. He asserts a fourfold rationale for this plan: first, so the whole
25   world might not observe what was carried on in the city by the Pazzivillani, especially by the Senators; second, to defend and augment the
city; third and finally, for warding off the cold. When this has been accomplished he desires the loftiest bridge to be constructed from solid
rock, extending from the peak of the old mountain to the new one to
30   serve for promenading and transportation. Another jumps up and,
smiling, asks how, in the end, a valley can produce a mountain. And
besides, if this were conceded to be possible, so large a bridge would be
exposed to all dangers; for if an animal or a traveler might be the slightest
bit unsteady, not Salus herself could prevent that one from falling;
35   indeed, he would inevitably perish immediately, and, besides, what is
worse, not without an arm or a leg miserably broken. Choose something

---

1 *A white wall is a fool's writing paper.*

else that carries more dignity with it, no danger, and not so much labor. Therefore, if his fellow citizens would kindly listen to his advice, it would seem to him the best plan by far that each house should erect a lofty spire, according to its size, on whose peak a bronze or silver cock with a golden comb would detect the ever-so-changeable breeze. And in every spire he would place a clock, and to every clock he would add a bell. Nor could it be described how elegant and pleasant a sight such a regular series of high towers would be to the arriving traveler and what a harmony so many little bells perpetually sounding through the hours would offer to the ear. Immediately, so suitable, easy, eminent, and highly desirable a suggestion is given unanimous approval, so that now any stranger who follows my footsteps in the future to that place will be a traveler about to cast an eye on a city far more elegant and refined.

Section 5. The District of Spesius

Next to this place lies the District of Spesius, extremely rich once upon a time, in which I saw nothing outstanding except Actaeonius Valley, Cubaea, an eight-cornered city, and Milana. All the inhabitants are certainly most liberal with their fortunes, and they contrive ingenious ways of squandering whatever they possess: certain ones on hunting dogs, others on hawks or kites, others exhaust an ample inheritance with an ivory cube or with painted cards. And, indeed, when only their clothes remain, either they auction them off or they pawn them to moneylenders so that they can pursue their pleasure to the end.

But whether this region belongs to Moronia Fatua or Moronia Felix is completely uncertain to me. Whoever it was once under the control of, the old inhabitants seem to me to have departed long ago, and whether or not this region might have maintained any lawyers or usurers in the past, I am certain this truly beautiful and fruitful land must have greeted its new inhabitants a long time ago.

People who have no more money either subsist at another man's table, or are perchance supported by the public. Azotium Promontory is renowned here, the haven of wretched debtors, where everyone takes refuge who has fled the marketplace because of misfortune. And here we know those able to pay who just mocked their unhappy creditors. If, by chance, these creditors pursue the fleeing debtor here and snatch him

---

14 *Land of prodigal fools.*   16 The three principal causes of prodigality: the dog, the dice, and the hawk.

back from this altar of refuge against his will, they are, indeed, themselves hurled down from the highest peak, being guilty of the sacrilege
that has taken place.

5   Here parents, even those still living, are more indulgent than ours
(so it seems), entrusting their entire inheritance to sons who are hardly
yet adults, and many men who are about to die are wont to bequeath
their whole family estate, fields, and household goods to their wives,
neglecting their children. In the event that their wives die first, they
lavish as much on their funerals as would be sufficient to settle a daughter
10   in marriage.

Section 6. *The People of Lisonica*

At the entrance to Moronia Felix dwell the people of Lisonica, the
strangest of all I ever saw, two faced, two tongued, their front half in the
shape of an ape, their rear in the shape of a dog, so that they all seem
15   composed of man, dog, and ape. Here let my witness be the grave author
Münster who described certain Indians of this shape in the other part of
the world. They are assuredly born to servitude, the greatest majority
giving themselves up voluntarily or selling themselves to the more
highly born men of a neighboring nation. And if they are so totally
20   stupid that not a single soul is able to conceive of anything praiseworthy
himself, they nevertheless know how perfectly to imitate what they have
observed anywhere. There is nothing that they wear, or do, or speak, of
which someone did not give them the example. While I was there everyone limped on one leg and constantly spat between paces, all because
25   Prefect Ciniflonius of Lisonica had broken his leg some time ago and
had long been afflicted with a cough.

Most of them are barbers, tailors, brokers, or, finally, pimps. And
there are some among them, so they say, who are courtiers, not to be
scorned in their position. No Spaniard is as perfect a mimic as these
30   Lisonicans. Speak to or look upon anyone; he, first bending his knee and
eagerly kissing your right hand, repeats the last word you spoke and,
mimicking your expression, fawningly echoes whatever he thinks will
be pleasing to you—not, however, without a great heap of titles. Then,
having kissed you with his other mouth, he gazes fixedly at your eyes,
35   anxious that his response will please you. Merely nod to him and con-

---

9 *Moresinus writes the same about the British in his book concerning the origin of the
papal religion.*   12 Land of flatterers.   21 *Oh imitators, you slavish herd!*

tinue speaking; whatever you say he copies into his notebook as if it were
a divinely given oracle, gazes up at the sky, and, bending down, worships
you. These men know no God except the person to whom they have sentenced themselves in servitude. To him, with altars, bended knees, and
prayers, these suppliants devote themselves. At least all these things are   5
done by *one* mouth, but no word ever emerges from this mouth that is
not retracted privately in the meantime by the other one (doglike, to be
sure).

In this region Louerium presents itself first of all, a lofty and remarkable city, but so flimsily constructed that it cannot hope to endure   10
for long. It is very often fertilized by the River Bugius and even now and
then submerged. And neighboring this is Babillarda, a buzzing village
whose citizens never hold their peace. Mountains rise from here and
project higher and higher all the way to Chatouilla, a truly renowned
district whose inhabitants are never not laughing. Connected to this is   15
the most charming Piacentian Plain, which finally ends in the Pipulian
Fen. This swamp terminates in the notorious city of Verguença, where
they exile all criminals and those they call Medrosi.

CHAPTER 7
Moronia Felix   20

Truly, whether you consider loveliness or richness, Moronia Felix is
easily preeminent in the southern continent. For if it were to possess as
much wealth as it claims, I fear this place might even snatch the prize
away from the northern hemisphere. But it is the custom of these people
to pretend to have what they do not have and show off very boastfully   25
whatever they do have. Bordered by a chain of mountains along its
length and width, this plain continues uninterrupted for 60 German
miles, which provides a most delightfully expansive site for Moronia
Felix. Through the foothills of the mountain, the most splendid river le
Sain meanders and nearly encompasses them.   30

As the Reader can easily comprehend, small cities are most pleasantly
scattered about on the sloping face of the hills which are so beautifully
linked together. From one part, you gaze upon a most flourishing valley
crossed by a quite graceful river; from another, upon a smooth and, by
Pollux, sufficiently spacious tract of pastures and fields, most conven-   35

---

21 Land of braggarts, or of conceited folly.

iently hedged. The cities here are not as populous as they are noble and well kept. Yet the buildings are exceedingly flimsy, and whatever their external splendor promises, on the interior they are sordid beyond measure. Here, where the Rodomantadian Hills offer an uneven path for the shoes of travelers, is the city of Vantarole, which is also called Salacona, superbly built but poor to the point of beggary.

Nearby is the village of Menosprecia, a very filthy town, to whose reputation that city of the Parisians has rightly yielded. Not far distant from here is the most lofty and famous Derrumbiadan Rock, not much different from the English Peak, whose summit is level and unbroken; its descent, however, is so abrupt and steep that if you look down from above, the smooth surface of the rocks looks like the highest tower constructed by human labor. Owing to its many funeral rites it is considered a fatal rock, so that I would believe no more people ever plunged from the Tarpeian Rock.

Occupying the rest of this small section of Moronia is the city of Antoia, very obnoxious because of its fires, so that even old Rome did not burn so often; this is believed to occur partly from the neglect of its citizens, and partly from building with oily material. And in this vicinity is the city of Putanium — which others call Villa Vitiosa — built from flint and the hardest stone. Thereafter, near the boundaries of Ucalegonium, the extremely broad Sin-obran Plain reveals itself, where the populace always vacations and where any who work are severely punished. Its principal cities are Jugaria and Risaglium, and on the eastern edge, where le Sain meets the River Oysivium, we see those Saltuares Islands (once known to Pliny, so it seems), which are said to be moved in harmonious rhythm to the beats of measured feet.

Section 2. The Customs of the People

Here there is no one who does not boast of his nobility, displaying statues of his ancestors and the insignia of his huge family line, showing his descent even from 10,000 years before the world was created (like those mentioned in Diodorus Siculus). There I saw some very long galleries where their family trees are depicted by straight, oblique, and transverse lines; whose neighbors, however, declare that their ancestors were tinkerers, colliers, or stableboys not long ago. There is no one who

---

7 *Cicero, Epistle to M. Fab. Gallus.*   10 The Torre.   22 "For the idle folk it is always a holiday," *Hesiod.*   26 Pliny, book 2, 95.

is not a nobleman, whom they call Scogidos. They even own suburban estates which are hired out to certain husbandmen commonly called Vellacos, and—to tell the truth—they employ many Lisonicans as servants. The Sennaladii, the most high-born of nobles, are themselves content with the most meager and inexpensive nourishment. However, there are some who, once a year, perhaps near the very end of December, hold the most splendid banquets, with great preparation and with so many guests and courses that it may be necessary for them to spend nearly everything they own for one of these feasts. Then they deny themselves for the rest of the year, so that, in fact, they nearly kill themselves from hunger. But the majority, despising their stomach and refusing to listen to it no matter how much it rumbles, squander all their money on anything that increases their wardrobe. However, they are so ashamed to acknowledge publicly their hunger that they dissimulate beautifully and, on the contrary, pretend to be full wherever they normally walk at lunchtime, wiping their mouths with napkins and freeing meat from their teeth with toothpicks, looking as though they had just left the remains of a meal.

None of these people has any treasure or land as valuable as his sword and the cloak he wears. There isn't a single one of these who doesn't feed and clothe a hundred or more Mange-guadagnos (these are servants). Whatever they possess, however, like that man in Plautus, they have bought with a loan bearing interest, and they have hired their clothes for the day from an agent. And I saw one man who built himself a truly royal stable, constructed of stones sought from a great distance, marble columns, and much ivory; in the meantime he actually inhabited a mean, narrow, little sod hut.

They fashion themselves the most exceedingly long names, which they delight in heaping up for people, for places, and for lineage and kinship. But not content merely to voice all these titles in one breath, they frequently use periphrasis in arranging their words. Here feathers, especially the longer ones, which they call struzzoliae, are sold at no less a price than furs are by modern-day Russians. Moreover, others fasten silver bells to their heels which, ringing out distinctly at every step, direct the eyes and allure the ears of passers-by to them.

Those few who are unable to deny their ignoble origin have a haughty spirit nevertheless and occupy their minds with the highest

1 *Or "escogidos," in Spanish.*   21 What the Italians ingeniously term their servants, in English *Eategaynes.*

thoughts. I remember reading the following inscription in a certain
vestibule:

> Miserable is he who is of low birth,
> But whose heart is born magnanimous and noble.

5 Among the rest, I was astonished by this one thing, and not without
reason. Most of the inhabitants feed neither on bread nor on food but on
the fume of an herb—not pleasant smelling or healthy, to be sure—
which they inhale through their mouth and exhale through their nostrils,
so that they seem in the meantime to have made so many chimneys out of
10 them. By Hercules, I do not know whether the Moronians learned this
custom from the Indians or the Indians learned it from them, for it is
related that a certain high-born but worthless nobleman, Topia-Warallador, obtained the source of this wretched vapor from a certain Indian
demon. There are those, however, who believe the originators to have
15 been certain Indian chiefs of the Torrid Zone, so renowned for smoking
that they had blackened their insides. It is clear that this color pleased
them, for it did not seem right that the inner part of their bodies should
differ in color from the outer. I do know that once the nostrils are filled,
the purses are emptied, and from this source many a generous inheri-
20 tance has evaporated in smoke and flown dishonorably away, out of the
owner's nostrils. And while their nostrils exhale smoke high in the air,
their kitchens have passed completely out of use.

In every city, especially Antoia and Putanium, every other house is
set up as a brothel, either for young men or for women, and these people
25 actually pay a yearly fee for their most agreeable profession. With them
this skill is practiced honorably; nor is anyone ashamed to greet the most
well-known male prostitute immodestly, either in the crowded forum
or, indeed, even with his wife's knowledge. And there are those who
compel their miserable little wives to receive their male prostitutes most
30 courteously.

Section 3. The Paradise of Moronia Felix

No other part of Moronia, or possibly of our world, has anything as
noble or as beautiful as the Paradise of Moronia Felix, without a doubt

---

3 *Written in a certain cave at the foot of a mountain at Fiesole, in the hand of Politian.*
7 *Tobacco.*   24 *The prostitutes of Rome pay Julian money to the pope, from whom
his wealth exceeds 40,000 ducats a year. Paul III had 45,000 whores on his books.*

an astonishing work and one whose sight will justify the weariness of so long a journey and abundantly recompense the cost. The glittering mountain draws the eyes from afar, and it is solid gold (either it is or, what is just as good, it appears so), fashioned once upon a time by an alchemist, so they say. However, if someone wishes to test the hardness of the rock with an iron rod, it vanishes into dust; if with a flame, it vanishes into vapor.

On the summit of the mountain there shines a crystal palace, formed (according to the estimation of the neighbors) not by human hands; for they claim that once upon a time Fortune, driven away from heaven and from the band of the gods, erected her throne here, an earthly equivalent of heaven. From here she assists mortals with her aid and with her gifts, and she bestows her inexhaustible wealth with so generous a hand that whatever worthy person will seek her with a trusting mind will not fail to obtain eventually whatever he desires, once he has waited long enough.

From all regions of the earth, from every age, sex, and rank of life, people flock together here; however, most frequently they come from Moronia Pia. There is scarcely anybody in the whole world either so impotent, or so extraordinary, who has not at some time gazed upon this mountain and ascended it, when he has been allowed. The Lady of Loretto, and the God of Compostela, and our Parathalassia of Desiderius are powerless, indeed, compared to this divinity.

Innumerable pilgrims lie prostrate in the valley, no differently than a layer of shining hailstones covers the roads after it has hailed, religiously awaiting the nod of the Good Goddess. Nor may anyone touch the sacred mountain with a bold foot until, the white flag having been extended by the priests of the castle, the Goddess signifies her willingness and her consent. Then all together the pilgrims exclaim, with a raucous shrillness that fills the heavens, "Madonna Scooperta," and they rush forward, complaining vehemently but vainly at the narrowness of the path and the door. And while they make great haste, first one pilgrim and then another blocks the way. Nor is it possible to tell how many brawls or even fights originate here, and at times not without bloodshed to be sure, for everyone wants to lead the way, no one wants to give way to his betters. They press down upon those standing; they envy those in front; they jeer at those behind.

I saw a few there, perhaps of weaker sides, who had almost grown old in this valley and who had not even yet been given permission to

---

10 *Fortune, the goddess of fools*, favors simpletons, *according to that old saying.* 18 *We have all been insane once.* 21 *Erasmus,* Our Lady of Walsingham. 29 *The cry of the Italians when the statue of the Virgin Mary is uncovered.*

enter. You ask, Reader, and wonder what business all these people carry on. Certainly, desire for worldly goods summoned them all here, and hope keeps them here: all offering prayers to the Goddess so that they may be allowed to attain their long-sought desire. I noticed one praying

5   here for denied loves; another for some domestic tranquillity; another for honors; another for wealth. This one asked for an uncle's death, now too long lived; that one asked to jump ahead of three others when a position became vacant. Here, near the gate, most recently arrived, a certain haughty Lord of property, seeking—as his final action—to obtain

10   his next monarchy, so they say. Here, a crowd of deformed wenches seeking the return of beauty; there, shriveled old women hoping to return to adolescence; here, the barren seeking children; there, a female slave seeking freedom; everyone contemplating something, each something different.

15   The signal having now been given, those who are able make their way forward, about to ascend the mountain not on foot (this is instantly a sin) but on their hands and knees. Once they have reached the middle of the mountain with great effort, one of the priests kindly receives each petitioner, wanting to know his name and country. Once this informa-

20   tion is received, while you stand still he pronounces the name in a Stentorian voice. He does this partly so that he may advise his companions and the Goddess herself what sort of guest they are going to have, partly so that he might know, having first consulted the Goddess, whether you have brought sufficient faith and purity with you before you advance any

25   farther. For if you are a little too impure, or a little too weighed down under the burden of heavier crimes, the omniscient Goddess signals you with a red banner to be banished to her cloister (placed nearby for purgation) and stay there until, lighter of purse and cleaner of mind, you are better prepared to continue the journey.

30   But if by chance your name should please her, once you have been well instructed, the attendant sends you on your way with a leaden token as a good omen, solemnly murmuring three words in your ear first: "Hope, trust, and expect." Joyful and well disposed of mind you proceed, and when you almost reach the palace steps, an iron door appears

35   with the inscription:

If you hasten to devour fortune avidly,
It is necessary that you digest it badly.

---

36 *An inscription of Sannazaro.*

A very stern doorkeeper obstructs the access to this most narrow passage, who, however, readily grows mellow with money and opens for you not so much a door as a hole. When with much effort you have made your way stooping into it, you behold structures nearly equal to those of heaven, gleaming with gold and pearls wherever you turn, whose out- ward appearance seems to promise nothing less in good fortune. The habits, offices, and rites of the priests and the form of the temple I pru- dently omit (lest I be tedious).

Finally (because one has the leisure to gaze upon everything only for a certain time) another flamen approaches and takes your hand and at the same time binds your entire face and eyes with a linen blindfold. Then he leads the blindfolded guest through many a maze, wherever he wishes; though the credulous think that on the contrary he leads them into the temple of the Good Goddess. Naturally, profane eyes are not allowed to gaze upon the divine deity. Here you are ordered to fall down on your face and kiss the sacred pavement and not move your hands or feet until the Goddess addresses you by name: then you boldly reveal whatever you desire and satisfy whatever she commands without delay or distrust, and the deed you have requested will be accomplished, no matter how difficult.

But what is the reward of such a religion? you ask. What is the con- clusion of this veneration? Mockery, indeed, and one that excites the spleen even of those who have not been ridiculed. The illusion is well simulated to everyone and multiplied, indeed, by art: but so secretly that although everyone is dismissed destitute, yet everyone chooses to blame his own inertia, or his incredulity, rather than the trustworthiness of the Goddess.

Once his request has been made (assume that an office has been requested), the Goddess kindly nods assent and commands that the sup- plicant first drink the sacred potion, as it is called, after first waiting a few hours, by which means his impurity of mind will be better cleansed away and he will be made more worthy to obtain whatever happiness he has longed for. After this let him recline for a while, until she addresses him a second time: then, if he patiently awaits her voice and quickly under- takes her commands, let him not doubt that he will leave this place having obtained his wish. When all these thoughts will have mounted up so greatly—in accordance with his desire—he may believe that he will remain eternally in the same condition and remember the deity's beneficence with a grateful mind.

Now, accepting the chalice, the pilgrim most gratefully and will-

ingly drinks it, silently praising the taste of the sacred liquor, not
knowing meanwhile that the draft given him to drink is actually sleep
inducing, compounded of honey wine, poppy, opium, lettuce, and such
kinds of herbs. This drink lulls the person to sleep, and just like a dead
5   man he is carried to and fro throughout the palace. Finally, having been
made the butt of the spectators' laughter for a long while, he is borne
away, at last, to a most elegant couch in a small chamber, decorated in
kingly fashion indeed with an ivory floor, golden beams, and carpets so
costly that neither the tapestries of Campania nor the tapestries of
10   Alexandria, embroidered with animals, are comparable. At the door are
posted the most well-bred ministers, to be sure, attired with signet rings
on chains, in the manner of courtiers, awaiting the time when this new
Endymion will awake (which is usually after three days). When finally
awakened, he gazes about amazed at the appearance and richness of the
15   place and never ceases to be astonished at the ministers' attire. All serve
him in succession on bended knees, salute the awakened one as King,
worship the auspicious day, and courteously inquire what sort of courtly
dress he would prefer today. Finally they present clothing of almost
boundless value: "They give gems for his fingers; they present a long
20   chain for his neck" and place a crown covered with pearls on his head.
When, at last, clothed and ornamented, he resolves it is time to eat, they
procure a sumptuous banquet. With masques, games, and a musical
concert they consume the remainder of the day. And he is feasted in a
manner that is more than royal (if that is possible). However, the feast is
25   ended, without his knowledge, with the same potion under which he
was lately oppressed by the soundest sleep. From his chamber that good
day-old king, "as soon as he is filled with food, and overwhelmed by
wine," is dragged out through the back door and set forth miserably in
the highway, in his own attire, but that made even filthier than before.
30   When he comes to he is astonished once again about who he is and where
he was long ago, and as his mind once again recalls the recent bliss, now
lost, he cries out miserably, blaming himself either for sluggishness
because he has not paid heed the second time to the voice of the so powerful Goddess (since he remembers having it in his instructions) or for
35   ingratitude because he neglected to thank that donor's generosity, even
though he had been elevated to such unexpected dignity. Therefore he
goes away weeping and wailing, preoccupied both in his mind and in

9 *Plautus, Pseudolus.*   19 *Ovid, Metamorphoses,* 10.   21 *Plautus, Epidicus.*   27 *Virgil, Aeneid,* 3.

his mouth with that one phrase, "We were Trojans," exhorting everyone
else to pursue the Goddess resolutely and offer obedience to her. He
claims to have been the happiest of mortals a short while ago, but he has
fallen by his own fault alone: whence others, promising themselves a
more favorable outcome, rush to the same place more eagerly.   5

CHAPTER 8
Moronia Pia

On the west, Moronia Pia bounds Moronia Felix and Moronia Fatua:
certainly a region quite fertile and elegant because of its innate virtue;
however, it is absolutely squalid because of its inhabitants' neglect. It is   10
divided into Credulium and Doxia, the former longer and broader, but
the inhabitants occupy themselves so completely with certain rotten and
ridiculous rites that they abandon all care of their own concerns, esteem-
ing the deed pleasing to God.

The best and most populated villages here are Lipsanium, Mara-   15
villa, and, not far away, Crocetta, Rodillia, and Bascia. The outer region,
which has scarcely known any inhabitants, is nearly deserted. In this
district Ceniza, D'ayuno, Gymnopodilla, and Fouetta are nearly abandoned, perhaps because the site is too unhealthy, except that once a year,
on a certain day sacred to Venus, they are visited by all the Moronia   20
Pians. Not to be omitted here is a poorhouse on Mount Bagnacavallino,
"The Hospital of the Incurable Pazzi," the most spacious and splendid
in the whole world, constructed and maintained at the expense of the
whole region, whose current prefect is Garzonius, a completely sensible
and solicitous man, who has neatly divided this body of citizens into   25
certain classes. There is no region of Moronia that has not dispatched
some colonies of unmanageables here.

In fact, I might have believed there were no other towns except for
the cloisters, which are numerous here; you glimpse nothing else except
the most sordid little huts, just like that Westphalian Inn described by   30
Lipsius. In this region no one possesses an inch of land, for all surrender
their fathers' fields to the altars and sacred fires of their gods and inden-
ture themselves to the Cloister of the Morosophers.

---

7 Land of superstitious fools.   11 *All are insanely religious and labor either under*
superstition or under novel and heretical ideas. From these sources originate the two fac-
tions of Moronia.   22 Hospidale di pazzi incurabili, *written—not very felicitously—*
by Tomaso Garzoni of Bagnacavallo.

Briefly, I might say that I did see four types of buildings here: temples, monasteries, hospitals or poorhouses, and little cottages, since, except for the religious, everybody either begs or serves. All are most devoted to a certain religion, but what they believe, or what God they 5 worship, they neglect to inquire. It is enough for them to follow the tracks of their forefathers and to occupy the temples of their traditional deities.

Even when they walk along they delight in crossing themselves: for they move their feet in such a way that one foot placed across the other 10 reproduces the shape of the cross. And in the same manner they position their arms entwined in a sorrowful gesture. They have, indeed, the most well-cared-for temples. Still they prostrate themselves in the fields before any sort of stone or twig, and they carry beads of wood and amber. There are not as many people as there are gods in this place. The old Roman 15 gods that Varro counted were a handful compared to these, nearly all of which are made of stone, wood, or some other material. And there are still those who substitute horses, hogs, and dogs in this calendar. Every day they create new gods for themselves, sometimes even two hundred in one day in one temple.

20 Everywhere here we observed something that we read the ancient Egyptians used to practice: the abodes of the living are neglected, the burial and the monuments of the dead are honored. Indeed, I saw 800 pounds of wax expended on the funeral of a man of no account. I want to be buried here myself, and I order by this testament that my heirs have 25 me taken there. And I want to be joined by whoever either condemns this travel of mine, or praises it more than is fitting, or resolves to imitate it in the future. At their funerals, for example, in addition to torches, they employ the burning of incense round the body, kisses, the sound of little bells, and the sprinkling of holy water, rites which are believed to profit 30 the soul of the lately deceased not a little. Two attendants, according to the law of the place, guard the dead one—in order to keep flies away from his body—with two flyswatters made of black silk, depicted with the coat of arms of the deceased, even if it should be wintertime when all the flies lie no less dead than the embalmed body.

35 No one touches anything that has not been exorcised first: water, oil, salt, wax, balsam, military swords. With great solemnity they bless

---

22 *They normally expend so much on a cardinal's funeral, Sacrarum Caeremoniarum, book 1.*   33 *These are the very words of the first book of Sacrarum Caeremoniarum concerning the funeral of a cardinal.*

golden roses; they baptize ensigns and bells. But what is more astonishing is that in the city of Maravilla it is certain that stones hear, weep,
laugh, extend feet and retreat, cure diseases, sweat blood, and daily
prophesy everything that may be done either by men, or by the Semones,
or by the Daemones.   5

Section 2. Doxia: The Other Province of Moronia Pia

Doxia, the other region, displays much variety but little elegance. Here
no town, no house is built according to the same form; every one adopts a
new fashion differing from the rest as much as possible. Nowhere did I
see more monuments of the past, monuments less obliterated by age.   10
The city of Chronia is here, and the seven pyramids, slightly ruined,
erected once upon a time by the Saturnians in memory of the seven
angels who, as the inhabitants believe, built the whole world against
God's will. Next is the city of Abraxia, the onetime seat of the Basilidians,
which consisted of 365 houses because of an ancient decree; nor is it   15
lawful either to add one more or, in truth, to demolish one. Not very far
from here is the Canton of the Borborites, where they display 30 statues
half devoured by time, right hands joined, to be sure. Eight, however, are
larger than the rest, the stones inscribed with Hebrew letters. And,
indeed, there is a rather woody desert here, in which they say the Elcesaites 20
or Ebionites used to live long ago. Certain remnants of an old altar
remain here where they made forced sacrifices to their pagan gods. On
the left, tombs of the Heracleonites could be discerned, still drenched
with oil and balsam. On the right, the Ophitica Valley, where are the
cave of the sacred serpent and the altar which it, called out so many times 25
by incantations, is said to have ascended. Even the little subterranean
homes of the Cainites—placed nearby Hell, so it is thought—stand

---

6 Land of heretical fools.   12 *The Saturnians taught that seven angels made the
heavens without the knowledge of God.* Augustine.   14 The Basilidians *believed there
were 365 heavens, according to the number of letters in the word* ἀβραξας.   17 The
Gnostics—*rather filthy*—*are so named because of the extraordinary shamefulness of their
mysteries. They are also called* the Carpocratians. *Irenaeus, book 1, chapter 24.*   17 *The
Valentini believed there were 30 Aeons out of which the eight eldest (in the words of
Irenaeus) were preeminent and the origin of the rest. These heretics generally used many
Hebrew words in their rites. Irenaeus, ibid.*   20 *Identical, according to Epiphanius.
These people (according to Eusebius) teach those under persecution that they should
renounce their faith and retain it in their hearts.*   23 *A new method of ransoming the
dead was provided by oil, balsam, water, and Hebraic invocations.*   24 *The Ophites say
that Christ was a deceiving serpent, and they keep a snake who emerges at the incantations
of the priest, licks the offerings, and retreats.*

open to visitors here, in which Cain's cudgel and Judas's halter are
solemnly preserved.

   At the bank of the Hygri Pond, attached to a stake by an iron chain,
is the bowl of the Severians, from which those men, formerly abstainers,
5 used to take water. And in the same place are the extremely narrow beds,
and smaller tables, of the Tacians. And scattered about lie the deadly
cakes of the Montanists, the stony testicles of the Valesians, the very
thorny fields of the Manichaeans, the Psallians' praying cells, the crosses
of the Patricians, the little wombs of the Ascites, the statues of Harpocra-
10 tes of the Pattalorinchites, the cups of the Aquarians, and whatever
monuments there were of the old heresies.

   However, no age previously saw a thing so splendid as the Palace of
Rhetorius, clearly built on the model of ancient buildings, considering
that it seems nevertheless to maintain a form peculiar to itself. Finally,
15 there still remain the spotless walls of the Abelians, who adopted children and publicly display the family tree and sacred relics of somebody
else's father. Here, not long ago, wandering fanatics whom they call
Enriconicolaitae and Georgo-Davidici built here the foundations of a
new but inauspicious city. And certain Virginian exiles wrongly believe
20 this republic will endure here.

---

4 The Severians *did not drink wine because they claimed it was sprouted from Satan and the
earth. Augustine, De Haeribus.*   6 The Tacians *held marriage equal to fornication;
therefore they used small beds, and even smaller tables, for they ate no meat. Ibid.*   7 *Those
heretics make bread from the blood of year-old infants, blood extracted from punc-
ture wounds, mixing this blood with flour. Ibid.*   7 The Valesians *castrated themselves
and their guests, hoping that they had performed a deed pleasing to God.*   8 The
Manichaeans, *among other of the greatest absurdities, believed plants sense and suffer
pain; therefore it seemed abominable to them to rid their fields of thorns.*   8 *These were
also called* Euchites; *they were at no time not praying, so that it seemed unbelievable (says
Augustine) to those who heard this about them.*   9 The Patricians *believed their flesh
was not made from God but from the devil, which they therefore hated so much that some
killed themselves.*   9 The Ascites *called themselves new vessels filled with new wine;
they carried a barrel about at their revels.*   10 *So called from* $\left| \begin{matrix} \pi\acute{\alpha}\tau\tau\alpha\lambda o\varsigma \\ \acute{\rho}\acute{\iota}\gamma\chi o\varsigma \end{matrix} \right|$ *denoting a
finger by a stake, who placed their fingers in front of their lips and noses and were
furthermore so zealous about silence. Augustine prefers to call them "dactylorynchites,"
"fingernosians."*   10 *They offered water in the sacramental chalice.*   13 Rhetorius,
*as Philastratus notes, though it appears incredible to Augustine, asserted that all heretics
walk rightly and speak truly.*   15 The Abelians *did not couple with their wives; however, they did not desire to live without their wives. Thus they adopted the children
procreated by other men throughout the neighborhood, who freely surrendered their
wretched offspring to the hope of being a stranger's heir. Augustine, loc. cit.*   18 Henry
Nicholas *and* George David, *the founders of that most foul sect of Anabaptists which
others call* Libertines, *we call* The Family of Love.   19 Brownists, *Englishmen truly
banished to Virginia.*

Allow me to warn all rulers, kings, and emperors of the world, if they wish rightly to preserve their own tranquillity and the well-being of their subjects, to relegate here all heretics, sworn enemies of the public peace, and agitators.

CHAPTER 9
The Status of the Moronian State

The government of each city is, indeed, midway between an aristocracy and a democracy. The people themselves elect the number of senators they wish, who hold office neither for a year nor for life; rather they are selected and retain their office according to the will of the electorate. If the people should suspect one of too much prudence, perhaps, they immediately eject him from office by severe ostracism.

However, all the provinces at least nominally acknowledge one leader, at that time called *Il Buffonio Ottimo Massimo*. His place is in Moronia Felix, near Moronia Pia, named Papagallium. He, midway between an emperor and a priest, sits looking distinguished, crowned and mitered at the same time. Instead of a staff, a key with a sword is carried before him, a clear emblem of riches and power. To be sure, the key teaches that all the treasuries of Moronia are laid open to him, the sword that he is permitted to plunder the possessions of others to defend his own. To those arriving he extends the great toe of his right foot to be kissed fondly, a custom which they report has prevailed for a long time, since it originally arose because certain of the ancient kings suffered from gout in their hands.

In truth, that man is not born to his position but elected: not, however, before he is of advanced age, lest he too long burden the populace, which is most eager for novelty. Yet, in front of the Chapel of St. Sapa there are two thrones of porphyry, where the person to be elected to this office must be seated, so that in the dung an examination of his virility may secretly be made. He is commonly carried on the shoulders of his attendants, not on a horse or a mule, in order to signify he is as far superior to other rulers as men are to other animals, and he always travels under a *baldachinus*. But this custom is of the sort that can be practiced by others, too. Some customs that he demands are peculiar to

15 The chamber of parrots, *the place in which the Pope is elected. Sacrarum Caeremoniarum.* 28 *These are the very words of the author of Sacrarum Caeremoniarum in the consecration of a Pontiff.*

himself, not to be shared by any ruler in the entire world. From his subjects he never exacts any tribute for himself, but whatever they have
offered him, he accepts with a willing hand and collects abundantly. He
never decrees anything which any of his high officials opposes. He
5   fashions many laws but obeys none. Nor does what he sanctions endure a
long time; if any law will have endured two winters, it is obsolete. He
greets his slaves quite familiarly and regards them as fit to dine at his
own table: and when he pleases, he even prefers them to his own great
counselors. He gives his parasites the power of daring to do whatever
10   pleases them, of violating whatever law they wish, or of coining money
and inscribing it with his own image and name. I could have easily
observed more of the same here, had not this kind of courtier's life always
been abhorrent to me.

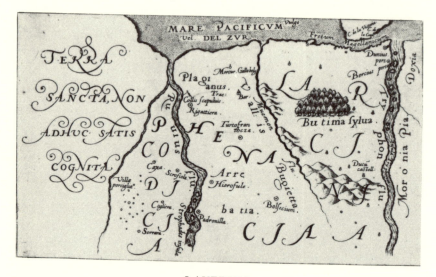

LAVERNIA

BOOK FOUR
LAVERNIA

CHAPTER 1
The Location of Lavernia

Lavernia is bounded on the west by the Ocean of Magellan, on the east by   5
Moronia Pia and some part of Crapulia. It is a land so utterly worn-out
and sterile (if you will except one province) that it seems the daughter of
Ceres was abducted by Pluto in antiquity from here, rather than from
that well-known Trinacria. Neither shepherd nor farmer lives in this
place. Nevertheless, the inhabitants are so flooded with all sorts of sup-   10
plies that no race in the whole world has seemed to me richer or (so far as
the fierceness of their nature permits) more luxurious: for whatever
object anywhere on earth is considered splendid or somewhat rare, they
will seize and carry off for themselves, either by deceit or by force, and
guard their plundering with like violence.   15

However, the eastern region normally enriches itself the most by
spoils from Moronia Pia and Moronia Felix; the maritime region, to be
sure, partly by treasures from the Indies, and partly by the common
piracy it busily engages in. There are two parts of Lavernia: Larcinia
and Phenacia. The former borders upon Moronia and the corner of   20
Crapulia; the latter lies more to the west and, contrary to the customary
wandering of the Larcinians, keeps to itself within its own boundaries.
Both are completely barbarous and inhospitable.

CHAPTER 2
The Customs of the Larcinians   25

The Tryphonian River separates Larcinia from both parts of Moronia,
whose very winding currents have created no fewer islands than the
Raleana River of Guiana. The entire region is so woody and mountainous that it rather deserves the name of a desert and, as Strabo remarked of
a certain city, seems more fit for insurrection than habitation. In their   30
speech I noted a certain Welsh vocabulary, which I should imagine
originated from the unknown travels of our countrymen.

---

5 Land of thieves, *whose goddess is Laverna.* "Fair Laverna, give me the power to deceive
and speak falsely," *Horace.*   19 *Just as there are two forms of this art: robbery and
imposture.*   25 Land of bandits.   26 *Tryphon was a famous bandit among the
Egyptians.*

The population of the Larcinians is, indeed, rather large, but it is no commonwealth. Everyone believes he is born for himself; he lives by himself; he esteems only himself; and he may retain possession of as many goods as he is able to steal and able to guard what he has stolen; and the more powerful he becomes, the more he is feared. He exerts power over many people, not so much over obedient subjects as over slaves. The inhabitants are divided into certain families, each offspring willingly obeying its most powerful member. Everyone spares those of his own family and sticks by them; all the rest he ravages most freely. Moronia Pia and Moronia Felix would have each been despoiled by the raids of these people a long time ago, had not the wiser governors purchased their safety—along with their freedom—every year from all the leaders of the families through the power of a great quantity of gold.

They differ from us scarcely at all in their bodily form, except that all (save the islanders) have hooked claws as though they were hawks: that is common to all Lavernians. The tribe Sbanditica dwells in the mountainous part where the Butinia Forest sheds its truly appropriate and beneficial shade, in comparison to which that Hercynia of Germany, surrounded by ten thousand highwaymen, looks like a narrow orchard, or even, as it were, a simple hedge.

Here you can observe castles scattered about, not overly splendid, by Hercules, but both numerous and exceedingly well fortified, where the leaders of each family may safely dwell and, under a sound roof, preserve their loot from the danger of their neighbors. Meanwhile, the inexperienced common people every day bed themselves down under any tree, in the manner of the Tartars, and prepare constant ambushes for travelers: those, stripped of everything valuable, they do not kill on the spot, as the Italian and German bandits are said to do (to be sure, they are afraid of nothing, for the commission of robbery has no penalties), but they lead them bound up to the castle of their leader and oblige them to swear that they will serve him in perpetual fidelity. If one of them either violates his faith, or pilfers nothing whatever a few times each month, or without a greeting willingly passes by a traveler with any valuables, he is condemned to the noose. Thus, day after day their power increases, and for this reason a Phenacian law has been enacted that younger sons should be immediately disinherited and the firstborn pro-

---

15 "His hands terminate in a point," *as Lucian describes Mercury.*

moted, which spontaneously aids in no small measure the increase of
even more noble adults.

Moronia Pians do not cherish crosses as much as these people
despise them. Therefore, in consequence of a treaty made with the
Lavernians from the beginning, they are able to remain safe only at   5
home; if, however, any Moronians should wander out here, most of them
will lose their lives by hanging, on the mere grounds that the Moronians'
very use of the cross is seen as a reproach to the Lavernians' use of the
gallows.

Among the heads of the tribes internal wars never cease to spring   10
forth as long as someone seeks property for himself and holds back from
others, which certainly turns out well for the rest of the world, for truly,
one ought to be fearful lest the combined strength of such a multitude of
foul people, daily increasing in number, might conspire toward the ruin
of the rest of the nations of the world. It is exactly for this reason that the   15
more prudent Phenacians both create and nourish quarrels among those
people.

Even for tiny children it is no very small distinction to steal cun-
ningly (as Caesar once said about the old Germans), since their parents
imbue them from the most tender age with principles and examples   20
which they term Hermetic. You will see little infants, even as they hang
from their mother's breasts, stealing little pins or coins as though they
were doing this while daydreaming, and if they are not audacious enough
or sleight enough of hand, and have undertaken their larceny so that
they may be easily nabbed in the very act, their parents beat them on the   25
spot. However, when they reach adolescence it is necessary that they filch
either ducks, or geese, or something larger every day; nor do they pass a
day without punishment in which they augment their domestic hoard
by nothing. For if they are quite certain that a job strenuously executed
by them is incapable of equal success, it is necessary that they steal some   30
soil from a neighboring field, or a twig, lest they grow inept from lack of
practice.

But these things can be particularly observed on the borders of
Phenacia itself: between them and the Larcinians extends the very broad
Bugietta Valley, of which you will hear more in its place, after we have in   35
turn described the Larcinians of the seacoast.

---

19 *Caesar, The Gallic War, book 6.*

CHAPTER 3
The Larcinians of the Seacoast and the Islands

Here, either in the Straits of Magellan, or on its banks, or scattered about on the shores of the Tryphonian Islands, live amphibians, and they are
5   wealthier than the rest because they are busier than the rest. Furthermore, the best known of the narrow straits favor them not a little. Because they know that owing to the swiftness of the sea's current no sailors dare retrace their path, the Larcinians obstruct the passage with chains and small boats and thus ravage the ship and its passengers: owing to which
10   fact I believe that that strait clearly allows no return, not so much because of the strength of the waves as because of the number and ferocity of the pirates. None of the European sailors is more experienced than they in the changeable storms of this region or in the location and fitness of ports, winds, sand banks, and shoals. Not even the fish themselves
15   swim better or more effortlessly.

First here is Port Dunius, not, indeed, a very large or strongly fortified town but exceedingly daring and wealthier than any other city in the region because of its plunder. It is situated in the very corner of Larcinia, where this country is separated from Crapulia by the Tryphonian River.
20   They say this shore is strewn with magnets and pulverized lodestone, whose strength draws ships to it, no matter how remote, and holds them there fast. But those natives of Port Dunius accomplish no less themselves, who roam throughout the seas and attack ships far more well fortified than theirs. It is a miracle, indeed, how often these people, after
25   an unequal confrontation, have returned victors, thanks to their boldness. Others, however, prefer to attribute it instead to the blessed and baptized ensigns received from the Moronians. The standard of their city is the vulture, which feeds while it flies, with the words, "I enjoy but do not rest."
30   Right at the entrance to the Tryphonian River is Port Bercius, the ruler of the waves and all the nearby islands: for from those just passing by, even its own people, it exacts a not inconsiderable tax as the price of passage; and with certain large magnetic fishhooks, no differently than we lie in wait for fish, they lie in ambush for foreign vessels, and once the

---

2 Region of pirates.   26 *The Pope baptized the ensign of the Italians and the Spaniards in Flanders and named it* Margaret, *which afterward defeated the* Devil. *Moresinus, The Origin of the Papal Religion.*

hook touches, it fastens on and leads the boat in, no matter how much it resists.

In all of these most marshy islands or even on the banks of the river you will scarcely discern a little shack or a rowboat: partly because each person arranges whatever nest he chooses for him and his family in the   5
midst of the reeds (without a doubt the reeds here grow much higher and no less strong than those we have often seen in India); and partly because, owing to the nearness of the place, these people are very greatly interbred with the Moronians, none of whom, to tell the truth, wish to sail as much as to swim, whence it appears they know how to move by   10
rowing their arms like Daedalus. Thus they spend half of their life (a period which ought to be called Crocodilian) in the water, and they even dare to match their fleetness of motion with that of the swiftest rower.

The sailors are more terrified of these people than of any pirates whatsoever; for they unexpectedly overtake the ship and, sticking as   15
firmly as a remora, hold it fast and either position the hull so that it is submerged by water, or vehemently overturn it, or finally dash it on the reefs.

CHAPTER 4

How I Got into the Country. The Harpies   20

But the Reader will be astonished to learn how I obtained access to the place, or thanks to which concession I finally got permission to remain in it. Nor will he believe that anyone sound of mind would either dare to trust himself with so monstrous a people or finally return alive. Therefore understand, dear Reader, that, owing to a solemn custom, these   25
people celebrate a common Jubilee with the Moronia Pians every 50 years, during which time they are drawn into a truce with all nations and peoples of the world, and, while it lasts, it is a religious offense for these most thievish gluttons to violate the public or private peace. It is then that strangers flock here, who, however, freely bestow on the inhabitants   30
whatever they bring with them, so that I believe this voluntary peace of one year is more profitable to the Larcinians than the strife of four years. Very conveniently, I entered during this sacred year and with certain other of our fellow travelers wandered through the region.

While traveling in this country we were threatened with the greatest   35

---

4 *Like the Egyptian pirates, according to Heliodorus, book* 1.

danger by the Harpies, who do not, indeed, permit themselves to make a treaty with us. These (I don't know whether to call them flying creatures or demons) have received a home here from the Lavernians since the time when (according to tradition) they were driven from their previous resi-
5   dence by the sons of Boreas. They build nests for themselves in the midst of the strongest oak trees out of crisscrossed beams. In front they resemble an owl, in back and in their bodily size an ostrich, in their wings a porcupine, in their beak and claws an eagle. When I saw them I recalled to my mind those anonymous birds that superstitious Aristotle once described
10   who were always flying around the Diomedian Isle, who clung so fawningly to the Greeks but attacked everyone else. These most rapacious Harpies behaved the same way to us and to all other travelers: they accepted the inhabitants themselves on friendly terms, as if they knew them well, and always released them unharmed; us they attacked with
15   great fury. Whoever walks alone through the wastes of Butinia Forest itself is immediately seized by their claws and torn to pieces. Yes indeed, the journey of a division of travelers is scarcely safe without the protection of a troop of Larcinians.

CHAPTER 5
20   *Bugietta Valley. The Customs of the Phenacians.*
The City of Furtofrancheça. Bolsecium

Now I return to the Bugietta Valley, the farthest boundary of Larcinia; however, the land is common to both provinces. The River Mnemon, flowing through the middle of the plain, disperses its water equally to
25   both regions and furnishes the most convenient site for the Phenacian garrison towns. I am mistaken if I did not glimpse here certain monuments of the historians Pliny and Herodotus, but which can scarcely be deciphered now. Mercurius Gallo-Belgicus built himself an elegant house here; and not far away a certain Cardinal, a historian, laid the
30   most spacious foundations for a truly majestic castle. For since Spain invaded India, the neighbor of this region, even the Jesuits (who are the most meddlesome of all people) have been allowed to visit these shores and occupy the land abandoned by others because of the Larcinians' frequent raids.

---

9 *De Mirabilibus. On the other hand, consider that dog whose epitaph can be seen in a suburban villa of Bologna:* "I barked before thieves, and was silent before lovers, *etc.*"
20 Land of Impostors.

There are many schools of astrologers here, whom, by Hercules, the Phenacians are wont to favor above all other (except for poets and lawyers). In this very valley, to be truthful (for why should I lie?), I founded a school, where I—as the omniscient soothsayer—boldly wrote the truest prophecy of this age. The Phenacians are far more sociable than the Larcinians; or at least they execute their cruelty more secretly, for what the Larcinians do visibly and in the open, these do without witnesses at home.

These people subject themselves to the laws and the authority of the Golden Prince (for that is what they call His Majesty). Furtofrancheça, the part nearest to Bugietta, is the best of all the regions of Lavernia, or at least it is the least wretched. Here, during the day they rest; at night, to be sure, they always carry on their business. Thus they despise the sun as the lighting most harmful to mortals; they worship the moon as the most bountiful of all heavenly bodies. The trees are by nature so viscous that whatever birds sit in their branches stick to them and are plundered by the wayfarers.

The biggest emporium of this province and the one most frequented by far is called Bolsecium. However, two villages in this city, Palatium and Fripperia, have more streets than those of any city I have ever seen. Palatium is, indeed, appointed for the controversies of lawyers, Fripperia for the business activities of traders. And truly, there is no place under heaven so abounding in lawyers who (as Plautus said) plant a dispute if there is nothing in dispute. The number of these people here is no fewer than in our capital of Westminster. Although, to be sure, every day new ones are begotten, even though that seems impossible, those who consider themselves Lynceus-like in political matters truly believe the number of these lawyers will diminish in the future. For when, through litigation, they have distributed the whole province among themselves (which has nearly happened already), finally their clients will necessarily be poor. When that happens the lawyers will in turn attack each other and, unwisely battling one another, disperse a portion to the common people and provide future generations of descendants an even more lucrative opportunity to practice this art. Their servants' clothes are always two-toned, so that by this they intimate themselves most eager to serve their clients on either side of a dispute. These people possess lawsuits in abundance, and also a wealth of moneylenders, and the Ruzius, the most violent of rivers, while running a headlong course among the Strophades Islands, now removes a large section of looser soil from this

19 *City of cutpurses.*   23 *Plautus, Poenulus.*

or that island and finally deposits it on a third. At another time, however, dissatisfied with its previous course, it seeks a new channel for itself, now carrying off the paternal lands of a most greedy landowner, now bestowing new lands on another.

5   Most of the inhabitants, like those people of the Alps, suffer from a tumor. Doctors call it Argyranchen, a disease which is so common that no one wishes to hide the affected spot or cure it. Nor do I know what secret virtue is attached to their skin that it attracts money to them no less than a magnet attracts iron; nor does their skin hold on to what it attracts

10   any less forcefully.

Fripperia is supplied with all kinds of artificers, and yet there are no workshops here. With a continuous clamor everyone hawks his skills and merchandise to the passing crowd and, once he has found a buyer, withdraws to show him the goods he has just praised. Here he produces a

15   copper necklace covered with thin layers of gold, and he swears neither Portugal nor the mines of India produce more gold. A second shows a fake musk testicle filled with the most agreeable odors. A third offers the clearest large pearls which, indeed, cannot be distinguished from genuine, natural ones either for brilliance, smoothness, size, roundness, or

20   weight (in this respect Pliny offers a criterion for every kind of stone), and he displays the very shells in which these specks of sand grew solid long ago. Nor is there a lack of gem cutters, who display stones counterfeiting the most precious stones of every kind: Cyprian diamond, Corinthian hephaestitis, Sicilian agate, Egyptian milkstone, Arabian asbestos,

25   Macedonian paeanite, Asiatic alabandine, Indian beryl, British jet, Persian aetite, African chalcedon, Scythian emerald, German cornelian, Aethiopian chrysolite, and Libyan carbuncle.

But also there are surely more than enough pharmacists here, all of whose fraud in compounding and mixing their little boxes can scarcely

30   be contained in a complete volume. Indeed, I cannot sufficiently express my astonishment and envy at the fact that every merchant mingles false and fabricated goods with the real merchandise; yet this can be detected by no sense; nor is any one of them afraid of any test of his merchandise — except the test of fire. If fraud occurs anywhere in public it is sufficient,

35   indeed, for that person to be beaten severely; to be certain, everyone zealously takes care that it not happen to him. And since each one's face, and clothes, and voice, and manner change daily, it is useless to complain today about yesterday's imposture.

---

6 *The disease of Demosthenes, in Latin,* "argentangina," "silver quinsy."   15 *Claves,*
Chrysopoeia, book 1, etc.

Here in the suburbs a public school was opened—not, by Hercules, uncelebrated—where this art termed Spagyric (forgive me, Alchemists, or be angry with yourselves, for having given the most praiseworthy name to a dishonest art) is read daily to the students. Naturally, this school possesses, in place of Alcoran, the most ancient *History of Mercury*, unknown to our remote world, which teaches how Cyllenius, while still an infant, successfully stole a trident from Neptune, a sword from Mars, a quiver and bow from Apollo, tongs from Vulcan, and a girdle from Venus; and how, "having begun the art of stealing almost in his mother's womb," as it were, he stole Jove's lightning. And thereafter the school supplies lessons in all kinds of cheating and stealing, teaching the novice in numerous ways how to draw the bar, how to unlock a door, how to move one's feet slowly, how to insert a sticky thread into an already locked chest, how to lift money from an untouched money purse, how to deny strenuously what you have done and not blush in the meantime, and a thousand of these sorts of tricks, secrets of the Cabalists which I scorned to inquire about.

The innkeepers are all, to a man, so untrustworthy that a stranger does not dare either to place gold under his pillow while he sleeps or to rely on a sack or a chest, no matter how ironclad. Instead, we learned to behave like the besieged Jews, who used to stow away valuables in their own stomachs when about to go to sleep and early the next morning draw them out again. In the villages you will scarcely see anyone except millers, tailors, and perhaps a few soothsayers.

CHAPTER 6
The Province of Plagiana

In the west can be discerned the most spacious region of Plagiana, where the city of Rigattiera, not new, indeed, but newly renovated, borders the Scapulius Hill. He who is observant will discover here not a few remains, hoary with age, of critics, and especially of poets. Though nothing seemed more improper, I am certain I saw a stone inscribed with Homeric verses but ascribed to another author. Among these were:

Goddess, sing for me the wrath of Demeter, bringer of splendid fruits. Orpheus.

---

9 *Lucian.*   21 *Josephus, The Wars of the Jews.*   29 *Having stolen his dictionary from Stephanus, Scapula proclaims: "But I contend this Lexicon to be new."*   33 *Homer alters this verse of Orpheus, according to Justin Martyr, writing in Protrepticus ad Gentes.*

And immediately afterward:

> For there is nothing more shameless or dreadful than a woman.
> Orpheus.

> One generation of men springs up and another passes away.
> Musaeus.

> And as a man reareth a lusty sapling of an olive tree. (Orpheus)

> In a lonely place, etc. Homer, *Iliad*, 17.

On the other hand, I have found many small verses in Virgil which are an almost word-for-word plagiarism from Homer and Hesiod, and I don't know how many pages are carried over to Petrarch from a certain vernacular Tuscan poet.

Next to here, on the south, comes Arrebatia, a deformed plain and full of rubbish. Troy was once here, as the piles of demolished stones indicate, which they say their ancestors tore down so that out of the many little villages (of which there remain today a few pyramids and other traces) they might build two absolutely magnificent cities, Patronilla and Hierosule. Thus, where there were once courtyards and temples, you may now glimpse fields and stables. Nor, indeed, does the violent boiling of the Ruzius spare the land itself but, tearing away with injurious waves, bestows it upon either the Plagianans or the Codicians.

CHAPTER 7
Codicia

Monstrous men inhabit the province of Codicia, whom Münster and Mandeville depict with a hog's head. They walk like quadrupeds, face always downward, so that they don't neglect anything worth picking up; nor do they ever look up at the sky. In terms of their speech, they grunt, indeed, rather than talk. No one is to tarry in this place, except the old; the inhabitants wear out the prime of their life either in Butinia

---

2 *Homer*, "for there is nothing worse and more vile than a woman."   6 *From a lost work on Dionysus.*   115/33-116/7 *Theodore Canter, in Variae Lectiones, part 2, chapter 3, numbers these among the robberies of Homer. He does so unjustly, for Homer imitates Orpheus and Musaeus, he does not plagiarize.*   23 Land of greed.

Forest (if their disposition is more courageous) or, if they are more studious, in the schools of Bolsecium. Only metal workers, farmers, and merchants live here. They nearly always dine on earth (as is said of the wolf about to fight or a starving fox). Among them are those who live and grow strong solely from gazing on gold and silver. They almost never sleep, the same as the lion.

They are superstitiously devoted to their god, namely Chrysius Deus; until they have seen him and worshiped him they will never rest or eat. Here I saw the cities of Scrofiola (a completely loathsome village and, in the word of Cato, *cloacal*), Cogliera, Serrara, and Caxa, which— even though I wanted to observe them—I was not permitted. Each and every one of the citizens carries his own key so that no stranger may enter. All the rest of the people, scattered throughout the Porciglian villages, are not as content with homes as with lairs.

These men, these customs, and these cities I gazed upon, was astonished by, and laughed at; and after 30 years, weakened by so much labor of traveling, I returned to my homeland.

A TRAVELER, formerly an Academic

---

7 The god Gold.   10 *Festus.*

INDEX OF PROPER NAMES

Actaeonius Valley: *from Actaeon, a great hunter, who (as is customary) was eaten up by his dogs.*

Amazonia: *a well-known name, once an American region but now ours, thanks to the manly spirit of our inhabitants.*

Antoia, town: *Spanish [antojo] for "lust," a city always burning. "Love burns," Virgil.*

Anylos, forest: *from the Greek [ἀν- "not," plus ὕλη- "wood"], in English, "wood-less."*

Aphrodysia: *Greek, from Αφροδιτη, "Aphrodite," or "Venus"; she is truly from the foam [ἀφρός], born of the sea. Here is the city of Amantina, whose name we take from a region on the Danube.*

Arrebatia, province: *Spanish from* arrebatar, *"to steal by force."*

Artopolis, Artocreopolis: *Greek, derived from a compound of* αρτος, κρὲας, πόλις, *"bread," "flesh," "city."*

Assadora, city: *Spanish [asador] for a "roasting spit," said to be from* assando [asado], *"roasted."*

Assagion, river: *see margin* [p. 24].

Auffzeichner: *German for "registrar."*

B

Beachera, city: *German for "goblet" [Becher], from which we say "a beaker" in English.*

Baldachinus: *thus the Italians term the* canopy *under which the Pope rides, according to the testimony of Sacrarum Caeremoniarum,* elevated

118

by eight spears. *(Consequently, the ceremony of the sacrament has the same name in the language of the Barbarians.) Sacrarum Caeremoniarum, Book 1.*

Bascia, *city: Italian for "given to kissing," from the French* baiser, "to kiss."

Batillum, *city: from the Latin "batillum," "chafing dish."*

Baveria, *province: meaning "nonsense" in French.*

Bercius, port: a well-known name in Flanders, &c.

בֵּח לֶחֶם: *"House of Bread," the name of our most famous prison.*

Bolsecium, *city: composed from the Spanish* bolsa, "small money bag," *or* bursa, "purse," *the* r *altered into an* l, *and the Latin* seco, "to cut." *Let that worthless, lying rascal Bolsec now thank me for the origin of his name.*

Bubonia, *forest: Latin, from "bubonum," "full of owls."*

Bugius, *river: Italian [bugia] for "a liar."*

Bugietta Valley: *This valley is irrigated by the river Mnemon. "To be a liar, a good memory is essential."*

Buscadores: *Spanish for* Inquisitors, *from* buscar, "to inquire."

Butinia, *forest: French* butin, *meaning "plunder"; whence the English* booty.

C

Cadilla, *city: Latin diminutive, from* cadus, "wine jar."

Calavernius, *mountain: from the Spanish* calaverna, "skull," *said to be from the Latin "calvus," "bald."*

Candosoccia: *[L. Junius] Columella, book 5, chapter 4. The far-reaching vine shoots in a vineyard, which we call* megros, *the French call* candosoccos, "a layer of a plant."

Saint Carniceria: *Spanish for* laniena, "butcher's stall"; *the home of an Inquisitor is nothing else.*

Caxa, *city: Spanish for "chest"; hence the English* cask.

Ceniza, *city: Spanish for "ashes."*

Chagrin: French for *"sorrow," "melancholy."*

Charbona, *city: from the French* charbon, "coal," *a subterranean village.*

Chatouilla, *city: French* chatouiller, "to tickle."

Cheminea, tower: *French [cheminée], see margin [p. 23].*

Chytraea, *city:* χύτρα, *Greek for "goblet."*

Cibinium, *city: in the region of the Danube: from the Latin "cibus," "food."*

Ciniflonius: *Latin "ciniflones,"* "hair curlers." Horace.

Cogliera, *city: Italian* cogliere, *"to gather"; just like* Gatherington.

Coledochia, *swamp: from the Greek* χολήγ δὲχεφας, *"to contain bile"; see margin* [p. 86].

Kotzunga, *city: German* koken [*kotzen*], *"to vomit"; hence* kotzunga.

Duke of Courroux: *French for "angry," "furious."*

Crapulia: *Latin* [*crapula*, "excessive wine drinking"], *see margin* [p. 19].

Creatium, *city: Greek* κρέας, *"meat."*

Crocetta, *city: Italian, "[little] cross."*

Krugtopolis: *from the German* Krugt, *"amphora,"* [and the Greek πόλις, "city"].

Cubaea, *city: Greek* [κὐβος] *for "die."*

Cucina, *city: Italian* [for "kitchen"], *see margin* [p. 23].

Cuillera, *city: French* cochlear, *"spoon"; hence a "wooing voice."*

D

D'ayuno, *city: Spanish* [*ayuno*] *for "fasting."*

Derrumbiada: *Spanish* [*derrumbadero*] *for "a precipice."*

Desuergona, *city: from the Italian word* [*svergognato*] *that means "shamelessness."*

Devoracum, *city: from the Latin "devorando," to "gulp down," "devour."*

Di-Marza: Italian *for "corrupted blood," "sanies."*

Diente: *from the Spanish* [*diente*] *for "tooth."*

Doxia: *from the Greek* Δόξῃ, *"belief."*

Dudosa, academy: *Spanish* [*dudoso*] *for "doubtful," the* b [of the Latin *dubia*] *altered into a* d.

Dunius, port: Dunkerk [Dunkirk].

Duricoria, *city: Latin "ficus duricoriae,"* Pliny, [*HN*], *book 15, chapter 18,* [figs] *which have a hard skin.*

E

Erotium, *city: Greek* [ἔρος], *synonymous with* Amantina.

Eugynia, *region: Greek* [εὐ- "good," *plus* γὐνή- "woman"]. Land of good women.

F

Farfellia, *city: Italian* farfello, *meaning "butterfly."*

Faessera, *city: German [Fässer] for* "city of casks."

Favillia: *from the Latin "favilla," "glowing ashes."*

Tierra del Fuego: ["land of fires"], *the c in the Latin [focus] altered to a g.*

Fourmagium, *city: from the French* fourmage [fromage], *"cheese."*

Fouetta, *city: French for* "place of scourging."

Fripperia, *village: from a certain section in Paris.*

Frivianda, *province: see margin* [p. 22].

Frugiona: *Latin [frux, frugis, "fruits of the earth"], see margin* [p. 22].

Furtofrancheça, *city: compounded from the Latin* furtum, "theft," *and the French* franchise, *"freedom."*

G

Garilla, *city: from the Latin "garriendo," "chattering."*

Gesundheits: *German for our English* "Healths."

Gola, *city: Italian [and Spanish, gola] for* "throat."

Golosinius, *district: Spanish [golosina, "delicacy"], see margin p.* [24].

Gorga: *Italian [actually Spanish, gorja] for* "throat."

Gorganta, *city: Spanish [garganta] for* "throat."

Gutiges, *birds: German [gütig] for* "beneficent"; *hence* good *in English.*

Gruessa, *moat: Spanish [grueso] for* "fat"; *assuredly from the Latin "crasso," hence the Italian* grasso *and the Spanish* g[ru]esso.

Gynaecopolis: *Greek* γυναίκοπόλις, *"city of women."*

Gymnopodilla, *city: Greek* γυμνοὶπόδες, *"bare feet."*

H

Hambria, *island: Spanish [hambre] for* "hunger," *see margin* [p. 23].

Hierosule, *city: Greek* ἱερῶν σύλη, *"sacrilegious plunder."*

Houbelonia, *province: from the French* houbelon, *"hops."*

J

Jugaria, *city: from the Spanish* jugar, *"to joke."*

L

Labriana, *city: from the Latin [labrum, labri], "lips."*

Lardana, *city: from the Latin for* "bacon."

Larcinia, *province: French* larrecin, *meaning "thief."*

Larmium, *river: French* larme, *a shortening of* [the Latin] *"lacryma," "a tear."*

Lavernia, *land: Latin* [Laverna, the patron goddess of gain; hence the protector of rogues and thieves], *see margin* [p. 107].

Lecanica, *plain: Greek, see margin* [p. 24].

Lecho, *city: Spanish* [*lecho*] *for "bed."*

Licoris, *river: Spanish* licor *from the Latin "liquor," "to be fluid."*

Linguadocia, *province: from the Latin "lingua," "tongue," because women are, for the most part, very talkative, in imitation of the French province Languedoc.*

Lingastrum, *city: from the Latin "ligendo," "licking."*

Lipsanium, *city: Greek* λείψανα, *"relics."*

Lirona, *city: in Spanish,* [*lirón*] *means "dormouse."*

Lisonica, *province: Spanish* [*lisonja*] *for "flattery."*

Livenza, *river: "fluid."*

Liviana, *valley: Spanish* [*liviano*] *for "light."*

Loçania, *province: Spanish* [*lozania*] *for "luxuriance."*

Louerium, *city: French* [*louer*] *for "laudatory."*

Lupulania, *province: from the Latin "lupulus," "hop."*

Lyperia, *province: Greek* λυπηρὸς, *"sorrowful," "melancholy."*

M

Mange-guadagnos: *Italians jokingly call their servants this* [from *mange,* "to eat," and *guadagnare,* "to earn"]. *See margin* [p. 95].

Maninconica, *land: Italian* [*malinconico*] *for "melancholy,"* n *replacing the* l.

    Cave of Maninconicus

Manteca, *city: Spanish for "butter."*

Maravilla, *city: Spanish* [*maravilla*] *for "miracle," from the French esmerveiller, "to marvel"; hence the English* marvel.

Marmitta, *city: Spanish* [*marmita*] *for "cauldron."*

Marza-pane, *city: Italian for "march-pane."*

Menturnea: *once a city of the Samnites; I pretend that the name is derived from "mentum," "chin."*

Medrosi: *Spanish* [*medroso*] *for "timid ones."*

Meionium, *river: from the Latin* meiendo, *"making water." Cyprus once enjoyed this name, Stephanus.*

Menosprecia, *city: Spanish* [*menospreciar*] *for "despised."*

Methius, *lake: from the Greek* μεθύειν, *"to get drunk."*

Milana, *city: French* [*milan*], *as it were, for* "*kitelike*," "*rapacious*"; *a city of kites and hawks.*

Mnemon, *river: Greek* [μνήμων] *for* "*memory.*"

Μωρονία [Moronia]: *from* μῶρος, "*stupid.*"

Mortadella, *city: Italian for* "sausages."

Muerius, field: *from the French* muer, "*to alter,*" "*cast off.*"

N

Novizza, *city: Italian* [*novita*] *for* "novelty."

Nuchtermagen: *German* [*nüchtern* + *Magen*] *for* "*empty stomach.*"

O

Ochietto, mount: *Italian diminutive from* ochio, "*eye.*"

Oenotria, *province: from the Greek* οἶνος, "*wine.*"

Offulia, *city: from the Latin* "*offula*" *for* "*little morsel.*"

Oglium, *river: Italian* [*oglio* in the sixteenth century; now *olio*] *for* "*oil*"; *we soften the* g *into a* y, Oyle.

Olmii, *hills: Italian and Spanish* [*olmo*] *for* "*elm tree.*" "*the grape vine* [clings to] *the leafy elm,*" *Virgil.*

Omasius, giant: *from the Latin* "*omasum*," "*stomach.*"

Orgilia, *province: from the French* orgueil, *meaning* "*arrogance.*"

Oysivium, *river: French* [*oisif*] *for* "*idle.*"

P

Patronilla, *city: Italian* [*patron*, "patron," *plus Latin diminutive*]. *But we should rather term it the* "*village of patrons.*"

Pampinola: *Latin; the same city in* Greek *is* Ampelona, *in imitation of the Spanish city* Pampelona.

Pazzivilla: *Italian* [*pazzo*, "crazy," *plus* *villa*, "village"] *for* "*city of fools.*"

Phenacia, *province: Greek* φένακες, "*imposters.*"

Piacentia: *Italian for* "*pleasantness.*"

Pipulia, *swamp: Latin. Plautus uses the word* [*pipulus*] *for* "*wrangling*": "I'll disturb you with wrangling in front of the house."

Pythonos-come: *Greek, see margin* [p. 27].

Ploravia, *province: from the Latin* "*plorare*," "*to weep.*"

Ponfinia, *province: see text* [Book 1, part 2], *chapter* [2].

Porcestria, *city: from the Latin "porcus," "pig."*
Porciglia, *village: from the word [porcilga] that means "pigsty" in Spanish.*
Putanium, *city: Italian for* "city of whores" [from the Italian *puttana,* "whore"].
Pyraenia, *province: from the Greek* πυρι, *"fire," and* οἴνω, *"wine."*

R

Risia major, minor, *provinces: from the Italian* [*riso*], *from the Latin "risus," "laughter."*
Risaglium, *city: from the Italian* risaglia, *"laughter."*
Rodomantadii, *hills: The southern French (if I remember correctly) call discursive speeches* rotomantades, *perhaps from the Spanish* romance[ar], *"to circumlocute."*
Rodillia, *city: from the Spanish* [*rodilla*] *meaning* "knee."
Roncara, *city: see margin* [p. 33]; *from* [the Greek] ρεγχειν, *"to snore."*
Ruzius, *river: from the French* ruse, *"fraud," "cunning."*

S

le Sain, *river: French* [*sain*], *"sound."*
Sbanditica, *tribe: all too well known to the Italians,* "outlaws" [from *bandito,* "bandit."]
Sans-eau, *river: French for* "waterless."
Sarcoboscum, *city: from the Greek* σαρκὸς, *"flesh," and* βόσκειν, *"to eat."*
Scrofiola, *city: from the Latin "scrofa," "sow." A pig is the most naturally greedy animal. It always looks toward the ground. Not a person in this place appears before evening.*
Scarpellino: *Italian* [*scalpellino*] *for* "stonecutter"; *the Latin* l *altered to an* r.
Scioccia, *province: from the Italian* sciocco, *"stupid."*
Schlauchberga, *city: from the German* Schlauch, ["wineskin," and *Berg,* "mountain," adding an a].
Scogido: [invented] *Spanish for* "noble," [from] escogido, *"elect."*
Schaum, *river: German for* "foam."
Sennaladii: *Spanish* [*señalado*] *for* "of eminent birth."
Seplasium, *city: Latin, from* Seplasia, *the perfumery marketplace of*

Capua, whose delights broke down the Carthaginians.
Serrara, *city: from the Latin "serando," "to be fastened with a bolt."*
Sialon, *river: Greek* [σίαλον], *"saliva."*
Spesius, district: *from the Italian* spesa, *which means "expensive,";
hence the English* spend.
Spagyric, *art: Greek* [?], *said to be from "trahendo," "to extract."*
Strophades, *islands: from the Greek* στρέφειν, *"to turn," and even said
to be the same islands of* Plotoe.
Struzzoliae, *feathers: from the Italian* struzzolo, *"ostrich."*

T

Tarochium, *city: see margin* [p. 84].
Tenaille: *French for "a pair of tongs."*
Topia-Warallador: *Spanish and Indian.* Hallador *is Spanish for "dis-
coverer."*
Topia-Wari: *one-time king of Guiana.*
Torcolia, *valley: from the Italian "torcolo," "to press," from the Latin
"torcularis," "wine press."*
Traubena: *from the German* Trauben, *"grape," "a cluster of grapes."*
Traurigii, mountains: *from the German* traurig, *"sad."*
Troverense, *college: from the French* trouver, *"to find."*
Tryphonia, swamp: *from the thief Tryphon; see margin* [p. 107].

V

Vale-dolium: *Latin* [for "strong jar"], *in imitation of the Spanish name*
valedolio.
Vantarole: *from the Italian* vantar *and the French* vanter, *"to praise."*
Ucalegonium: *Greek* [οὐκ ἀλέγων, *"carefree"*] *meaning "idle city."*
Vellacos: *what the Spanish call their servants.*
Verguença: *Spanish* [vergüenza] *for "scandal," "shame."*
Viraginia: *Latin,* [from *virago, viraginis,* "a female warrior"].
Verulanium: *Latin,* [perhaps from *veru,* "spit," and *lana,* "lamb," or
lanio, "butcher"].
Vinicella: *Latin,* [from *vinum,* "wine," and *cella,* "storeroom"].
Vortunius: *Latin, from "vertendo," "to be turned about."*
Uscebatius, *region: from an Irish drink.* [Gaelic *uisgebeatha,* literally,
"water of life."]

Z

Zornus, *river: from the German* [Zorn] *for* "angry," "furious."
Zouffenberga: *from the German* zauffen [*saufen*], *which means* "to carouse" *in French.*
Zuckerii, *hills: German* Zucker, *for* "sugar."

COMMENTARY

In the commentary, head words are cited from the English text, preceded by the page and line numbers. Hall's marginal notes are here designated by the letter *m* following the page and line in the text at which they begin, even though they often continue down the page for several lines in the original. Quotations from a classical author are always from the text of the Loeb edition if one exists for the work cited; otherwise, the best generally available edition has been chosen. The bibliography includes abbreviations or short titles for those works referred to frequently. The abbreviations used to designate classical works are from the *Oxford Classical Dictionary*, 2nd ed., except when none was given there. For the Medieval and Renaissance authors quoted, unless a translation is specifically noted in the commentary, the translation is my own.

The *Mundus* is a highly allusive work, intentionally so; Hall provides nearly two hundred marginal notes of his own (giving authors, titles, or both) to alert the reader to echoes of other works. It has been my policy—in keeping with this spirit—to try to suggest the origin of as many other allusions in the *Mundus* as I can and, wherever I can, to provide the original text for comparison. Many of the actual chapters and lines for the authors Hall refers to in his marginal notes were first identified by Huntington Brown in his 1937 edition of *The Discovery of a New World*. When my use of Brown has been limited to these (which I have independently verified), in the interests of saving space I have not footnoted him. Those who are familiar with Brown's edition will recognize his identifications in about one third of my notes. I am grateful to him for his earlier scholarship and have tried to build upon his efforts: to suggest why Hall incorporated these authors; to show whether Hall has reworked or misunderstood his sources and why; and to provide parallels from Hall's later writings to emphasize how the concerns he voices here continued to engage him throughout his career. I have also endeavored to explain place-names and mythological legends, if obscure, in the belief that some readers would appreciate such information. If occasionally I have explained too much, I ask the reader's indulgence, having myself been more often frustrated by editors who have explained too little or not at all.

2/3-4 Henry . . . Huntingdon] The fifth earl, who succeeded to the title in 1604 and to whom Hall also dedicated *Heaven upon Earth* (1606) and *Contemplations* (1612).

3/13-14 moisture . . . seed] Hall agrees but believes vice is far more often propagated than virtue:

> Ah me! how seldome see we sonnes succeed
> Their Fathers praise in prowesse and great deed?
> Yet certes if the Syre be ill inclin'd,
> His faults befal his sonnes by course of kind.
>   (*Vd.*, 4, 3, 84-87)

Cf. *Holy Observations*: "Virtue is not propagated; vice is" (*Works*, 7, 523). His philosophy may be derived from Juv., 14, 1-41.

3/15-16 procreate . . . 6,000] The universe was traditionally believed to have been created about 4,000 years before the birth of Christ or, speaking very broadly, 6,000 years before the time Hall is writing.

4/2-4 Platonists . . . *world*] The Platonists believed in a transcendent world of perfection toward which our world strives but imperfectly mirrors. Hall sarcastically claims that this newly discovered southern continent is the archetype for the rest of the world: that depravity—not virtue—is the goal mankind seeks.

4/8 Cimmerian obscurity] The Cimmerians were a fabulous people supposed to have dwelt in perpetual darkness (Val. Flac., *Argon.*, 3, 397-401).

4/24-27 long . . . Muses] An exaggeration. Hall produced *Virgidemiae*, his six books of satires, in 1597 and 1598 and worked on *Mundus Alter et Idem* as late as 1605 (see note to 117/16). Though he received his B.D. from Cambridge in 1603 and had preached sermons in and around the university from approximately 1600, it is difficult to believe this assertion of his (or of his friend William Knight, whose signature at the end of the introduction makes this statement ostensibly his). No doubt Hall wished to make the *Mundus* seem a product of his earlier years, perhaps believing some people would find it incompatible with the solemnity expected from a divine.

9/8 for . . . Zeus] Hom., *Od.*, 6, 207-08.

9/13-14 true . . . wisdom] With reference not only to the Greeks as great scholars but also to students at Cambridge, which was commonly termed "Athens." Cf. note to 11/16 below.

9/15 Peter Beroaldus] Anderson's speculation (p. 110) that the name may come from François Béroalde de Verville (1556-c. 1612) is made almost certain by de Verville's *Thesaurus Incantatus*, a work concerned with alchemy, in which he is referred to as "Beroaldus Cosmopolita," "Beroaldus, a citizen of the world," the very posture Hall's Beroaldus adopts in this dialogue; see note to 10/3-4 below.

9/16 Adrian . . . Drogius] Hadrianus Cornelius Drogius, the author of two theological works: *Disputationum Theologicarum Vigesima-octava: de Adoratione Eucharistiae* (Lyons, 1597), and *Theses Theologicae, de Libertate Christiana* (Lyons, 1596).

10/3-4 obscure . . . Socrates] Meant ironically, for, as Diogenes Laertius notes, "unlike most philosophers, [Socrates] had no need to travel, except when required to go on an expedition. The rest of his life he stayed at home" (2, 22).

10/16-17 polypus . . . stone] Pliny claims the polypus "changes its colour to match its environment, and particularly when it is frightened" (*HN*, 9, 87). In his character of "The flatterer," Hall repeats this belief: "Like that subtle fish, he turns himself into the colour of every stone for a booty" (*Works*, 6, 114). Cf. the note to 76/11 below and additional references given there.

10/36 Camden . . . Britain] William Camden, English antiquary and historian, who wrote *Britannia*—a survey of the British Isles—in 1586. In *Quo Vadis?* Hall paraphrases Beroaldus's arguments in this paragraph but uses them as a reason to stay home, not to push farther into the unknown: "Let an Italian or French passenger walk through this our island; what can his table-books carry home in comparison of the learned 'Britain' of our Camden, or the accurate 'Tables' of Speed?" (*Works*, 9, 540).

11/6-10 French . . . superstitious] Such catalogues were common in the sixteenth and seventeenth centuries. John Florio, *His firste Fruites*, contains nearly a dozen. Compare these lines, and lines 17-20 on p. 11, with what Hall says in one of his *Epistles* (*Works*, 6, 153-54): "The soil is not so diverse as the inclination of persons. . . . The Italian, deep, close, and crafty; the French, rash; the German, dull. . . . There are long catalogues of peculiar vices that haunt special places, which, if they were not notoriously infamous, my charity would serve me to particularize. It were pity there should be fewer virtues, local and proper."

11/16 dwellings . . . Muses] Cambridge University, where Hall studied from 1589 to 1601. Hall was very proud of English universities: "I am sure the universities of our island know no matches in all the world" (*Works*, 9, 537).

11/24-25 illustrious . . . Junius] William Whitaker (1548-95), master of St. John's College, Cambridge, Regius Professor of Divinity, whose championship of the teachings of the Church of England, interpreted in their most Calvinistic sense, made him one of the foremost English divines in the sixteenth century; John Reynolds (1549-1607), president of Corpus Christi College, Oxford, famous for his lectures on Aristotle and one of the translators for the King James Bible; Francis Junius, or Du Jon (1545-1602), prominent Huguenot scholar, professor of theology at Leyden, best known for his edition of the Latin Old Testament. In one of his *Epistles* (*Works*, 6, 149-50), Hall pays tribute to all three: "Alas, how many worthy lights have our eyes seen shining and extinguished! . . . That honour of our schools and angel of our church, learned Whitaker, [and] . . . that famous and illuminate doctor, Francis Junius, the glory of Leyden. . . . Doctor Reynolds is the last; not in worth, but in the time of his loss. He alone was a well furnished library."

11/25-26 'travelers' . . . del Cano] In 1577 Drake undertook the second circumnavigation of the globe, returning in November 1580. The first circumnavigator was Sebastian del Cano, who in 1522 reached San Lucar de Barrameda, Spain (from where Magellan had sailed in 1519), in command of the *Victoria* after Magellan was killed in the Philippines in 1521 (*Biographie Universelle*, 7, 23-24). Thomas Cavendish, emulous of Drake's example, fitted out three vessels for an expedition to the South Seas in 1586. He returned to England in 1588 as the third successful circumnavigator of the globe (Hakluyt, *Principal Navigations*, 8, 48-74, 206-55).

11/29-30 Ferdinand . . . Moluccas] In 1509 Magellan joined Diogo Lopes de Sequeira on his voyage intended for the Spice Islands (Moluccas).

When the Portuguese were ambushed at Malacca in 1510, Magellan
fought bravely, was rewarded with the rank of captain, and in 1511
was sent on to discover the Moluccas (*EB*, 17, 302-03).

11/30-31 Francisco . . . Peru] Pizarro (1475-1541), the discoverer of
Peru, and Diego de Almagro (1475-1538), the governor of Chile.
Together with Hernando de Luque, they signed a contract on 10
March 1526 for the conquest of Peru, which they ruthlessly accomp-
lished between 1530 and 1537.

11/31 Hugh Willoughby] The leader of an expedition that set out in
1553 to discover a northern passage to China. Two of his three ships
reached the coast of Lapland where he decided to winter. Unfortunately, he and his men died of cold and starvation sometime early in
1554. Several years later his remains were discovered, and his journal
was published in Hakluyt's *Principal Navigations*, 1, 244-54.

11/35 heroic venture] Some aspects of this conversation, in particular
the question of how to attain glory and the variety of dispositions
among the various European nationalities, seem to derive from
Erasmus's *The Lover of Lies* (*Colloquia*, tr. pp. 364-71).

12/24-25 *Terra . . . Incognita*] For a survey of the early history on Antarctica, Hall's "unknown southern continent," see Rainaud, *Le continent austral*.

12/34-35 trusted . . . sea] Although Hall indents three lines in the text,
only these two come from Horace: "[Oak and triple bronze must
have girt the breast of him who first] committed his frail bark to the
angry sea" (*Carm.*, 1, 3, 9-11).

13/14m Chinese proverb] "And therefore thei seyn hem self, that thei
seen with 2 Eyen; and the Cristene men see but with on: because that
thei ben more sotylle than thei. For alle other Naciouns, thei seyn,
ben but blynde in conynge and worchynge, in comparisoun to
hem" (*Mandeville's Travels*, p. 219).

13/33-34 Patagonian Polyphemus] Polyphemus, a cyclops, devoured
whoever reached his shore. The Patagonian natives were considered
giants by the early explorers: "He was so tall that the tallest of us
only came up to his waist" (Pigafetta, *Magellan's Voyage*, 1, 46);
"They [are] very mightie men of bodie of ten or eleven foot high,
and good bow-men, but no man-eaters" (Hakluyt, *Principal Navigations*, 8, 178). Cf. Peter Martyr's account in *De Orbe Novo*, 2, 154,
and Thevet, *Newfounde Worlde*, fol. 88v.

14/1 Cape . . . Hope] The southern tip of Africa, discovered and named
by Bartholomew Diaz in 1488, named on the map facing p. 19.

14/7-8 sent . . . heaven] An allusion to Columbus, whose last name means "dove" in Latin.

14/14-15 *Discoverer . . . conqueror*] Perhaps directed at the Spanish explorers, though more probably a slap at Sir Walter Raleigh, who is satirized in this work as Topia-Warrallador, and whose last name is glossed (125/13) as "Spanish for 'discoverer.'" Raleigh, banished from Elizabeth's court in 1592 after secretly marrying one of her maids of honor and desperate to recover favor, exalted discovery as Beroaldus does: "Discovery was not only an end in itself, there was the spur of fame: the fortunate discoverer might become 'as famous and powerful as Cortes or Pizarro'" (V. T. Harlow, ed., introduction to Raleigh, *Discoverie of Gviana*, p. xlv).

14/17 tragedian Seneca] *Medea*, lines 375-77.

14/39 golden Ophir] The place to which the ships of Hiram and Solomon sailed from Ezion-geber, at the head of the Gulf of Aqaba, and after three years returned with gold, silver, precious stones, costly woods, ivory, apes, and peacocks. It is not specified that Ophir was the source of all these products but simply that such articles were brought back at the end of a three-year cruise (Hastings, *Dict. Bib.*, p. 626). The primary biblical references to Ophir are: Gen. 10:28-30; 1 Kings 9:26-28, 10:11, 22:48; 2 Chron. 8:18, 9:10. Modern authorities lean toward southeastern Arabia as Ophir's location on the supposition that the place called Ophir was named for Ophir the son of Joktan and therefore located in the area settled by the Joktanites mentioned in Gen. 10:28-30, and on the strength of the gold-producing qualities attributed to it. See Martinière, *Dictionnaire géographique*, 7, O62-73 (paginated by letter).

15/2 five . . . opinions] Beroaldus's discussion comes mainly from the treatise by Gaspar Barreiros, *Commentarius de Ophyra*, sigs. H6v-L4v.

15/3 Hrabanus . . . Lyra] Barreiros, *Commentarius de Ophyra*, sig. H7. Cf. Hrabanus Maurus, *Commentaria in Libros II Paralipomenon*, · 3, 8 (in *PL*, 109, 472), and Nicolas de Lyra, *Biblia Latina*, 2, 146v, gloss on 3 Regum 9.

15/4 Raphael of Volaterra] Barreiros, *Commentarius de Ophyra*, sig. H7v. Cf. Volaterra, *Commentarii Urbani*, fol. 168v.

15/5 Abraham Ortelius] Ortelius, *Thesaurus Geographicus*, s.v. "Ophir."

15/6-7 doubtful . . . Venice] Hall's "unknown Ludovico of Venice" (apparently his rendering of Barreiros's "Ludovicus quidam Venetus" [*Commentarius de Ophyra*, sig. H7]) may be Ludovico de

Varthema, for he wrote *Novum Itinerarium Aethiopiae, Aegypti, utriusque Arabiae, Persidis, Siriae, ac Indiae* in 1511. Though he makes a fleeting reference to Sofala and its gold, Ludovico de Varthema does not specifically connect it with the land of Ophir (*Novum Itinerarium*, in Grynaeus, *Novus Orbis*, p. 303; tr. p. 291).

15/7 Gaspar Barreiros] "If anyone will diligently compare the maps of Ptolemy with those of our geographers, . . . he will discover a gold and silver region [Pegu] placed between the Bay of the Ganges [now called Bengal] and the Golden Chersonesus. . . . The greatest argument in this matter is the enormous supply of other goods in Pegu that Solomon carried back besides silver and gold. For no place in India except Pegu sells gems of such a precious variety. It possesses many apes and peacocks, a prodigious amount of ivory, and forests of the most precious woods" (Barreiros, *Commentarius de Ophyra*, sigs. I3v-I4v).

15/9 Francisco Vatablus] Barreiros, *Commentarius de Ophyra*, sig. I2. Cf. Vatablus, *Sacra Biblia*, 1, 286, note to 1 Kings 9:28.

15/9 Peter Martyr] "According to Columbus, Hispaniola is the island of Ophir mentioned in the third book of Kings" (*De Orbe Novo*, 1, 86-87).

15/11 Postellus] *Cosmographicae*, pp. 32-33.

15/11 Goropius . . . Montano] Ortelius, *Thesaurus Geographicus*, s.v. "Ophir."

15/15-16 Barreiros . . . refuted] *Commentarius de Ophyra*, sigs. I2-L2v.

15/18-19 Sumatra . . . Chersonesus] Sumatra is an island located in the Indian Ocean to the west of the Peninsula of Malacca (today the Malay Peninsula). The golden Chersonesus, according to Martinière (*Dictionnaire géographique*, 8, Q23), was the name given by the ancients to the Peninsula of Malacca, but he speculates that it might also include part of the western coast of Burma and thus be the same region as that named Pegu (the area north of Rangoon, Burma). Hall's map, facing p. 19, correctly places the city of Malacca on the Malay Peninsula but omits the island of Sumatra.

15/21 Tyre] The capital of ancient Phoenicia, a seaport on the Mediterranean in southern Lebanon.

15/37-38 transpose . . . ambiguous] The Hebrew words Hall gives in the margin stand for "Ophir," WPR ופר and "Peru," PRW פרו. By moving the *W* from the beginning to the end of the word "Ophir," Beroaldus is attempting to prove that the two places are really one.

16/19-20 time . . . elapsed] "The whole period from the accession of

Hirom to the foundation of Carthage thus amounts to 155 years and eight months; and, since the temple at Jerusalem was built in the twelfth year of King Hirom's reign, 143 years and eight months elapsed between the erection of the temple and the foundation of Carthage" (Joseph, *C. Ap.* 1, 18).

16/21 Carthaginians . . . avows] "In the sea outside the Pillars of Hercules they say that a desert island was found by the Carthaginians, having woods of all kinds and navigable rivers, remarkable for all other kinds of fruits. . . . As the Carthaginians frequented it often owing to its prosperity, and some even lived there, the chief of the Carthaginians announced that they would punish with death any who proposed to sail there, and they massacred all the inhabitants, that they might not tell the story" (Arist., *Mir. Ausc.*, chap. 84).

16/23 beyond Gades] A famous colony of the Phoenicians established on an island of the same name in southeastern Spain, today named Cadiz.

16/37-17/19 Behold . . . glory] Beroaldus's argument and his listeners' response seem to derive from the Ulysses passage in canto 26 of Dante's *Inferno*.

17/23 The Phantasia] See Introduction, p. lii.

17/36 Fortunate Isles] "The Fortunate Isles, or, as the Spaniards call them, the Canaries, . . . are distant from Cadiz about three hundred leagues. . . . In ancient times these islands were called Fortunate, because of the mild temperature they enjoyed" (Peter Martyr, *De Orbe Novo*, 1, 58).

17/36 Monomotapensi] Shown on Hall's map facing p. 19. According to Martinière (*Dictionnaire géographique*, 7, M442), this region was bordered on the north and west by the Zambesi River, on the east by the Indian Ocean, and extended nearly to the tip of Africa on the south.

19/5m Pliny] The correct reference is to *HN*, 23, 24.

19/5m πηλοῦ . . . wine] The Phocian Hall names is apparently the Athenian general and statesman of the fourth century B.C. condemned to death in 318 (*OCD*, p. 826). Liddell and Scott do give as one definition for πηλός, "thick or muddy wine, lees" (*A Greek-English Lexicon*, p. 1401), designating it as a poetic usage, but neither the life by Cornelius Nepos (ed. John C. Rolfe [London, 1929], pp. 596-605) nor the one by Plutarch (*Vit.*, 8, 143-233) attributes any such saying to Phocion.

19/6m Without . . . Bacchus] Expanded, the quotation reads: "Without

Ceres and Bacchus, Venus is a-chill" (Ter., *Eun.*, line 732; Eras., *Adagia*, 2, 521-22; tr. fol. 341).

19/7m fat . . . mind] In one of his sermons (*Works*, 5, 294-95), Hall expresses a similar belief: "The Psalmist describes some wicked ones in his time by *sepulcrum patens guttur eorum, Their throat is an open sepulchre,* Psalm v. 9. How many have buried all their grace in this tomb! how many their reputation! how many their wit! how many their humanity!" The saying is proverbial in the Renaissance, appearing in Lyly (*Campaspe*, 1, 2, 79) and Shakespeare (*Love's Labor's Lost*, 1, 1, 26) among others, according to the *Oxford Dictionary of English Proverbs*, p. 247. Their source, and Hall's, is probably Erasmus (*Adagia*, 2, 853), who derives it from Saint Jerome.

19/9 RUC] Hall apparently draws his information on this fabulous beast, especially its strength, from Marco Polo; see note to 35/7 below. In the *Arabian Nights* (6, 16-19), Sinbad the Sailor is borne aloft twice by a similar bird named "rukh."

19/16 Pamphagonia] See Hall's fanciful derivation of this name on p. 22 below. The name actually derives from the Greek πᾶν, and φαγεῖν, "to eat." The name also echoes "Pamphlagonia," an ancient province in Asia Minor noted for its fertility (Strab., 12, 3; Xen., *An.*, 5, 6, 6).

19/19-20 two Germanies] Upper and lower Germany, named according to the two army commands stationed on the Rhine in the time of Germanicus Caesar (first century after Christ). The upper command was headquartered at Mainz, the lower one at Vetera, near Xanten.

21/3m ibis . . . image] Conrad Gesner, *Historia Animalium* (3, 549, 46-50), mentions the ibis and its feet. His treatment follows Plutarch (*Quaest. Conv.*, 4, 5, 670), who says the ibis "forms an equilateral triangle by the position of its outspread feet and bill." Plutarch specifically calls such a belief irrational and nowhere explains why the Egyptians hold the ibis in such high esteem; yet it is likely Hall took his information from Plutarch, since the lion sleeping with his eyes open and the pig showing mankind how to plow, mentioned later in the *Mundus* (see notes to 32/30-31 and 117/5-6 below), appear in this very question.

21/9 Ortolani and Beccafici] "*Ficedulae,* 'fig-peckers,' and *miliariae,* 'ortolans,' are named from their food, because the ones become fat on the *ficus,* 'fig,' the others on *milium,* 'millet'" (Pliny, *HN*, 37, 156). Both are delicacies artificially fattened for the table.

21/10-11 from . . . produced] In his note Hall calls them Barnacles, the

same name he gives to them in *Vd.* (4, 2, 139-40), where he says they
are generated from worms. His source is probably Andreas Libavius,
to whom Hall mistakenly refers in his following note on the vegetable lamb: "fruits of Scottish trees, from which worms are first produced, and afterward birds" (*De Judicio Aquarum Mineralium,* 1,
29, 307). In his *Description of Scotland,* William Harrison, translating Hector Boethius, also talks of "geese which are ingendred by
the sea": "All trees cast into that element in processe of time become
wormeaten, and in the holes thereof are the said wormes to be
found. . . . In the beginning, these worms doo shew their heads and
feet, and last of all their plumes & wings. Finallie when they are
come to the iust measure and quantitie of geese, they flie in the aire
as other foules doo" (p. 17). Earlier, in his *Description of Britaine*
(p. 38), Harrison also calls this creature a barnacle.

21/13 world . . . lamb] Hall's first marginal reference is to J. C. Scaliger
(*Exoticarum,* exercise 181, fol. 248v): "The principal tribe of the
Tartars is the Zavolha. . . . In their fields a fruit similar to a melon
grows, but shorter in length, from which a plant arises, which
they call Borometz, that is, a lamb. This phantom of a lamb grows
nearly three feet tall, which it counterfeits in its legs, hooves, ears,
head, all except its horns." Sigismund, Baron von Herberstein
(*Rerum Muscoviticarum Commentarii,* 2, 74-75) in a similar description calls it both a "boranetz" and a "Samarcandeos" and adds
that "it bore very fine wool. . . . The plant,—if plant it could be
called,—had blood in it, but no flesh; but in lieu of flesh, there was a
kind of matter very like the flesh of crabs; it also had hoofs, not
horny like those of a lamb, but covered with a hairy substance resembling horn. Its stem came to the navel, or middle of the belly; it
continued alive until the grass around it was eaten away, so that the
root dried up for want of nourishment." Libavius mentions no
vegetable lamb in his writings, but see the preceding note on geese.
Hall elsewhere refers to the "Samarcandian lamb, which growing
out of the earth by the navel grazeth so far as that natural tether will
reach" (*Quo Vadis?, Works,* 9, 541-42).

21/18 Nero's turbot] Juv., 4, 68-69.

21/21 Charon's boat] "If an epidemic or a war sends me down a large
batch, I can then make a profit, by overcharging on the fares in the
rush" (Lucian, *Dial. Mort.,* 342).

22/7 Frugiona] Hall's marginal note should be Varro, *Ling.,* 5, 104.
Here Varro points out how words become extended in meaning,

showing the variety of words that have sprung from the verb *fruor.*
He does not specifically connect it with clothing.

22/9 Saturn's age] Saturn, an early king of Rome, civilized the people
and taught them agriculture. Mild and beneficent, his reign was regarded as the Golden Age. Hall devotes the first half of satire 1 in
book 3 of *Vd.* to describing the austere tranquillity of Saturn's reign.
See Hes., *Op.,* 111-20.

22/20-21 Promontory ... Continent] This cape is, in fact, placed exactly
at 42 degrees south latitude on the world map of Abraham Ortelius
(*Theater,* map 1).

22/25 promontory ... Black] Hall's references to Pliny are, in modern
notation, *HN,* 3, 1, 4; 5, 17, 76. The first white cape, according to
Rackham (*HN,* 3, 1, 4n), is probably Punto del Sarinas in Morocco,
across the Straits of Gibraltar from Spain. The second, still called
the White Cape (Ras el Abiadh in Arabic), is situated on the coast of
Tunisia, northwest of Tunis, near Bizerte. Note also that Hall includes a C. Blanco on the coast of South America on his map of
Pamphagonia.

23/2 Tierra del Fuego] The island at the southern tip of South America
discovered by Magellan in 1520. He called it the "Land of Fire,"
either from now-extinct volcanoes or from the fires kindled by the
natives along parts of his course.

23/5 Cacuchina] Apparently compounded from the Greek κᾱκός, "bad,"
and the Italian *cucina,* "kitchen." Compare Peter Martyr's city of
Campeche, where the houses "are built of lime and bitumen" (*De
Orbe Novo,* 2, 10).

23/12 Cheminea Tower] In addition to the note Hall gives, this tower's
name and his reference to Memphis in the preceding line appear to
come from Diodorus Siculus (1, 63, 3-4): "The eighth king, Chem-
mis of Memphis, ruled fifty years and constructed the largest of the
three pyramids, which are numbered among the seven wonders of
the world. . . . By the immensity of their structures and the skill
shown in their execution they fill the beholder with wonder and
astonishment."

23/19 Hambrians . . . Apuleius's] Apuleius mentions a thief named
Haemus, who may well be the source for Hall's name: "Yet think
you not that I am an abject or a beggar, . . . for I have been a captain
of a great company, and wasted all the country of Macedonia; I am
the renowned thief Haemus the Thracian, whose name whole countries and nations do greatly fear" (*Met.,* 7, 6).

23/27 Culliera] See note to 120/14.

23/30 fountain . . . Peak] Hall is conflating two accounts in Harrison:
"The third place wherein hot baths are to be found is neere vnto
Buxton, a towne in Darbishire, situat in the high Peke" (*Description of England*, p. 214); "There is a well in Darbieshire called
Tideswell . . . whose water often seemeth to rise and fall, as the sea
which is fortie miles from it dooth vsuallie accustome to ebbe and
flow" (*Description of Britaine*, p. 131).

24/9m Scarcely . . . Galen's] In fact, Galen specifically discusses the
properties of sugar in *De Simplicium Medicamentorum Facultatibus, Libri 2*, fol. 55E: "But sugar [sacchar], as they name it, which is
brought from India and Arabia Felix, collects in reeds, . . . congeals,
and is itself a type of honey, certainly excessively sweet compared to
ours, but resembling it in its strength even if dried and powdered.
Just like our honey it is not harmful to the stomach; yet it differs to
the extent that it does not cause thirst."

24/10m Pliny] "Arabia also produces cane-sugar, but that grown in
India is more esteemed. It is a kind of honey that collects in reeds,
white like gum, and brittle to the teeth" (*HN*, 12, 17).

24/21 honeydew] "A sweet sticky substance found on the leaves and
stems of trees and plants, held to be excreted by aphids: formerly
imagined to be in origin akin to dew" (*OED*). Davenport notes:
"This honey on oak leaves is usually mentioned in poetical descriptions of the Golden Age. See Ovid, *Met.*, 1, 1, 104 sqq.; Virgil, *Ecl.*, 4,
30" (*Poems*, p. 184).

24/29 Cibinium] According to Brown (*Discovery*, p. 228), "Cibinium
can be found on the map of Europe (at 50 degrees E. Long. and 46
degrees N. Lat.) preceding the first chapter of Book 13 of André
Thevet's *La Cosmographie Universelle*, 2 vols., continuous pagi-
nation (Paris, 1575), fol. 469," a work I have not been able to consult.

25/1-2 Apicius . . . crab] "Marcus Apicius, named by Pliny as the most
extraordinary glutton, wrote books on gluttony according to Suidas
and squandered his vast sums on his palate. When he heard that
marine crabs grew in Africa which weighed much more than those
in France, he sailed there" (Volaterra, *Commentarii Urbani*, 13, fol.
182r-182v). Athenaeus reports that the place in Africa was Libya:
"When he drew near these regions, fishermen sailed to meet him . . .
and brought to him their best prawns. On seeing them he asked if
they had any that were larger, and on their answering that none

grew larger than those they had brought, he bethought him of the prawns in Minturnae and told the pilot to sail back by the same route to Italy without so much as approaching the shore" (Ath., 1, 7).

25/3 testimony of Seneca] Contrary to Hall's fanciful suggestion that Apicius died of intoxication in Pamphagonia, Seneca writes that he died in Rome: "After he had squandered a hundred million sesterces upon his kitchen, . . . he began to examine his accounts. He calculated that he would have ten million sesterces left, and considering that he would be living in extreme starvation if he lived on ten million sesterces, he ended his life by poison" (*Dial.*, 2, 453).

25/28-29 academies . . . mother] I.e., Cambridge and Oxford. See Introduction, p. xvi and n. 8.

25/32 Saturn's age] See note to 22/9 above.

26/6 Verolamium] Spenser's city of Verlame, a symbol of desolation. Verulamium, near the modern town of Saint Albans—containing a Roman theater, palatial townhouses, and three monumental arches—was built from the first to the fourth century after Christ. In the late fifth or sixth century the site became deserted, and the ruins were much pillaged for the monastic buildings of Saint Albans in the early Middle Ages (*OCD*, pp. 1114-15).

26/24m Strabo] "Now August Caesar concerned himself about such impairments of the city, organizing for protection against fires a militia composed of freedmen, whose duty it was to render assistance, and also to provide against collapses, reducing the heights of the new buildings and forbidding that any structure on the public streets should rise as high as seventy feet" (Strab., 2, 403-05).

26/26 Seneca] Despite Hall's suggestion, neither Seneca nor Juvenal (note following) says anything about stairs; rather, they criticize the unsoundness of the buildings themselves. "First, if you wish to start there, the very buildings: these they have raised to such a height that though houses are meant for use and protection they are now sources of danger, not of safety; such is the height of the structures, so narrow are the roads, that there is no guarding against fire—and no escape in any direction from collapsing buildings" (Sen., *Controv.*, 2, 1, 11).

26/26 Juvenal] "Who at cool Praeneste, or at Volsinii amid its leafy hills, was ever afraid of his house tumbling down? . . . But here we inhabit a city, supported for the most part by tender props: for that is how the bailiff patches up the cracks in the old wall, bidding the inmates sleep at ease under a roof ready to tumble about their ears" (Juv., 3, 190-96).

27/32 Pythonos-come] Hall's note refers to Pliny (*HN*, 10, 31): "There is a place in Asia called Pythonos Comen [village of snakes] with a wide expanse of plains where cranes meet in assembly to hold a palaver, and the one that arrives last they set upon with their claws, and so they depart." Brown (*Discovery*, p. 209) says that Solinus (*Polyhistor*, 40, 25) copied this story and was ridiculed by Albertus Magnus (*Opera*, 6, 618a–b). Strabo refers to a town of Phriconian Cume twice in his *Geography* (13, 1, 3 and 13, 3, 3), a place founded by the inhabitants of Phricium, a mountain above Thermopylae, but this is clearly unconnected with Pliny's place. Why Hall should include Strabo in his note cannot be answered with certainty, but I would venture that it is deliberate nonsense. Hall loves to play on words with similar sounds (see, for example, his derivation of Pamphagonia, p. 22, and the notes to 23/19 and 92/25) and to provide references that either give an ironic twist to what has been said or— as here—parody pedantic scholarship.

27/33-34 pot . . . reserved] "[The Sybarites] were the first to invent chamberpots, which they carried to their drinking parties" (Ath., 519e).

28/6 in Petronius] There are two such examples in Petronius: "Following the dogs came servants with a tray on which we saw a wild sow of absolutely enormous size. . . . Clustered around her teats were little suckling pigs made of hard pastry, . . . intended to show that ours was a brood-sow" (*Sat.*, p. 37); "The slaves went scurrying about and promptly appeared with a barbecued calf, with a cap on its head, reposing on a huge platter—it must have weighed 200 pounds at the least" (*Sat.*, p. 58).

28/9m Philoxenus . . . *Ethics*] "A certain gourmand [Philoxenus] prayed that his throat might become longer than a crane's, implying that it was the contact that he took pleasure in" (Arist., *Eth. Nic.*, 3, 10, 10); "Therefore gluttons pray not for a long tongue but for the gullet of a crane, as did Philoxenus" (Arist., *Eth. Eud.*, 3, 2, 12).

28/18 Wilfred's Needle] "'Within the Church [at Ripon, Yorkshire], Saint Wilfride's Needle, was in our grandfathers remembrance very famous. A narrow hole this was, in the Crowdes or close vaulted roome under the ground, whereby women's honestie was tried: For, such as were chast did easily passe through, but as many as had

playd false, were miraculously, I know not how, held fast and could
not creepe through' Camden, *Britain,* transl. Philemon Holland
(London, 1610), p. 700E. Belvoir or Bever Castle, together with a
small abbey adjoining, is described by Camden on p. 536B, C, but
without mention of the relic. Of course it may have been at Belvoir
[once] as Hall says, but I learn, through the kindness of Mr. C. G.
Aldus, secretary to His Grace the Duke of Rutland that there is no
record of it ever having been there" (Brown, *Discovery,* pp. 167-68).
Hall refers to Wilfred's needle in a letter (*Works,* 6, 144-45) ridiculing those who believe that "St. Wilfred's needle opened to the peni-
tent, and closed itself to the guilty."

28/22 of Adonis] The tradition of an actual garden of Adonis comes
from Pliny's remark "that nothing was admired in antiquity more
than the gardens of Hesperides, and those of the kings Adonis and
Alcinous" (*HN,* 19, 19) (Josephine Waters Bennett, "Spenser's Garden of Adonis," *PMLA,* 47 [1932], 69-70), later picked up by Justus
Lipsius (see note to 28/22-23 below). Spenser, however, was the first
to describe it in detail (*The Faerie Qveene* [London, 1596], 3, 6,
29-49).

28/22 Alcinous] The prosperous king of Phaeacia who entertained Odysseus during his return from Troy, whose fruit garden was lush with
vegetation throughout the year (Hom., *Od.,* 7, 114-22).

28/22-23 of Langius] In *De Constantia* Justus Lipsius describes Langius's garden in Vienna: "You have here *Langius* a Heaven rather
than a Garden. . . . Talk we of the Gardens of Adonis or Alcinous?
compared with these, they are doubtless inconsiderable trifles. . . . I
speak with all seriousness imaginable, the *Elysian* Fields, are less so
than these Gardens of yours. . . . Within the narrow limits of this one
place, Nature seems to have enclosed all the excellencies, which
either this of ours, or that other World is able to boast of" (2, 1; tr.
pp. 139-41).

28/25-26 radishes . . . muskmelons] The fertility of the soil in Pamphagonia reminds one of Peter Martyr's description of Hispaniola:
"Everything in Hispaniola grows in extraordinary fashion. I have
already related that the vegetables, such as cabbages, lettuces, salads,
radishes, and other similar plants, ripen within sixteen days, while
pumpkins, melons, cucumbers, etc., require but thirty days" (*De
Orbe Novo,* 1, 364).

28/27 Pythagoreans] "The Pythagoreans trained themselves in the exercise of self-control in the following manner. They would have

prepared for them everything which is served up at the most brilliant banquets, and would gaze upon it for a considerable time; then, after . . . they had aroused their natural desires with a view to their gratification, they would command the slaves to clear away the tables and would at once depart without having tasted of what had been served" (Diod. Sic., 10, 5, 2).

28/34-35 Island of Sorbonia] Derived from the Sorbonne in Paris, apparently because of the meager diet of the poor students there.

29/21-22 Virgil . . . napkins] Verg., *G.*, 4, 377; *Aen.*, 1, 702.

29/32 Archisilenius] A name apparently compounded by Hall, meaning "head drunkard," from ἀρχι, "chief," and "Silenius," one of the older satyrs generally termed Sileni and a prominent member of the retinue of Dionysus, "from whom he is inseparable, and whom he is said to have brought up and instructed" (Smith, *Dict. Gr. & Rom. Myth.*, 3, 892).

29/33-34 a certain Apicius] Hall's note refers to Suidas's *Lexicon*, but nowhere in that work is it asserted that Apicius wrote books on gluttony. Brown (*Discovery*, p. 168) notes that Hall likely received his information on Suidas from Volaterra (*Commentarii Urbani*, p. 300), for Volaterra does ascribe such a statement to Suidas; see note to 25/1-2 above.

30/7-8 Asclepiades objects] "Asclepiades, one of the first of all physicians, and superior to all, Hippocrates excepted, was the first one who used wine as a remedy for the sick" (Apul., *Flor.*, 19). Besides his liberal use of wine, his great popularity depended "upon his not only attending in all cases, with great assiduity, to everything which contributed to [his patients'] comfort, but also upon his flattering their prejudices and indulging their inclinations" (Smith, *Dict. Gr. & Rom. Myth.*, 1, 382). Hall's sarcastic comment is directed at just such behavior, for since the most severe cure to impose on a glutton would be to purge him of food, it is a cure a doctor as indulgent as Asclepiades would never recommend.

30/8 Celsus] "To cause vomit on getting up in the morning, he should first drink some honey or hyssop in wine, or eat a radish, and after that drink tepid water" (*Med.*, 1, 3, 22).

30/9-10 Whatever . . . treasury] An alternative translation is: "Whatever is vomited up in this manner is an object for the public treasury."

30/14m Plato Comicus] Clement of Alexandria quotes Plato Comicus, *Festa*: "Hereafter 'twere well to kill no beast but swine, for they are excellent eating, and we get nothing out of them but bristles, and mire, and squealing" (*PG*, 9, 446B-C; tr. p. 57).

30/14-16 swine . . . table] "O woful, woful condition of those godless men; yea, those epicurean porkets, whose belly is their God, whose heaven is their pleasure, whose cursed jollity is but a feeding up to an eternal slaughter!" (Hall, *Works*, 5, 154).

30/24-26 corn . . . Venetians] Though I have not found a specific reference to the Venetians, such a practice is known among other nationalities: "Like the twentieth-century Eskimos, [paleolithic man] may have regarded the partially digested stomach contents of his kill as a special treat" (Reay Tannahill, *Food in History* [New York, 1973], p. 28).

30/37-38 beginning . . . banks] A sarcastic reference to the gluttonous feasts at the New Year and before Lent, when people stuff themselves and, consequently, swell the rivers with their refuse.

31/18 Fortune . . . inferior] Hall's saying seems to echo Manilius's that "Fortune does not always favor the most worthy" (*Astronomicon*, 4, 96). Cf. note to 97/10m below.

31/32m Virgil] The name of the old men in *Aen.*, 2, 311; also in Juv., 3, 199. Salyer notes that "noster Dunaeus" in Hall's note apparently refers to Andrew Downes, Regius Professor of Greek at Cambridge from 1585 to 1624 ("Joseph Hall," p. 235).

32/4 lead . . . Monk's] Erasmus devotes an entire section of *Moria* to the "felicity . . . [of] the men who generally call themselves the religious and monks" (4, 471-75; tr. pp. 98-101). His satiric remarks on such people parallel similar passages in the *Mundus*, such as pp. 70-72, and p. 102 above.

32/9 German miles] "A distance of between 4 and 5 English miles" (*OED*).

32/13m castle in Scotland] "The place to which [Hall] alludes is clearly 'the Basse castell,' a high rock rising sheer out of the sea beside the Isle of May at the entrance to the Firth of Forth, now known as the Bass Rock" (Brown, *Discovery*, p. 169).

32/27 Apuleius's meaning] *Flor.*, 2, 31.

32/29 Sybarite law] "The Sybarites were also the first to forbid noise-making crafts from being established within the city, such as blacksmiths, carpenters, and the like, their object being to have their sleep undisturbed in any way" (Ath., 12, 518). Hall's snide slap at the French is meant to refer to the noisiness of their cities; he makes a similar comment about Paris on p. 69 above.

32/30-31 farmers . . . Egyptians] "There are no men . . . who get their produce with so little labour; . . . the river rises of itself, waters the fields, and then sinks back again; thereupon each man sows his field and sends swine into it to tread down the seed, and waits for the harvest; then he makes the swine to thresh his grain, and so garners it" (Herod., 2, 14). Similarly, Plutarch says the pig taught man the function of a plowshare, for "it was the first to cut the soil with its projecting snout" (*Conv. Sept. Sap.*, 4, 5, 670).

32/32 servants . . . richer] This description expands upon one in *Mandeville's Travels*: "For he hathe every day, 50 fair Damyseles, alle Maydenes, that serven him everemore at his Mete, . . . thei kutten his Mete, and putten it in his Mouthe: for he touchethe no thing ne handlethe nought" (p. 210).

33/2-3 inhabitants . . . sleeping] See note to 32/29 above; Hall uses the phrase "sleepy *Sybarite*" in *Vd.*, 5, 2, 58.

33/3 Pliny . . . bears] "For the first fortnight they sleep so soundly that they cannot be aroused even by wounds; at this period they get fat with sloth to a remarkable degree . . . [and] live by sucking their forepaws" (Pliny, *HN*, 8, 54, 126-27). In *Christian Moderation (Works*, 6, 407) Hall refers to this belief: "If a bear or a dormouse grow fat with sleep, I am sure the mind of man is thus affamished."

33/10 To . . . order] Hall's note mentions Synesius; however, a careful search of Synesius's writings collected in *PG* does not reveal this saying.

33/10m This . . . ones] The opposite of the saying given at 80/3; see note to 80/3m below.

33/18 eat . . . streets] "[The Egyptians] relieve nature indoors, and eat out of doors in the streets, giving the reason that things unseemly but necessary should be done in secret, things not unseemly should be done openly" (Herod., 2, 35, 3).

34/1m Suetonius, *Claudius*] "He is even said to have thought of an edict allowing the privilege of breaking wind quietly or noisily at table, having learned of a man who ran some risk by retaining himself through modesty" (*Claud.*, 32).

34/14 House of Bread] Bethlehem (= "House of Bread") Hospital, better known as Bedlam, the first English lunatic asylum, was founded in 1246 as a priory for the clergy of Saint Mary of Bethlehem (Stow, *Suruay of London*, p. 166).

34/15-16 outside . . . Plutarch] "Why is the shrine of Aesculapius outside the city? Is it because they considered it more healthful to spend their time outside the city than within its walls?" (Plut., *Quaest. Rom.*, 4, 141).

34/20 Chambers of Meditation] Possibly a sarcastic reference to the treatment of the English envoys who in 1599 journeyed to Rome to protest the behavior of the English Jesuit Robert Parsons:

> The envoys who were come to appeal against the doings of Parsons were arrested by him to prevent their access to the Pope; and, to make security surer, were imprisoned under the roof and in the custody of their enemy. . . .
>
> Bishop [explains] how they were treated: "In the college we were locked up apart in two little close chambers, much more like the worst than the best in the house, with poor scholar's fare, and in smoky-coloured gowns such as servants wear; . . . for the most part kept without fire, being very cold, and for twenty days not suffered to go out not so much as to hear Mass upon New Year's Day or the Epiphany." (Taunton, *History of the Jesuits in England*, p. 249)

34/24 Aristotle . . . antiquity] "Many barbarian tribes . . . do not go beyond exchanging actual commodities for actual commodities. . . . Exchange on these lines therefore is not contrary to nature, nor is it any branch of the art of wealth-getting, for it exist[s] for the replenishment of natural self-sufficiency" (*Pol.*, 1, 3, 12–13).

35/2-3 God . . . things] Hall is probably thinking of Ovid's phrase *tempus edax rerum*, "time devours things" (*Met.*, 15, 234; *Pont.*, 4, 10, 7). The Titan Kronos (χρόνος = "time"), in Greek mythology, swallowed both of his children when they were born because he had been warned that one of them would overthrow him. The fact that Kronos is identified with Saturn in Roman mythology helps explain Hall's subsequent mention of Saturn's statue being sculpted on his sons' tomb.

35/7 RUC] "And at a certain time of the year a marvelous species of bird appears, which is called RUC, having, indeed, the appearance of an eagle, but immense in size. . . . In truth that bird has such great strength that it may alone seize an elephant without any help, and carry it aloft, and let it fall back to earth, by which means it is able to enjoy its flesh" (Marco Polo, *De Regionibus Orientalibus*, 3, 40). Cf. a similar description in Peter Martyr, *De Orbe Novo*, 2, 326. In *Quo Vadis?* (*Works*, 9, 542) Hall mentions the RUC as one of the "loud lies" readers learn from travel tales, and in *Vd.*, 4, 6, 68 he repeats Marco Polo's tall tale "of the Bird *Ruc* that beares an Elephant."

36/13-17 giant . . . Cambridge] Brown (*Discovery*, p. 171) quotes William Cole's ms history of Cambridgeshire, in which he comments on

Hall's passage: "When I was a boy, about 1724, I remember my
Father or Mother . . . always used to stop and show me and my
Brothers and Sisters the figure of the giant carved on the Turf; con-
cerning whom there were then many traditions, now worn away.
What became of the two said Teeth I never heard" (Smith, *The
Cambridge Portfolio*, 1, 196).

36/17-18 tooth . . . Sigebertus] "Today on the African shore near Utica
a giant tooth was found, so large that if it were cut down to the size
of our teeth, a hundred could be made from it" (Sigebertus Gemblacensis, *Chronicon*, fol. 7r); Harrison (*Description of Britaine*, p. 9)
repeats this but gives his authority as Augustine (*De Civ. D.*, 15, 9).

36/19 Orestes . . . Pliny] "The records attest that the body of Orestes dug
up at the command of an oracle measured 10 feet, 6 inches" (*HN*, 7,
16). Hall may very well have received his information from Harrison
(*Description of Britaine*, p. 11), who mentions all four of these
giants; see following notes.

36/19-20 Orion . . . Plutarch] Hall has confused authors, for Plutarch
says nothing of Orion's size: "*Plinie* telleth of an earthquake at
Creta, which discouered the body of a giant, that was 46. cubits in
length after the Romane standard, and by diuerse supposed to be the
bodie of *Orion* or *AEtion* [Otus]. . . . The said *Plinie* also addeth that
the bodie of *Orestes* was seuen cubits in length" (Harrison, *Description of Britaine*, p. 11; Pliny, *HN*, 7, 73).

36/20 Antaeus] "*Plutarch* telleth how *Sertorius* . . . caused his souldiers
to cast downe the hill made sometime ouer the tombe [of Antaeus],
and finding the bodie in the bottome coffined in stone, after the
measure thereof taken, he saw it manifestlie to be 60. cubits in
length" (Harrison, *Description of Britaine*, p. 11; Plut., *Sert.*, 9).

36/21-23 Boccaccio . . . Drepanum] "The like hereof also dooth *Iohn
Boccace* set downe . . . that in the caue of a mountaine, not far from
Drepanum . . . the bodie of an exceedingly high giant was discouered,
three of whose teeth did weigh *100.* ounces. . . . By the proportion of
the bone of his thigh, the *Symmetricians* iudged his bodie to be
aboue 200. cubits" (Harrison, *Description of Britaine*, p. 9; Boccaccio, *Genealogia*, 4, 68). Drepanum is a cape and town on the west
coast of Sicily.

36/27 delusion of Pythagoras] Namely, metempsychosis: "Pythagoras
believed in the transmigration of souls and considered the eating of
flesh as an abominable thing, saying that the souls of all living

creatures pass after death into other living creatures" (Diod. Sic., 10, 6, 1). Hall mentions the "erroneous opinions" concerning "Pythagorean transanimation" in his sermons (*Works*, 5, 17).

36/30 Mohammed . . . Turks] Hall may be thinking of the following incident in Ludovico de Varthema: "These old men began to cry out . . . like fanatics, 'Mohammed, messenger of God, arise from the grave, oh Prophet, oh God, Mohammed arise from the grave.' . . . Our captain and we, hearing this noise, immediately ran with our arms in our hands, thinking they were Arabs who wanted to rob the caravan, . . . for they made just such a noise as is heard amongst us Christians when a saint performs a miracle" (Grynaeus, *Novus Orbis*, p. 199).

36/33 Colossus of Lysippus] "We see enormously huge statues devised . . . [such as] the 60 ft. high statue at Taranto made by Lysippus. . . . Though it can be moved by the hand, it is so nicely balanced . . . that it is not dislodged from its place by any storms" (Pliny, *HN*, 34, 18).

36/33m statue . . . height] One of the seven wonders of the ancient world was "the colossal Statue of the Sun at Rhodes made by Chares of Lindus, the pupil of Lysippus. . . . Sixty six years after its erection, [it] was overthrown by an earthquake, but even lying on the ground it is a marvel. Few people can make their arms meet round the thumb of the figure, and the fingers are larger than most statues" (Pliny, *HN*, 34, 18).

37/3-4 but . . . stone] Ov., *Fast.*, 5, 131-32.

38/3-4 Mentones . . . Palatini] Fictitious tribes made up in imitation of real tribes such as the Palatines and the Mentores, which both appear in Pliny, *HN*, 18, 13, and 3, 139. Mentones comes from *menton*, French for "chin"; Buccones from *bucca*, Latin for "cheek"; Ventricones from *venter, ventris*, Latin for "belly," "paunch"; Palatini from *palatum*, Latin for "palate."

38/18 Nothing . . . excess] The opposite of Erasmus's famous dictum, *Ne quid nimis*, "nothing too much," *Adagia*, 2, 259-60; tr. fols. 19v-20r. Erasmus devotes nearly a page to this proverb, citing its use from Homer to Plautus. Hall himself discusses the concept thoroughly in *Christian Moderation* (*Works*, 6, 387 ff.), using the very same motto of Erasmus, emphasizing that without moderation "there can be nothing under heaven . . . but mere vice and confusion" (p. 388).

38/32 goddess Carnea] Carna, or Carnea, was a Roman divinity "whose

name is probably connected with *caro*, 'flesh,' for she was regarded
as the protector of the physical well-being of man" (Smith, *Classical
Dict.*, p. 198).

39/4-5 no one . . . Greeks] According to Anderson, pp. 95-96, although
"to imitate the Greeks" would normally mean "to live effeminately,"
as the Romans would say the Greeks did, here it probably means "to
avoid eating enough." Hall may be alluding to the well-known
starving Greek who appears in Juv., 3, 78, or to the Spartan diet.

39/13m Cagastrum . . . Iliastrum] "There are two seeds of disease, the
Iliastric and the Cagastric. The first is the substance from the beginning, the second is generated out of putrefaction. Dropsy and gout
are Iliastric; plagues, fevers, pleurisy, etc., are of cagastric origin"
(Waite, *Writings of Paracelsus*, 2, 358).

39/15 ostrich . . . sword] The notion that ostriches could digest iron was
widespread: "When he is killed and slaughtered, stones and occasionally iron are said to be found in his stomach, which are much
diminished in size by his digestion" (Münster, "De Struthione," in
Cosmographia, p. 1319). Cf. Bright, *A Treatise of Melancholie*, pp.
16-17. In *Meditations and Vows* (*Works*, 7, 493) Hall refers to the
ostrich's power to digest iron as something we "can scarce credit";
in *Quo Vadis?* he terms parents who are unmindful of their children's welfare "careless ostriches" and asks: "Have your stomachs
resolved to digest the hard news of the ruin of your children?"
(*Works*, 9, 531).

39/16 Digest and Conquer] A parody of Philip of Macedon's motto,
Divide et impera, "Divide and conquer" (Stevenson, p. 1014). Hall
refers to this twice in his *Works*: "For a prince, that he may have
good success against either rebels or foreign enemies, it is a sure
axiom, 'divide and rule'" (7, 459); in his sermons he calls "divide
and rule" "that old Machiavelian principle of our Jesuits" (5, 15).

39/29 Famelica Island] From the Latin *famelicus*, "famished."

39/31 Cabo Blanco] Cabo Blanco appears on modern maps just slightly
south of Cabo Tres Puntas on the Atlantic coast of southern Argen-
tina, at approximately 65°, 30' west longitude, 47° south latitude,
roughly where it appears on Hall's map of Crapulia, facing p. 21.

40/6-9 Ceres . . . grow] Ceres, in her vain search for her daughter Proserpine, finally came to Sicily where she discovered Proserpine's girdle.
Though she did not know where her daughter was, she blamed
Sicily most of all and accordingly made the land barren (Ov., *Met.*,
5, 384-525). Hall's mention of a shipwreck is his invention.

40/20 rule of Aristotle] Probably the discussion in Aristotle's *Politics* of the relationship between a country's size and its ability to support its population: "In laying down the laws, the legistor must have his attention fixed on two things, the territory and the population" (2, 3, 4); "There must be a limit fixed to the procreation of offspring" (7, 14, 10).

40/26 Nuchtermagen] This animal's habits seem to derive from Peter Martyr's description in *De Orbe Novo*: "When twilight falls, it leaves its hiding place in the woods and comes into the town, where it prowls about the houses, wailing loudly. Those who are ignorant of the animal's subtlety would believe a child was being beaten. . . . The wild beast, lying in wait, then springs upon the unfortunate creature, and in a twinkling of an eye tears him to bits" (2, 374).

40/30m Cercopitheci . . . tails] "The somewhat greenish [monkey] we call *Catus Maimonus* is mischievous. I saw this species devour the extreme end of its own tail . . . because he enjoys flesh now and then" Scaliger, *Exoticarum*, exercise 213, p. 680).

41/18 two Germanies] See note to 19/19-20 above.

42/4 Oenotria] The ancient name for the extreme southeastern part of Italy, "called Oenotria either because of the excellent wine, . . . or, as Varro claims, from Oenotrus, king of the Sabines" (Servius, *Commentarius*, 1, 163). Hall gives two conflicting derivations for this word: one in the marginal note to this line; the other in the Index of Proper Names.

42/4 Zythaenia] From ζῦθος, "beer." "The Egyptians also make a drink out of barley which they call *zythos*, the bouquet of which is not much inferior to that of wine" (Diod. Sic., 1, 34, 9).

42/12 Ampelona] See Pampinola in the Index of Proper Names.

42/22 Raleana] Actually the Orinoco; see note to 107/27-28 below.

42/28 Sprukwall] The fish is, in fact, called a Springwal by Gesner: "I remember Olaus the Great taught that this species of whale is called Springwal by the northern Germans. . . . By the English the monster is called a Whirlpoole, which spouts water through its head: two or three of which were captured in the Thames in the year 1550" (*Historia*, 4, 750). Compare the fish in Lucian (*Ver. Hist.*, 1, 7), which, when cut open, are full of wine lees.

43/17 ἤ πίθι ἤ ἄπιθι . . . gone] The inscription upon the Dolphin in Cambridge, according to John Healey (p. 48), who translated the *Mundus* in 1609 as *The Discovery of a New World*.

44/3 painted . . . Britons] "All the Britons, indeed, dye themselves with

woad, which produces a blue color, and makes their appearance in
battle more terrible" (Caes., *BGall.*, 5, 14).

44/4 Centaurs . . . Tragelaphs] Both were mythical creatures, the first a
combination of a man and a horse, the second of a goat and a stag.

44/4-5 doves . . . drunken] "It is a peculiarity of this species and of the
turtle-dove not to raise the neck backward when drinking, and to
take copious draughts like cattle" (Pliny, *HN*, 10, 52).

44/20 way . . . Romans] A libation, the pouring out of wine or other
liquid as a ceremonial act in honor of a god, which formed part of
the Roman's daily ritual.

44/22 statue of Bacchus] Salyer ("Joseph Hall," pp. 242-43) notes that
this statue was probably inspired by a stone figure of Hercules on Sir
Robert Drury's estate in Hawstead (where Hall was chaplain from
1601-1608), which urinated into a carved basin (Nichols, *Progresses
of Queen Elizabeth*, 2, 121).

44/23-24 Virgil . . . sister] *Moretum*, line 28.

44/37-38 Plautus . . . goblets] "People with piles of money can drink
out of . . . embossed beakers and tankards and fancy goblets" (*Stich.*,
lines 693-94).

45/1-2 solemn . . . song] In his note Hall gives the drinking song; the
references he gives should be: Plut., *Quaest. Conv.*, 3, 9; Ath., 10,
426; and Plaut., *Stich.*, line 707.

45/24-25 Horace . . . wine] *Carm.*, 2, 14, 26-27.

46/3m Horace . . . verses] *Sat.*, 2, 7, 117.

46/3m dithyrambs . . . *Birds*] Ar., *Av.*, line 1388. The sense of Aristophanes' lines differs greatly from what Hall gives here, but no other
instance of the word "dithyramb" occurs in any of his plays.

46/4 Plutarch . . . *Symposiacis*] "And so philosophers, whenever they
plunge into subtle and disputatious arguments at a drinking party,
are always irksome to most of the guests, who cannot follow; and
these in turn throw themselves into the singing of any kind of song,
the telling of foolish stories, and talk of shop and market place"
(*Conv. Sept. Sap.*, 1, 1, 614).

46/9m Nonius] Nonius Marcellus, early fourth-century lexicographer
and grammarian. His encyclopedic *De Compendiosa Doctrina* is
the chief authority for many fragments of early writers. Henry
Stephanus, ed., *Fragmenta Poetarum Veterum Latinorum, quorum
Opera non Extant* (n.p., 1564), p. 139, reproduces this saying of
Laberius and cites Nonius as his source.

46/12 Anacreontian verses] "Anacreon, who made all his poetry depend upon the subject of intoxication, is a singular case. For he is maligned for having given himself over in his poems to laxity and luxury, though many do not know that he was sober while he was engaged in composing . . . and merely pretends to be drunk" (Ath., 10, 428). Anacreon's poems, chiefly light songs of love and wine, done in iambic (i.e., short) verse, lead to Hall's sarcastic remark about such verses being "a fitting cover for such a small dish"— meaning this drunkard's song was insubstantial in both matter and form.

46/18m writer . . . elephants] I cannot find the author Hall alludes to in his note.

46/22-23 notary . . . Auffzeichner] "So great was the luxury of older times in regard to their sumptuous entertainments that they had wine-inspectors as well as wine pourers. . . . These wine-inspectors superintended the arrangements at dinners to see that the members of the company drank equal quantities" (Ath., 10, 425).

46/27-31 Trinkenius . . . Saturio] Trinkenius, from the German *trinken*, "to drink." Bibulus and Biberius, from the Latin *bibo, bibere*, "to drink." Dipsius, from the Greek διψάς, Latin *dipsas*, "a kind of serpent whose bite causes violent thirst." Drollius, from the English *droll*, "a buffoon." Zaufenius, see the Index of Proper Names. Oesophagius, from the Greek οἰσοφάγος, "gullet." Leinius, from the Latin *Lenaeus*, an alternate name for Bacchus, derived from ληνίς, "maenad." Saturio, from the Latin *satur*, "full of food."

47/10 Ariadnes . . . thread] Hom., *Od.*, 9, 322; Ov., *Met.*, 8, 152.

47/20 that . . . Lucian] "You can't blame wine or Dionysus for such things, but drinking to excess, and swilling down neat wine beyond what's decent" (*Dial. D.*, 249).

47/24 golden barrel] Perhaps modeled on the great tun of Heidelberg built between 1589 and 1591, 27 feet long and 18 feet high at the middle, which is described in *Coryats Crudities* as having been "once drunke out in the space of eight dayes, at the time of a certain noble meeting of Princely Gallants at the Court" (p. 492).

47/32m custom . . . Helots] It is unclear whether Hall is referring to the custom the Spartans had of slaying the Helots or of forcing them to drink excessively. Since Plutarch speaks of both in *Lycurgus*, 28, Hall probably wishes to evoke both: "In the daytime [the secret service of the Spartans] scattered into obscure and out of the way places, where they hid themselves and lay quiet; but in the night they came down into the highways and killed every Helot whom

they caught. . . . And in other ways they were harsh and cruel to the
Helots. For instance, they would force them to drink too much
strong wine, and then introduce them into their public messes, to
show what a thing drunkenness was."

49/3 Stilliard] The name given by Stow to the Steelyard merchants of
Germany who were granted liberties by Henry III to import grain
into England. By the reign of Edward VI these merchants were importing so much grain "that the occupiers of husbandry in this land
were inforced to complaine of them for bringing in such an abundance, when the corne of this realme was at an easie price: where-
upon it was ordained by Parliament, that no person should bring
into any part of this Realme by way of Marchandise, Wheate, Rie, or
Barly, growing out of the said Realme, when the quarter of wheate
exceeded not the price of 6. shillings 8. pence, Rie 4. s. the quarter,
and Barley 3. s. the quarter, vpon forfeyture the one halfe to the
king" (*Suruay of London*, pp. 232–34).

49/7 well-known tumors] The tumors are goiters, a disease traditionally
associated with mountainous regions, whose inhabitants normally
lack iodine since they do not eat sufficient quantities of fish. In Book
4 (p. 114 below), Hall connects these tumors with the wealth of the
Swiss and says that their necks swell because their skin "attracts
money to them no less than a magnet attracts iron." Here, however,
Hall tries to suggest that their necks have swelled from drinking too
much.

49/10 saying . . . Lucian] "Imagine what he would be like if sober, when
he can do this when tipsy?" (*Dial. D.*, 249). In this dialogue Jupiter
is praising his son Bacchus's conquest of India and defending his
drunkenness.

49/17 Apuleius . . . Antigenides] "Antigenides was a certain flute-player,
a honeyed modulator of every tone. . . . Being thus a most distinguished flutist, he used to say that nothing so vexed and fretted his
mind as that the horn-players at funerals were called flutists" (*Flor.*,
4). Hall's marginal note to *The Golden Ass* is incorrect.

49/20 parasites . . . others] In *Vd.*, Hall deprecates such poetry:

> Nor can I crouch, and writhe my fauning tayle
> To some great Patron, for my best auaile.
> Such hunger-staruen, trencher Poetry,
>
> (1, 1, 11–13)

49/24 poet . . . starved] Spenser, whom Hall admires above all other
English poets. He repeats this accusation in "To Camden":

> Sidney ye Prince of prose & sweet conceit
> Spenser of numbers & Heroick Ryme
> Iniurious Fate did both their liues defeate
> For war & want slew both before their time
>
> (*Poems*, p. 105)

49/27-28 shift . . . Irish] Though I find no specific reference to underwear being termed Irish armor, "Irish" used as an adjective is often derogatory: Irish daisy = dandelion; Irish apricot = potato; Irish man-of-war = barge; Irish draperies = cobwebs (*OED* and *Supplement*, s.v. "Irish," 2.b., 2.c.). Partridge, ed., *A Classical Dictionary of the Vulgar Tongue*, p. 200, claims this usage became frequent only after 1690, and the *OED* lists none contemporary with Hall, but Hall's use seems to indicate it began earlier.

49/32-33 wine . . . boldness] Possibly a remembrance of Ovid's *vina dabant animos*, "wine gave them courage" (*Met.*, 12, 242).

50/4-6 window . . . neck] Possibly suggested by the death of Elpenor in Hom., *Od.*, 10, 555-60: "he was heavy with wine. He heard the noise and the bustle of his comrades as they moved about, and suddenly sprang up, and forgot to go to the long ladder that he might come down again, but fell headlong from the roof, and his neck was broken away from his spine, and his spirit went down to the house of Hades."

50/8-9 draped . . . cypress] "The cypress has held the place of honour throughout the ages in connection with death" (B. S. Puckle, *Funeral Customs, Their Origin and Development* [London, 1926; rpt. Detroit, 1968], p. 168).

50/12-13 pieces . . . Lucretius] Hall refers to nothing more than the phrase *thuris glaebis* in Lucretius, *De Rerum Natura*, 3, 327.

50/17-18 The . . . you] These lines, apparently invented by Hall, are then supplemented in his marginal notes by real inscriptions just as ludicrous. Both appear in Schrader, *Monumenta Italiae*, the first on fol. 95r, the second on fol. 96r.

51/10 Tricongius] A congius is one eighth of an amphora, or nearly six pints English (Lewis and Short, p. 419).

51/11 Cantharidi] Hall probably derives the family name from *cantharus, i*, "a large, wide-bellied, drinking vessel with handles," Plaut., *Asin.*, line 906, *Stich.*, line 710 (Lewis and Short, pp. 280-81).

51/22-23 travelers . . . crosses] "When papist travelers and others addicted to superstitions encounter [crosses] along the road, the multitude adore them—as well as the sanctuary doors and the nails on the doors—prostrate, with their heads uncovered and knees bent, . . .

make a votive offering, set down a piece of fruit, and encamp for a while" (Moresinus, *Papatus*, pp. 46-47).

51/35 Bacchus Pyrodes] The discoverer of fire, according to Pliny, *HN*, 7, 56.

51/35 Ardens Chapel] From the Latin *ardens*, "on fire," "glowing."

52/2 snatched . . . womb] Semele, loved by Zeus and pregnant with Dionysus (Bacchus), was persuaded by Zeus's jealous wife Hera to ask Zeus to appear to her in all the splendor of a god. He, who had sworn to refuse Semele nothing, consented and appeared in his chariot surrounded by thunder and lightning. She was consumed in the flames, but Zeus rescued her unborn child from the ashes and placed him in his thigh, from which in due time he was born (Ov., *Met.*, 3, 260 ff.).

53/1 Port Aqua Fortis] Latin for "strong water"; the early scientific name for dilute nitric acid but used figuratively for anything powerful: "Mony is that *Aqua fortis* that Eates into many a maiden head" (Middleton and Dekker, *The Roaring Girle*, 3, 156).

53/14-15 Palinurus's fate] Verg., *Aen.*, 5, 853; 6, 337-81. Palinurus, the pilot of Aeneas, was drugged with sleep while at the helm and tumbled overboard. Hall's allusion suggests that Palinurus drowned; actually he was able to reach the shore near Velia where he was murdered by the inhabitants.

54/2 Glacialis Island] From *glacialis*, "frozen," "full of ice." After Zeus had rescued Bacchus from Semele's womb (see note to 52/2 above), he entrusted him for rearing to the nymphs of Nysa. When he grew up Bacchus was persecuted by those who refused to recognize his divinity, but he overcame them and extended his conquests far into Asia. See, for example, Diod. Sic., 4, 2 ff. Hall's account, that Bacchus's father Zeus punished those who treated his son badly, is an invention, though Hall seems consciously to be borrowing from the legend of Ceres (see note to 40/6-9 above), attempting to create a mirror image of Sicily, with its perpetual heat changed to perpetual cold, its Mount Aetna changed from the place where sinners are tortured to the place where those who lived too soberly are punished.

54/16m the year 1000] Hall apparently takes his information from Moresinus: "Abbot Odilo established [the feast of All Souls] from the fact that he believed the souls of sinners were purified in Mount Aetna, since he had himself heard the raging murmurings of the tossing sea and the casting upward of fire. He made that regulation about the year 1000, so that our forefathers might at length recover their complete piety" (*Papatus*, p. 12). Peter Martyr, *De Orbe Novo*,

2, 86, has a similar description of a mountain, in the midst of whose flames "Kings who have governed ill during their lives . . . are purged of their crimes, and where they have only wicked demons for their companions."

54/29 drink . . . flames] Lucian's description of the Moon-people is analogous: "And while they are cooking, they sit about . . . as if at table, snuff up the rising smoke and gorge them" (*Ver. Hist.*, 1, 23). Cf. Herod., 1, 202; Strab., 15, 1, 57.

54/31-32 Francis . . . fire] In 1587 Francis Drake went to Lisbon with a fleet of 30 ships. There receiving intelligence of a great fleet being assembled in the Bay of Cadiz and destined to form part of the Armada, he courageously entered the port and burnt upward of 10,000 tons of shipping—a feat he afterward called "singeing the king of Spain's beard" (*EB*, 8, 474).

57/6 New Gynia] New Gynia ("Land of new women") appears on Hall's world map (facing p. 19) just southwest of Insula Hermaphroditica. On maps by Ortelius, however (*Theater*, maps 1 and 3), the region called Nova Guinea is the large rectangular salient of land corresponding to a similarly shaped salient on Hall's map lying northeast of Insula Hermaphroditica and extending from approximately 170° to 190° east longitude. On Ortelius's first map it is connected to the continent, but on his third map it appears as a rectangular island, separated from the mainland by a narrow strait.

57/6m Maletur . . . Beach] On Ortelius's map of the world (*Theater*, map 1), Maletur and Beach lie close together at 140-50° east longitude, 30° south latitude, and 160° east longitude, 15° south latitude, respectively. If transferred to Hall's world map (facing p. 19), they would both lie to the southwest of Hermaphroditica Island, near where Aphrodysia is marked, not one on either side as Hall claims.

57/7 Land of Parrots] On Ortelius's map of the world (*Theater*, map 1), "Psittacorum regio" appears directly south of the Cape of Good Hope (C. Bonae spei), approximately 50-70° east longitude and 50-60° south latitude. The legend next to it says the region was "named this by the Portuguese because of the incredible number of birds there." Mercator's map of the world (*Drei Karten*, map 3, fol. 16) places it between 40° and 50° east longitude and annotates the name similarly.

57/13 Rixatia] From the French *rixe*, "quarrel," "scuffle."

57/14 Hermaphroditica Island] Derived from the bisexual divinity Hermaphroditus (Ov., *Met.*, 4, 285-388).

57/17 Psudium] From the Greek ψεῦδος, "falsehood."

58/18 Gynaecium] From the Greek γυναικεῖον, "the inner part of the house where the women dwelt."

58/21m England ... horses] A saying current in the 1590s, appearing in Florio, *Second Frvtes*, p. 205, as "England is the paradise of women, the purgatory of men, and the hell of horses," and, according to Henderson (*Scottish Proverbs*, p. 126), in the form Hall uses c. 1595.

58/27-30 so lecherous ... entirely] Diodorus Siculus attributes similar behavior to the Celts: "Although their wives are comely, they have very little to do with them, but rage with lust, in outlandish fashion, for the embraces of males" (5, 32, 7).

58/32-33 gathering ... thread] The Amazons, as described by Diodorus Siculus, treat their men the same way: "To the men [were assigned] the spinning of wool and such other domestic duties as belong to women" (2, 45); "They kept in their hands the administration of all the affairs of the state. The men, however, like our married women, spent their days about the house, carrying out the orders which were given them by their wives; and they took no part in the military campaigns or in office or in the exercise of free citizenship in the affairs of the community" (3, 53).

59/1 Juno's altar] "The marriage of Jupiter and Juno was viewed as the pattern of those of mankind, and the goddess was held to preside over the nuptial union. Hence she was surnamed the *Yoker*, the *Consecrator*, the *Marriage-Goddess*" (Anthon, p. 704).

59/31m Erasmus, *Colloquia*] See his "Senatulus, sive Γυναικοσυνέδριον," in *Colloquia*, 1, 842-44; tr. pp. 441-47.

60/7-8 Hundred Women] A feminine version of the *Centum-viri*, "Hundred Men," "one of the two permanent courts of plebeian judges, instituted probably by Servius Tullius and exercising jurisdiction until the fall of the Western Empire" (Smith, *Dict. Gr. & Rom. Antiq.*, 1, 404-05).

60/24m Vetulonia ... Italicus] "Vetulonia, once the pride of the Lydian [Etruscan] race" (Sil., *Punica*, 8, 483). The Latin *vetula* is a contemptuous term, meaning "little old woman" (Lewis and Short, p. 1983).

60/28 Lauriotian owls] Ar., *Av.*, lines 1106-08:

> Little Lauriotic owlets shall always be flocking in.
> Ye shall find them all around you, as the dainty brood increases,
> Building nests within your purses, hatching little silver pieces.

"The Owl was stamped on Athenian coins; in Laureium were the silver mines" (note to Ar., *Av.*, 2, 236). The connection of the owls with money leads Hall naturally into the bribery of the judges in the following sentence.

61/9 Gynandria] From the Greek γύνανδρος, "of doubtful sex," applied to women with masculine characteristics; hence the English word "gynander."

61/9 Amazonia] This legendary nation is usually placed on the river Thermodon in Asia Minor (Diod. Sic., 2, 46; 3, 53-55). But Peter Martyr (*De Orbe Novo*, 2, 18) locates this race in South America, which explains Hall's sarcastic comment in the Index of Proper Names, p. 118 above, that Amazonia was once an American territory but is now British (literally, "ours") because of the manly temperament of England's women.

61/26 Amantina] From the French *amant*, "lover." Under "Aphrodysia" in the Index of Proper Names, Hall says, "Here is the city of Amantina, whose name we take from a region on the Danube." The site of the ancient town of Amantia is not known (Smith, *Dict. Geog.*), but Volaterra (*Commentarii Urbani*, p. 188) observed that, "according to Ptolemy, the Amantians conquered by Tiberius lived in Pannonia, of which province the Danube formed the northern boundary" (Brown, *Discovery*, pp. 213-14).

62/1-6 material . . . transparent] The juxtaposition of the glass houses and the delicate clothing suggests that Hall may be borrowing from Lucian's description of the Cork Islands: "For baths they have large houses of glass, warmed by burning cinnamon. . . . For clothing they use delicate purple spider-webs" (*Ver. Hist.*, 2, 11-12).

62/3 custom . . . Moscovites] The custom was, in fact, quite British: "Bearing in mind that [Elizabeth I's] pale complexion was the inspiration for contemporary beauty, it is not surprising that white powder was the foundation on which the rest of the cosmetic treatment was applied. Unfortunately, one of the most successful means of creating a white powder was by using . . . white lead, which . . . if used constantly, had a harmful toxic effect on the individual" (Fenja Gunn, *The Artificial Face: A History of Cosmetics* [Newton Abbot, England, 1973], p. 76). Hall complains of the "painted faces and manishness and monstrous disguisedness of the [female] sex" in his sermons (*Works*, 5, 76; 5, 288).

62/19-21 stallions . . . love potions] Cf. Hall's description in *Vd.* (4, 1, 110-13):

   . . . chaister dames can hyre,

> Some snout-faire stripling to their Apple-squire:
> Whom staked vp like to some stallion-steede
> They keepe with Egs and Oysters for the breede.

Hall uses "Apple-squire" in the sense of "gigolo."

62/32 Guinea . . . Moluccas] The name Moluccas in its wider sense includes all the islands of the Malay Archipelago between Celebes on the west, New Guinea on the east, Timor on the south, and the open Pacific Ocean on the north (*EB*, 18, 681).

62/32-33 Cape . . . Promontory] On Ortelius's map of the world (*Theater*, map 1), Cape Hermosa appears at the northwest corner of a rectangular land mass labeled "Nova Guinea"; for its placement, see note to 57/6. For Beach Promontory, see note to 57/6m.

63/3-4 clothing . . . sexes] Hall condemned the idea of one sex adopting the clothing of the opposite sex in *Vd.* (4, 6, 1-18) and in his sermons (*Works*, 5, 76; 5, 296; 5, 305): "What shall we say to the dames, yea to the hermaphrodites of our times, whom it troubles that they may not be all man? . . . [Their] prodigious deformity of attire [leads] to the scorn of other nations, to the dishonour of their husbands, to the shame of the Gospel, to the forfeit of their modesty, to the misshaping of their bodies, to the prostitution of their souls, to the just damnation of both" (*Works*, 5, 296).

63/18-19 young . . . Cybele] According to Ovid (*Fast.*, 4, 183-246), a Phrygian boy named Attis consecrated himself to Cybele, a goddess of the powers of nature, and promised to be a boy forever and guard her temple. However, meeting the nymph Sagaritis he broke his oath. In retribution the angry goddess slew the Naiad; Attis went mad with despair and castrated himself. His example set a fashion, and the priests of Cybele, named Corybantes, in celebrating the festivals of their goddess, "ran about with loud cries and howlings, beating on timbrels, clashing cymbals, sounding pipes, and cutting their flesh with knives" (Anthon, pp. 378-79).

63/20-21 sodomites . . . Rome] Both the ancient Romans, such as Julius Caesar, and the Catholic priests of modern Rome. In *Vd.*, 4, 7, 38-40, Hall accuses the priesthood of fornication with animals as well as with men:

> Trudges to open stewes of eyther kinde:
> Or takes some Cardinals stable in the way,
> And with some pampered Mule doth weare the day.

63/26 cattle . . . mules] The mule, a hybrid produced from the mating of a he-ass and a mare and exhibiting some of the characteristics of both, is particularly appropriate for a people who like nothing of a single nature.

63/27 beasts . . . hares] "Archelaus . . . says that the hare is a hermaphrodite and reproduces equally well without a male" (Pliny, *HN*, 8, 81).

63/27-28 fish . . . shellfish] Shellfish were popularly reputed to be aphrodisiacs: "The polyp, while it is an active aphrodisiac, is tough and indigestible" (Ath., 356e). In *Christian Moderation* (*Works*, 6, 392) Hall claims that "shell-fishes are more powerful to stir and inflame nature than other duller . . . viands of flesh." Cf. *Vd.*, 4, 1, 113.

63/32*m* Land of Shrewes] Hall's marginal note (one of the few notes in English and printed in black letter) may have been inspired by Harrison's marginal reference in black letter to an "Ile of Shrewes" off the coast of Scotland (*Description of Britaine*, p. 40).

64/11-13 breeches . . . weaving] See notes to 58/32-33 and 63/3-4 above.

64/14*m* Augustine . . . heresies] "The Pepuzians . . . grant leadership only to women so that among them women receive the dignity of the priesthood, for they say that Christ was revealed to Quintilla and Priscilla under the appearance of a woman in that same city of Pepuza" (*De Haer.*, chap. 27).

64/16-17 Aristotle's time] "Yet among barbarians the female and the slave have the same rank" (*Pol.*, 1, 1, 5). In his sermon, "The Women's Veil," Hall condemns the behavior of men who have allowed the rule over their wives to degenerate "into a stern tyranny; according to the old barbarian fashion in Aristotle's time, which holds even still, their wives are their slaves" (*Works*, 5, 538).

66/23 Sibyl] The Sibyl of Cumae, who could foretell the future and who guided Aeneas into the underworld (Verg., *Aen.*, 6, 36).

66/24 Tuberonian Mountains] From the Latin *tuber*, "a bump" or "a protuberance."

66/27 honorable women] Hall's description seems to borrow from a similar one in Peter Martyr's *De Orbe Novo*, 2, 18: "A number of other islands lie off the coast of Coluacan, which are inhabited only by women. . . . Some people think they live as did the Amazons, but others who have studied the question more closely believe they are virgins dedicated to God, who take pleasure in solitude, just as those amongst us; or in ancient times, did the vestals or the priestesses of the Bona Dea."

69/5 Moronia . . . populous] "The world is full of fools" (Cic., *Fam.*, 9,

22); repeated in Eras., *Moria*, 4, 490; tr. p. 118; Garzoni (*Hospitall*, p. 3) gives an alternative saying, "infinite is the number of fooles," and cites Ecclesiastes as his source.

69/19 Pygmies . . . Arctic] "Beyond the Lapps in the region between the northwest and the north, a region burdened by perpetual darkness, the Pygmies are found, . . . a timid folk who speak a chattering language, so that they seem as close to monkeys in body and mind as they are remote from normal men" (Mercator, *Atlas*, p. 42). Aristotle explains that animals in cold countries are "smaller and shorter lived," since the moisture in their bodies congeals easily and "the frost robs them of growth" (*Gen. Corr.*, 5, 466*b*23 ff.).

69/33-70/1 Variana] From the Latin *varius*, "changeable."

70/1 Moronia Mobilis] From the Latin *mobilis*, "easily moved," "inconstant."

70/1 Moronia Aspera] From the Latin *asper*, "harsh," "violent."

70/2 Moronia Felix] From the Latin *felix*, meaning both "fertile" and "fortunate," probably in imitation of Arabia Felix, ancient name for the southern part of Arabia. See, for example, Diod. Sic., 2, 54.

70/2 Moronia Fatua] From the Latin *fatuus*, "simple."

70/3 Moronia Pia] From the Latin *pius*, "devout."

70/5*m* Homer] *Il.*, 2, 219.

70/8-10 entertain . . . table] Diodorus Siculus describes the Celtiberians' customs toward newcomers in the same way: "[Those] who come among them they one and all entreat to stop at their houses and they are rivals of one another in their hospitality" (Diod. Sic., 5, 34, 1).

70/22-23 contemptuous . . . naked] Hall may well be thinking of the Indians described by Peter Martyr: "The natives are very lazy, for they shiver with cold among their mountains in the winter, without ever thinking of making clothes for themselves" (*De Orbe Novo*, 1, 91).

70/31 Morosophers] More uses the term in *Utopia*, p. 64, glossed by the editors as:

> "Foolish in their wise-ness," a Greek term from Lucian's *Alexander* 40 ("our learned idiots"). In *The Praise of Folly*, Erasmus uses the Greek form, which Lister proceeds to gloss as follows: "Μωροσόφους.) The expression is composed from stupidity and wisdom, as if you were to say foolish wisemen" (*Moria*, sig. b3). The Latin form is given as an example of a *Verbum*

> *novatum* in [Erasmus's] *Copia* I.II (ed. 1541, p. 26). (*Utopia*,
> note to 64/2, p. 322)

In a sermon Hall says "wise folly" describes "all figure casters,
palmisters, physiognomers, fortunetellers, alchymists, fantastic projectors, and all the rabble of professors of those . . . not so much
curious as *idle arts*" (*Works*, 5, 160).

70/32 Bonzi] According to Hakluyt, the Chinese call their priests "Xe-
quiam" or "Cen," while it is the Japanese who call them "Bonzi"
(*Principal Navigations*, 2, 579-80).

70/35*m* Morelloscuro . . . valley] The order whose name is derived from
the motherhouse, Vallombrosa ("shady valley," as Hall notes), situated 20 miles from Florence. Noted for its austerity and penitential
character: "severe scourging was inflicted for any breach of rule,
silence was perpetual, poverty most strictly enforced. The rule of
enclosure was so strict that the monks might not go out even on an
errand of mercy" (*Cath. E.*, 15, 262-63). Hall leaves half of his made-
up name undefined, for while *morello* does signify "dark-colored"
in Italian, he neglects to mention that the ending may derive either
from the Italian *oscuro*, meaning "dark," or from the Latin *scurra*,
meaning "buffoon." This ambiguity is reinforced by having the
word end with an *a* in the text and with an *o* in the marginal note.

70/36*m* Lateran . . . rules] Two reform movements. The Lateran rule,
formed soon after the Lateran Synod of 1059, conformed to the so-
called Rule of Saint Augustine, which prescribed the strict community life of the Apostolic Age, such as the Bishop of Hippo had
supposedly practiced in his episcopal house (*EB*, 2, 911). Cluny,
during the Middle Ages the largest church in Christendom, started
drawing other monasteries under its influence in the late eleventh
century. The supervisors of such houses were subject to the Abbot of
Cluny and were his nominees, not the elect of their own communi-
ties, as was the custom (*Cath. E.*, 4, 73).

70/36 Licetani] Apparently invented by Hall from the name of Francesco
Lichetto (1518-70), second General of the Reformed Order of Franciscans. Lichetto and his successors diligently enforced the rule that
members were to hold no property in common and to renounce all
vested incomes and accumulation of goods (*Cath. E.*, 6, 284-86).

71/1 Zoccolanti] The order known as Observants: "As a protection
against the snakes so numerous in the districts, wooden slippers

[named] *zoccoli* ['clogs'] were worn by the brothers, and, as their use continued in the order, the Observants were long known as the Zoccolanti or ['wooden feet']" (*Cath. E.*, 6, 284).

71/1 Cercosimii] Composed from κέρκος, "tail," and *simius*, "ape." Hall's gloss, Certosini, however, refers to the Carthusian monastery of Certosa di Pavia, one of the most magnificent in the world: "The Carthusian monks, to whom the monastery was entrusted by the founder [Gian Galeazzo Visconti], were bound to employ a certain proportion of their annual revenue in prosecuting the work till its completion, and even after 1542 the monks continued voluntarily to expend large sums on further decoration" (*EB*, 20, 970-71). It is undoubtedly this splendor that incurs Hall's anger.

71/1m Capuchins] Moved by the need for reform in the Franciscans, Matteo di Bassi, in 1525, began a more austere life, choosing a form of garb resembling that of Saint Francis. The name *capuchin*, Italian for "hood," was given to the new Franciscan monks by the people because of their long, pointed hoods. Their hermitages or monasteries were to be erected, if possible, outside the cities or towns, and no more land was to be taken than in keeping with their humble estate. They were never to lay in a store of food but were to rely on daily alms (*Cath. E.*, 2, 344; 3, 321).

71/1m Celestini] Named after Saint Celestine V, whose love of wilderness led him to be a hermit. His discipline was rigorous: "He fasted every day except Sunday; each year he kept four Lents, passing three of them on bread and water; the entire day and a great part of the night he consecrated to prayer and labor" (*Cath. E.*, 3, 479). Hall refers to Celestine V in *Christian Moderation* (*Works*, 6, 416), noting that his reign as pope was destined to be short since he "would only ride upon an ass, while his successors mount on shoulders." Hall ridicules this practice of riding on the shoulders of men (see 105/30 above).

71/1 Della mercede] Italian for "of the reward." Founded in Barcelona in 1218 by Saint Peter Nolasco, the Mercedarians were a congregation of men devoted to the ransom of Christian captives from the Moors (*Cath. E.*, 10, 197).

71/1-2 Della vita commune] Italian for "of the common life," founded by Geert de Groote about 1380. "The members took no vows, neither asked nor received alms; their first aim was to cultivate the interior life, and they worked for their daily bread" (*Cath. E.*, 4, 166).

71/7 lead . . . parchment] Indulgences were written on parchment, and a

lead seal was attached, often stamped with the seal of the order. See
Lambarde, *Perambulation of Kent* (1596), p. 333.

71/9m well-known . . . Dominican] "Presumably a Franciscan, being
under the vow of poverty, begs of a Dominican, who being under
the vow of silence, turns him a deaf ear" (Brown, *Discovery*, p. 179).

71/12-13 revive . . . Spartans] "The boys in Sparta were lashed with
whips during the entire day at the altar of Artemis Orthia, frequently
to the point of death, and they bravely endured this, cheerful and
proud, vying with one another for supremacy as to which one of
them could endure being beaten for the longer time and the greater
number of blows" (Plut., *Inst. Lac.*, chap. 40, in *Mor.*, 3, 443-45).
Cf. Lucian, *Anach.*, 38; Philostr., *VA*, 6, 20. Hall refers to the custom
again in *Christian Moderation* (*Works*, 6, 425): "We may not so ob-
dure ourselves as to be like the Spartan boys, who would not so
much as change a countenance at their beating."

71/18m Hugh . . . illumination] Hall's note refers to Hugh of St. Victor,
"De Tonsura Ecclesiastica," in *De Sacramentis*, 2, 3, 3 (*PL*, 176,
422), who claims tonsuring was a Nazarene custom and that those
who are tonsured signify their dedication to God. Hrabanus Maurus,
"De Tonsura Clericorum," in *De Clericorum Institutione*, 1, 3 (*PL*,
107, 298-99), agrees and adds that tonsuring recalls the ring of
thorns with which Christ was crowned by the Jews. Robert Bellarmine, "De Habitu et Tonsura Monachorum," in *De Monachis*, 2, 40
(fol. 245E-246A), says that according to Isidore, Hrabanus Maurus,
and Hugh of St. Victor, the third and fourth reasons for tonsuring
are that "the hair, which is a superfluous part of the body, should be
cut to signify that clerics and monks ought to cut off everything
superfluous—and especially any vicious desires—so that the crown
(i.e., the mind) might remain free and receptive to heavenly contemplation and illumination."

71/23 ingeniously . . . Scaliger] Hall's note refers to some sarcastic
saying by Joseph Justus Scaliger, apparently in a book of Janus
Dousa's, curator of the University of Leyden and a close friend, who
persuaded Scaliger to take a post there, which he held from 1593 to
his death in 1609. Scaliger's modern historical method undermined
the authenticity of many Catholic documents, and the Jesuits replied with vicious attacks on his work (especially Gaspar Scioppius's
Scaliger Hypobolimaeus), his reputation, and even his supposedly
princely heritage. It is probably these attacks that called forth from
Scaliger the statement to which Hall refers. I cannot, however, find

it among Scaliger's published works. On Scaliger and the Jesuits, see Pattison, *Essays*, 1, 150–60, and Nisard, *Le triumvirat littéraire au XVIe siècle*, pp. 254–308.

71/28 dying . . . oil] Anointing the sick with oil was a primitive form of medical treatment; see, for example, Luke 10:34. However, it is more likely that Hall is ridiculing the Catholic practice of extreme unction, in which the gravely ill are anointed with blessed oil, a custom that Popes Innocent I and Felix IV made a sacrament to encourage wider use (Moresinus, *Papatus*, p. 179).

71/33–72/2 consider . . . shell] Hall's own beliefs on the wisdom of ocean travel seem to mirror those of his Morosophers: "I bethought myself how fondly our life is committed to an unsteady and reeling piece of wood" (*Works*, 6, 138).

72/9–13 body . . . ancients] "The dead bodies, especially those of nobles, are stretched on mats, woven partly of reeds, and are gradually dried at a fire of special herbs. When all the moisture is evaporated, the body is hung inside the house and treated as a *penate*" (Peter Martyr, *De Orbe Novo*, 2, 396). Hall's reference to the burial rite of the ancients apparently refers to the Egyptian practice of mummifying the dead.

73/34m Virgil] There is no such statement in Virgil; the closest is the following passage in Ovid which, although it describes water frozen over, is (in the context of the frozen rivers mentioned at 74/12–13) a plausible source for Hall's apparently invented quotation: "Where ships had gone before now men go on foot and the waters congealed with cold feel the hoof-beat of the horse. Across the new bridge [of ice], above the gliding current, are drawn by Sarmatian oxen the carts of the barbarians" (*Tr.*, 3, 10, 34).

74/7 Papilionia] From the Latin *papilio*, "butterfly."

74/11m More . . . Anydrus] See *Utopia*, pp. 41, 117–19.

74/12–13 river . . . path] See note to 73/34m above, and compare the description in Diodorus Siculus: "For example, there are countries where, because of the excessive cold, the greatest rivers are frozen over, the ice sustaining the crossing of armies and the passage of heavily laden wagons" (3, 34, 1 ff.).

74/19 I . . . me] The Wise Greek was Bias of Priene. Valerius Maximus records the story in *Dictorum Factorumque Memorabilium Exempla* (7, 2, #3; tr. p. 312): "*Bias*, when the Enemy had invaded his own native Countrey *Priene*, and that all people whom the ravage of War suffered to get safe away were upon their flight, laden with the weight of what they esteem'd most precious, being asked why he carried away nothing of his own Goods, I, said he, *carry all my Goods about me*. For he carried them in his Breast, not upon his Shoulders; not to be seen by the Eye, but to be prized by the Minde."

74/23 dressed . . . Indians] The main ideas in this paragraph seem to be borrowed from two descriptions in Peter Martyr's *De Orbe Novo*: "The natives also wear trousers decorated with bunches of various colored feathers; from the knee down their legs are bare, though many of them wear shoes, made for the most part of feathers. They mix plumes with woofs of cotton, and also skillfully employ rabbit's hair, of which they make their winter clothing and their bed covers. For the rest they are naked and leave one of their arms uncovered, except when it is very cold" (2, 198); "On [special] occasions they all adorn themselves by wearing clothes or head-dresses of various coloured plumes" (2, 251).

75/5-7 They . . . it] Compare Hall's character of "The unconstant": "He says, swears, renounces; because, what he promised, he meant not long enough to make an impression" (*Works*, 6, 113).

75/21m Aelia Laelia . . .] The entire inscription is given in Schrader, *Monumenta Italiae*, fols. 76v-77r; and in Fendt, *Monumenta Sepulchrorum*, no. 125. Turler, *De Peregrinatione*, sig. A7r, gives an abbreviated version. Each varies slightly from the others.

75/27 H. I.] The initials apparently stand for H[all] I[osephus], who betrays his name nowhere else in this work.

76/2-3 ERR. VAR. DUC.] In John Healey's 1609 translation he emends this to FBR. VAR. DUC., meaning "Fabricatus [a] Varianae Duce," "Made by the Duke of Variana" (*Discovery*, p. 86). However, if one considers the two faces of the coin, it may be that ERR. VAR. DUC. stands for "Err[or] Var[i] Duc[is]" "The error of general [P. Quinctilius] Varus," legate of the Rhine army, defeated in Germany about A.D. 9. The obverse, with Janus bifrons, probably suggests deception (or changeability), since elsewhere in the *Mundus* Hall describes the two-faced Lisconicans as liars. The reverse, with a rock poised above a tablet, may represent an agreement about to be broken. Both would apply to Varus, for when marching back with three legions from his summer camp near the Weser, he was treacherously attacked in difficult country by the German chieftain Arminius—a master of the surprise attack—after having been given assurances of Arminius's friendship (*OCD*, pp. 1108-09; Suet., *Aug.*, 23). From the evidence of the following two coins, I would expect

that Hall is actually satirizing a contemporary, but I can find no
sixteenth-century personage who fits.

76/8 CONST. LIP.] "A sarcastic description of Justus Lipsius (1547–
1606), the Belgian humanist, author among other things of a dialogue entitled *De constantia*, . . . who changed his front repeatedly
in the struggle of Catholic versus Protestant, openly joining the
Catholic Church at last, to which his sympathies appear to have
belonged from the beginning. His passion for dogs was a mania
which drew him not only the ridicule of his enemies but even the
reproaches of his friends" (Brown, *Discovery*, p. 181). Hall refers to
De Constantia; see note to 28/22–23 above. For an account of Lipsius's passion for dogs, see Nisard, *Le triumvirat littéraire au XVIᵉ
siècle*, pp. 137–39.

76/9–13 oval . . . Good] Hall's riddle here is more complex than the previous two instances. The French inscription—instead of Latin, as
in the two other coins—suggests a reference to a Frenchman, specifically a poet because of the garland of leaves. These two clues, plus
the physical features, point to Julius Caesar Scaliger who, though
of Italian birth, emigrated to France, where he spent the rest of his
life. Scaliger produced much poetry, as well as an important book
on poetics (*Poetices, libri septem*, 1561). Furthermore, a contemporary portrait readily discloses a long face with an aquiline nose.
Though Hall's suggestion that a good knowledge of antiquity is
necessary to discover this person's identity might suggest a classical
author, I rather think it is a satirical thrust at Scaliger's pretensions
to have descended from the noble Della Scala family of Verona,
which Scaliger himself claimed to have traced back to antiquity (cf.
Hall's mocking comments in *Vd.*, 4, 3, about people who make such
claims).

Scaliger's habit of contentiousness for its own sake often seems
to have led him to shift positions when confronting an adversary.
Charles Nisard notes that in his *Exoticarum Exercitationum* upon
the *De Subtilitate* of Cardan (1557) "il parut s'appliquer a nier ce
que Cardan affirme et a affirmer ce que l'autre nie" (*Les Gladiateurs
de la république des lettres aux XVᵉ, XVIᵉ et XVIIᵉ siècles*, 1, 370).
And his vicious attacks on Erasmus's *Ciceronianus* change to praise
of Erasmus's works after the latter's death. Thus, the representation
of the polypus fish on the coin.

Likewise, the inscription *Pour Bon* (and the coin itself) may be
connected to the Erasmus-Scaliger controversy. In *Ciceronianus*

Erasmus had proclaimed the archeological study of medals, coins, and inscriptions to be idle curiosity, and Scaliger in turn defended it in his *Oratio pro M. Tullio Cicerone contra Des. Erasmum* (1531). Unlike the other two coins, this third one is blank and, one cannot help but think, significantly so. Is the saying meant to read starting with *Pour, Pour Bon,* "For Good," or with *Bon, Bon Pour* [ ], "Good for Nothing"? Read the second way, the inscription could contain a slap both at Scaliger and at the folly of archeological investigation. Hall's dislike of archeology is expressed elsewhere in the *Mundus* in his ridicule of the Pazzivillani, who "prefer to dig up stones rather than bury them" (p. 89), and, perhaps, in his descriptions of the Codicians who walk with their heads toward the ground, lest they "neglect anything worth picking up" (p. 116).

76/11 polypus fish] "Theophrastus, in the book *On Animals that change Colour,* says that the polyp blends its colour only with that of rocky places, doing this through fear and in self-protection" (Ath., 7, 317). Pliny (*HN,* 9, 87) and Aristotle (*Mir. Ausc.,* no. 30) reiterate this belief. See also note to 10/16–17.

77/4 colleges . . . skeptics] "Those whom we call the Pyrronian philosophers are designated by the Greek name σκεπτικοί, or 'sceptics.' . . . [They] are always engaged in inquiring and considering what there is in all nature which is possible to decide and determine. And moreover they believe that they do not see or hear anything clearly. . . . They are in doubt as to the nature and character of those very things which cause them those experiences, and they deliberate about them: and they declare that in everything assurance and absolute truth seem . . . beyond our grasp" (Gell., *NA,* 11, 5, 1–4).

77/7m Diogenes Laertius] "Lacydes, son of Alexander, was a native of Cyrene. . . . Whenever he brought anything out of the store-room, he would seal the door up again and throw his signet ring through the opening, to ensure that nothing laid up there should be stolen or carried off. So soon, then, as his rogues of servants got to know this, they broke the seal and carried off what they pleased, afterwards throwing the ring in the same way through the opening into the store-room. Nor were they ever detected in this" (Diog. Laert., 4, 59). Hall refers again to this story in "The Deceit of Appearance": "We justly laugh at that sceptic in Laertius, who, because his servants robbed his cupboard, doubted whether he left his victuals there. What do we with eyes if we may not believe their intelligence?" (*Works,* 5, 157).

77/19-20 bubbles . . . reed] Hall gives the same image in one of his sermons: "Do ye not smile at the child, which when he hath raised a
large bubble out of the walnut-shell joys in that airy globe?" (*Works*,
5, 234). Cf. *Vd.*, 4, 4, 61-62.

77/22 from Mainz] Gutenberg, who printed the 42-line Bible in Mainz
around 1457.

77/26 Supermonical] According to the *Chymicall Dictionary* appended
to Michael Sendivogius's *New Light of Alchymie*, "*Supermonicum*
is AEnigmaticall*" (sig. Fff2v).

77/31 Cedurinus] "*Cedurini* are dull wits" (Sendivogius, *A Chymicall
Dictionary*, sig. Bbb3v).

77/33 ff. Earth itself . . .] Of the 50 terms given by Hall, all but two are
accounted for in the *Dictionarium Theophrasti Paracelsi*, the *Lexicon Chemicum* by William Johnson, or *A Chymicall Dictionary* by
Sendivogius. The two missing words are "Zeninephidei" and "Ro-
bolt."

79/20-21 extremely . . . climate] Black bile, the humor of melancholy, is
traditionally considered by writers on the humors to be cold and dry
(Burton, *Anatomy*, 1, 1, 1); cf. Bright, *A Treatise of Melancholy*,
especially pp. 102-04.

80/1 Cordolium] From the Latin *cordolium*, "sorrow at heart."

80/3m Ranzovian . . . Segeberg] Hall is referring to Henrik Rantzau
(1526-98), a Danish statesman and native of Segeberg, who recorded
the epitaphs of his numerous ancestors. The phrasing of this note
would seem to specify *Descriptio Sacelli prope Monasterium Sege-
bergense* (Leipzig, 1588) as the source of this saying, but I cannot
find it in this work or in three other of his collections of sayings:
Epitaphia in Orbitum Patris, Matris, Fratris, et Sororis (Leipzig,
1584); *Epigrammatum Historicus Liber . . . Insertis Elogiis & Epi-
thaphio quae in quorundam Ranzoviorum Monumentis Leguntur*
(Antwerp, 1581); *De Somniis . . . nonnulla Epitaphia, & Monumen-
torum quorundam Ranzouianorum Descriptiones* (Rostock, 1591).
Note that this saying is the exact opposite of the one given in the
note to 33/10 above. After a patient search for both, I am inclined to
believe that Hall—intent on frustrating source hunters—has made
both up.

80/20m Carthusian monks] The Carthusians spend most of their days
in silence, but "once every week, the monks go out for a walk together, during which they converse. This is known as the *Spatia-

mentum and usually lasts about three and a half hours" (*Cath. E.*, 3, 390).

80/20m *Hospital . . .* Garzoni] "The people of [Gamsofanti], inhabiters of one part of Libya, . . . were of so dead and fearefull a disposition, that they shunned the meeting with any one, neither coulde they be brought to conuerse with any men liuing, they thinking themselues halfe kilde in other mens companie" (*Hospitall*, discourse 7, p. 35).

80/25–28 imagining . . . disturbed] Burton, following Hieronymus Mercurialis, describes the behavior of those beset by melancholy thus: "Tis proper to all melancholy men . . . what conceit they have once entertained, to be most intent, violent, and continually about it" (*Anatomy*, p. 394).

80/32m Pisander . . . Rhodiginus] Hall's incorrect reference shows he received his information from Tomaso Garzoni: "And *Caelius* in the twentie six chapter of his ninth booke, recounteth one *Pisander* amongst these sorte of fooles, who thinking himselfe to be dead, was woonderfully afraide of meeting with his owne soule, which he esteemed to be a mortall enemie to his bodie, and that he might not come to haue anie thing to doe with it, hauing so iniuriously en-treated him, and trecherously borne itselfe towards him, in leauing his bodie" (*Hospitall*, pp. 17–18). Cf. Rhodiginus, *Lectiones Antiquae*, 17, 2(2, 457). In *Christian Moderation* (*Works*, 6, 433), Hall mentions him again: "There is no evil, whether true or fancied, but may be the subject of fear. There may be a Pisander so timorous, that he is afraid to see his own breath."

81/5 Furies . . . Pluto] The Furies, primeval avengers of crime, are in this case sent by Pluto, because no soul condemned to the lower world is ever allowed to escape.

81/23 Megaera] One of the three Furies. In *Vd.* (6, 1, 6) Hall refers to "foule Megaera."

81/27–28 insane Ajax] After the death of Achilles, Ajax and Ulysses dis-puted their claim to the arms of the hero. When they were given to Ulysses, Ajax became so infuriated that in a fit of delirium he slaughtered all the sheep in the camp under the delusion that they were his rival Ulysses and those who had favored his cause (Anthon, pp. 94–95).

81/32 Merlino's Cingar] In Merlino Coccaio's work *Macaronicon*, Cin-gar's nose suddenly grows to be seven cubits long—according to his friends, the result of sorcerers. At first he drapes it three times around

his neck, "like a beautiful gold chain," but later he grows fatigued
by its weight, and his friends take turns carrying it on their shoulders
(*Macaronicon*, pp. 209-10). Hall's mention that Cingar ties it to his
back does not appear in the work.

81/33-34 glass . . . nearby] Burton, possibly copying Hall, recounts the
same delusion: "[Some think] that they are all glass, and therefore
will suffer no man to come near them" (*Anatomy*, p. 386).

82/7-9 bear . . . paws] Pliny, *HN*, 8, 54, 127; see note to 33/3 above.

82/9-10 eyes . . . Caecilius] Hall's Latin parallels Caius Caecilius Statius's: *grammonsis oculis ipsa atratis dentibus* (*Scriptorum Romanorum*, p. 31). Lewis and Short (p. 822) emend this first word to
gramiosis, "full of matter or pus."

82/16-19 werewolves . . . shrieking] "Among these humours of melancholy, the Phisitions place a kinde of madnes by the Greeks called
Lycanthropia, termed by the Latines *Insania Lupina*; or wolues
furie: which bringeth a man to this point . . . that in Februarie he
will goe out of the house in the night like a wolfe, hunting about the
graues of the dead with great howling, . . . to the great feare and
astonishment of all them that meete him" (Garzoni, *Hospitall*, p.
19).

82/19 Gramia Valley] From the Latin *gramiae*, "rheum that collects in
the corners of the eyes"; cf. note to 82/9-10 above.

82/20 Melaena] From the Greek μέλας, "dark," an epithet of Demeter.

82/21m Melancholy . . . lionlike] Melancthon (*Commentarius de Anima*, p. 79v), discussing the humor of melancholy, says: "In the lion
his temperament is dominated by heavy bile, and he inclines toward
Melancholy." On the same page he gives the term *Asinina Melan-
cholia*, "asinine melancholy."

82/26 Cave of Maninconicus] Besides Hall's derivation of Maninconica in the Index of Proper Names, the word ultimately derives from
the Latin *manicon*, a kind of nightshade supposed to cause madness
(Pliny, *HN*, 21, 105, 179).

82/27 Cave del Pianto] From the Italian *pianto*, "weeping."

83/5 Chimaeras . . . Centaurs] The Chimaera, a fabulous monster, had
the head and neck of a lion, the body of a goat, the tail of a serpent,
and vomited forth fire (Hom., *Il.*, 6, 181). The Tragelaph, or goat-
stag, is named by Plato (*Resp.*, 488A) and Aristotle (*Mir. Ausc.*, 4, 1,
1) as a creature that exists nowhere. The Centaurs were a race of half
men, half horses (Hom., *Il.*, 2, 742).

83/18 Russian tyrant] Czar Ivan IV, whose reign of terror from 1560 to 1584 earned for him the epithet of "terrible."

83/19-20 infamous Caesars] See Suetonius's accounts of the emperors Nero and Domitian (*Ner.*, 26-37; *Dom.*, 10-15); and the note to 84/15 below.

83/20 Patagonians] The natives of Patagonia, discovered by Magellan in 1520, averaged about six feet in height. Both their height and their quarrelsomeness were exaggerated by later explorers, but I can find no record of the bloodthirstiness Hall suggests. More than likely he is generally connecting them with the cannibals found on these expeditions. See 13/33-34 above where he talks about a "Patagonian Polyphemus."

83/27-28 reaction of opposites] "Now we know that hot and cold have a mutual reaction on one another (which is the reason why subterranean places are cold in hot weather and warm in frosty weather). This reaction we must suppose takes place in the upper region, so that in warmer seasons the cold is concentrated within by the surrounding heat" (Arist., *Mete.*, 1, 12, 348b).

83/28-29 Africa . . . serpents] Aristotle, at least, does not claim any such thing: "The same kinds of animals are longer lived in hot countries than in cold, for the same reason as that which makes them larger. The size of animals which have a cold nature makes this obvious; so snakes, lizards, and reptiles with horny scales are large in hot countries, . . . for the warm moisture causes growth as well as life" (*Long. Brev. Vitae*, 5, 5-11). But Hall may be using *gelidissimas*, "coldest," in the sense of "most deadly"; if so, the connection between size and deadliness can be readily understood.

83/29m Mercurialis . . . *Lectiones*] "In the island of Cyprus in the copper smelting furnaces where copper ore is placed to be refined for many days, small insects are generated in the midst of the flames, a little bigger than flies, which leap through the fire and crawl about" (3, 14 [p. 18]).

84/1m Georg Agricola] *De Animatibus Subterraneis*, p. 479. In one of his sermons (*Works*, 5, 504), Hall says that when he was a young man, Georg Agricola was regarded as "the most accurate observer of these underground secrets of nature."

84/15 feed . . . flesh] Possibly inspired by the following passage in Suetonius: "It is even believed that it was [Nero's] wish to throw living men to be torn to pieces and devoured by a glutton of Egyptian birth, who would crunch raw flesh and anything else that was given him" (*Ner.*, 37).

84/27m Garzoni . . . Tarocco] Tomaso Garzoni's thirteenth discourse is entitled: *Pazzo da tarocco* (*Opere*, p. 43). As Brown notes, "The verb 'taroccare' in Italian, 'to become angry,' 'to speak angrily,' may have originated in quarrels at the card game of 'tarocchi,' according to Tommaseo and Bellini, . . . *Dizionario della lingua italiano*" (*Discovery*, p. 206).

85/10-12 Vitellius . . . lamprey] Suetonius describes Vitellius's gluttony thus: "Most notorious of all was the dinner given by his brother to celebrate the emperor's arrival at Rome, at which two thousand of the choicest fishes and seven thousand birds are said to have been served. He himself eclipsed even this at the dedication of a platter, which on account of its enormous size he called the 'Shield of Minerva, Defender of the City.' In this he mingled the livers of pike, the brains of pheasants and peacocks, the tongues of flamingoes and the milt of lampreys, brought by his captains and triremes from the whole empire" (*Vit.*, 13). Hall refers to this in one of his sermons where he condemns "the liquorous palate of the glutton [who] ranges through seas and lands for uncouth delicacies; kills thousands of creatures for but their tongues or giblets" (*Works*, 5, 346).

85/15m Diodorus Siculus] The story is in Diodorus Siculus as Hall indicates, but contrary to Hall's assertion, he sees Olympias's actions as less rather than more merciful: "She ordered certain Thracians to stab Philip to death, . . . but she judged that Eurydice, who was expressing herself without restraint and declaring that the kingdom belonged to herself rather than to Olympias, was worthy of greater punishment. She therefore sent to her a sword, a noose, and some hemlock, and ordered her to employ whichever of these she pleased as a means of death" (Diod. Sic., 19, 11).

85/30-31 blood . . . congeal] Paracelsus describes the process in *De Natura Rerum*: "So also flesh, and blood, which indeed are putrefied, and grow unsavory quickly, are preserved in cold fountainwater, and not only so, but by the addition of new and fresh fountaine-water, may be turned into a quintessence, and bee for ever preserved from putrefaction. . . . Now this blood is the balsome of balsomes, and is . . . of such great vertue, that it is incredible to be spoken" (pp. 15r-15v; tr. p. 21).

85/32 Massic . . . wine] Massicus, a mountain in Campagnia, and Falernus, the region at its base, both famed for their excellent wine.

85/33-34 Inquisition Chapel] The name given in the Latin refers to Libitina, the goddess of corpses, in whose temple everything pertaining to burials was sold or hired out and where registers of deaths were kept.

85/38 person . . . scars] The Germans, especially university students, were so fond of dueling that it had to be outlawed in the nineteenth century.

86/4 Meotis] Another name for the Sea of Azov, in Russia. Hall actually seems to be referring to the remarkable lagoons and marshes to the west known as the Sivash, or Putrid Sea, where the water is intensely salty.

86/15 most . . . Bacon] Possibly not Sir Francis Bacon but Sir Edmund Bacon, a close friend of Hall's, whom he accompanied to the Continent in 1606. A letter written by Hall about this time addresses itself specifically to Bacon's desire to retire from the world:

> To lie hidden was never but safe and pleasant, but now so much better as the world is worse. It is an happiness not to be a witness of the mischief of the times, which it is hard to see and be guiltless. . . . Every evil we see doth either vex or infect us. Your retiredness avoids this. . . . I do not so much praise you in this, as wonder at you. . . . I nowhere know so excellent parts shrouded in such willing secresy. The world knows you, and wants you; and yet you are voluntarily hid. (*Works*, 6, 160-61)

85/29 Scioccia] Although glossed by Hall as coming from the Italian *sciocco*, "stupid," the name is also meant to suggest *Sicilia*, "Sicily."

86/35-87/1 walks . . . quadrupeds] Hall is borrowing from Mandeville and Münster: "And in another Yle ben folk, that gon upon hir Hondes and hire Feet, as Bestes" (*Mandeville's Travels*, p. 206); "There are also said to be creatures there called Artapathitae, who go on their hands and feet like quadrupeds" (Münster, *Cosmographia*, p. 1319).

87/15 Arcadian beast] Arcadia, a pastoral country in the center of the Peloponnesus, next to Sparta. Among the Romans, as well as the Greeks, the expression frequently occurs because the rude Arcadians were thought to be simpletons. See Per., 3, 9; Plaut., *Asin.*, line 333; Pliny, *HN*, 8, 68.

87/24 always . . . intently] Hall says the very same thing in *Occasional Meditations* (*Works*, 10, 144): "When we would take aim, or see most exquisitely, we shut one eye."

87/29 towering . . . birds] Cf. Peter Martyr's description of the Indians in
an unnamed land 70 miles from Rio Negro: "The country, however,
has such lofty trees that the natives may easily build houses among
their branches" (*De Orbe Novo*, 1, 299).

88/1 Calais . . . Argonauts] Two brothers, the offspring of Orithyia and
Boreas, who were born without wings but grew them as they reached
manhood. They sailed with Jason and the rest of the Argonauts in
his quest of the Golden Fleece (Ap. Rhod., *Argon.*, 1, 211; 2, 240 ff.;
Ov., *Met.*, 7, 710 ff.). See also note to 112/5 below.

88/2 Thessalian Venetians] Thessaly, a country of Greece, considered to
be treacherous. According to Suidas (*Lexicon*, s.v. Θεσαλὸν σόφισ-
μα), *Thessalos sophisma* was a familiar term for trickery. Hall is
here thinking of Venice's notoriety as a haven for mountebanks; see
Coryats Crudities, pp. 271-75.

88/9m Libavius] Hall's note is ironic since Libavius, a serious student
of alchemy, would never have written such a rhyme. His work *Alchemia* begins with the statement that "Alchemy is the art of per-
fecting the powers of transmutation, and of extracting pure sub-
stances from impure ones by a separation of elements" (par. 1). *Pars
cum parte* is defined by both Libavius and Paracelsus as the process
of alloying silver and gold with baser metals (Libavius, *Alchemia*,
p. 176; *Dictionarium Theophrasti Paracelsi*, p. 73).

88/21 Villa Pratensis] The reference is to Jason Pratensis, a Belgian doctor who wrote several treatises on reproduction, particularly *De
Uteris, libri duo* in 1524. His interest in reproduction explains
Hall's sarcastic reference to the Italians, to whom large families are
well known, and who—to Hall—overindulge in procreation (Al-
berto von Haller, *Bibliotheca Medicinae Practicae* [Basel, 1776], 1,
511; *Biographisches Lexikon der hervorragenden Ärzte* [Munich-
Berlin, 1962], 2, 669).

88/24-26 ringing . . . storm] "Even now Italian women, fearful of im-
pending storms, burn foul-smelling manure in the open air: the
priests, however, in the Thracian manner (who, at the threatening
of a storm, are armed with unsheathed swords and bells, and rage
horribly at the clouds) gather together with resounding cymbals—
which are called bells—more confident in the power of those up-
roars with God, than in the prayers and fastings of their fellow
countrymen" (Moresinus, *Papatus*, p. 27).

89/8-11 Belgium . . . crocodile] Emblematic maps were exceedingly
popular in the seventeenth and eighteenth centuries, Famianus

Strada's *De Bello Belgico* going through over 90 editions between 1632 and 1794. Michael Aitsinger's *Leo Belgicus*, with Belgium in the shape of a lion, first appeared in 1583. Hall obtains the other resemblances from Postellus, *Cosmographicae*, pp. 5-6: "Strabo writes that the Peloponnesians are similar to the leaf of the plane tree, Italy to the tibia of a dead man, Spain to the shin of an ox. . . . I remember . . . each peninsula of the Atlantic region [compared to] the very membranes of fish lungs, . . . Asia . . . to a crocodile pelt, with the tail somewhat mutilated."

89/12 Colossus] See note to 36/33.

89/38 dig up stones] Excavations to uncover Roman ruins began in Italy as early as the fifteenth century when the Renaissance first focused on the remains of antique sculpture. The interest in antique monuments is witnessed by Aloisio Giovanni's *Vedute degli antichi vestigi de Roma* (Rome, 1616), a work of over 100 engravings with no text.

90/1m white . . . paper] This saying appears in Florio, *His firste Fruites*, fol. 20r, which he translates as "A white wal is a fooles paper." Italian buildings, from antiquity to the present, have frequently been covered by graffiti.

90/10-11 cities . . . proximity] Aristotle (*Pol.*, 7, 5, 4) says much the same thing: "Now it is not difficult to see that, if [excess population and immigration of undesirables] are avoided, it is advantageous in respect of both security and supply of necessary commodities that the city and the country should have access to the sea."

90/24 fourfold rationale] The Pazzivillani are apparently too stupid to note that the speaker provides only three reasons.

90/34 Salus herself] An old Roman goddess, the personification of health, later often identified with the Greek Hygieia, the attendant of Asclepiades" (*OCD*, p. 948).

91/6-10 add . . . ear] An ironic description. Cf. Rabelais: "A town without bells is like a blind man without a staff, an ass without a crupper, and a cow without cymbals" (*Gargantua*, 1, 19).

91/26-29 inhabitants . . . ago] The sense of these lines is unclear, but Hall seems to be saying that the earlier, more prudent inhabitants must have abandoned this place ages ago, for lawyers and usurers (who derive their livelihood from spendthrifts) seem to have been long established here.

91/31 Azotium Promontory] From the Latin *asotus*, "a dissolute man," and possibly also with reference to the city of Azotus, the place to

which the Philistines transported the captured ark of the covenant
for safekeeping (Joseph., *BJ*, 6, 1).

92/9m Moresinus . . . British] "See [in Blondus, *Triumph. Romae*] the
care for the dead and the sepulchral banquet, on which more is often
spent in England—as is well known—than in the marrying off of a
daughter, or (more truthfully) on the dole which ought to be given
to the poor every day in church" (Moresinus, *Papatus*, pp. 151–52).

92/16 Münster] Münster describes no monster exactly like this, but he
does show a picture of a monster generally human in shape, having
a tail, webbed feet and hands, a long, tail-shaped nose, eyes ringed
with feathers, two eyes on his stomach, four dog heads, one at each
elbow and knee, and two monkey heads coming out of his chest
(*Cosmographia*, p. 1057). Perhaps from this picture, and perhaps
also from Pliny's description of dog-headed people (*HN*, 7, 2, 23),
Hall composed his race of flatterers. Cf. the notes on Münster and
Mandeville at 116/23 and 116/24 below.

92/21m Oh . . . herd] Hor., *Epist.*, 1, 19, 19.

92/25 Ciniflonius . . . leg] Hall borrows the incident from Garzoni:
"*Clisophus* parasite to Philip K[ing] of Macedonia, . . . perceiving
that his master by chance had broken one of his legs, began likewise
to goe limping like him . . . imitating diligently and like an Ape, his
Lord and master in euerie thing" (*Hospitall*, p. 95).

92/34-93/2 gazes . . . worships] Cf. Hall's character of "The flatterer":
"He hangs upon the lips which he admireth, as if they could let fall
nothing but oracles; and finds occasion to cite some approved sentence, under the name he honoureth" (*Works*, 6, 114).

93/12 Babillarda] From the French *babillard*, "chattering."

93/21 Moronia Felix] See note to 70/2.

93/27-28 German miles] See note to 32/9 above.

94/5 Salacona] From the Latin *salaco, salaconis*, derived from the Greek
σαλάκων, "a swaggerer," "braggart."

94/7m Cicero . . . Gallus] *Fam.*, 7, 23. Hall's marginal reference (anno-
tating the town of Menosprecia, Spanish for "despised") cites a
"letter to M. Fab. Gallus," an apparent mistake for M. *Fadius*
Gallus, an acquaintance who is heaped with abuse for having
bought works of art for Cicero that did not meet with his approval.

94/10m The Torre] See note to 23/30 above for a description of the Peak
district in Derbyshire. The rock named by Hall is called both High
Peak and Mam Tor. Brown (*Discovery*, pp. 200–01) cites a Mr. F.
Williamson, who writes that "Mam Tor is unique so far as this

country is concerned, as the whole of one side of the mountain is cut away in a steep cliff consisting of soft sandstone and shales, presenting one smooth face many hundreds of feet high."

94/15 Tarpeian Rock] A celebrated rock at Rome whose steepest side overhangs the Tiber. From this rock, state criminals were thrown in the earlier Roman times.

94/20 Villa Vitiosa] From the Latin *vitiosus*, "wicked," "depraved."

94/22 Sin-obran Plain] From the Latin *sine*, "without," and the Spanish *obra*, "toil." Hall's marginal note is incorrect. The saying is not from Hesiod but from Theocritus (*Id.*, 15, 26): Ἀεπγοῖς αἰεν ἑορτά, "To the idle all days are holidays"; Erasmus (*Adagia*, 2, 586-87; tr. fols. 37v-38r) repeats it as "With sluggers . . . it is alwaies holy daye."

94/25-26 Saltuares . . . Pliny] "There are also small islands at Nymphaeum [a promontory in Illyria] called the Dancing Islands [Saliares], because they move to the foot-beats of persons keeping time with the chanting of a choral song" (*HN*, 2, 96).

94/30-32 showing . . . Siculus] Diodorus Siculus, in discussing conflicting theories regarding the origin of the world, says one group believes "the race of men also has existed from eternity, there having never been a time when men were first begotten" (Diod. Sic., 1, 6). Hall consistently criticizes those who boast of their noble ancestry without demonstrating it by their noble deeds:

> VVhat boots it *Pontice*, tho thou could'st discourse
> Of a long golden line of Ancestors?
> Or shew their painted faces gaylie drest,
> For euer since before the last conquest;
> Or tedious Bead-roles of descended blood,
> From Father *Iaphet* since *Deucalions* flood
>
> (*Vd.*, 4, 3, 1-6)

Hall also ridicules those who try to disguise their lowly ancestry:

> His father dead, tush, no it was not hee,
> He findes records of his great pedigree,
> And tels how first his famous Ancestor
> Did come in long since with the Conquerour.
>
> (*Vd.*, 4, 2, 133-36)

95/7-11 banquets . . . hunger] Cf. Hall's character of "The covetous": "Once in a year, perhaps, he gives himself leave to feast; and, for the

time, thinks no man more lavish. . . . And when his guests are parted
. . . [he] feeds his family with the mouldy remnants a month after"
(*Works*, 6, 117).

95/16-18 freeing . . . meal] Hall mentions this subterfuge twice; in his
character of "The vainglorious" Hall claims "he picks his teeth
when his stomach is empty" (*Works*, 6, 119), and he repeats it in *Vd.*,
3, 7, 4-6:

> And picks his glutted teeth since late Noon-tide?
> T's *Ruffio*: Trow'st thou where he dind to day:
> In sooth I sawe him sit with Duke *Humfray*.

Duke Humphrey was the popular name for a chapel in Saint Paul's:
"A penniless gallant who could not pay for his dinner would spend
the dinner-hour walking in St. Paul's, and then was said to have
dined with Duke Humphrey" (Davenport, *Poems*, p. 190; see further references given there).

95/22-23 Plautus . . . interest] The expression *foenere sumere*, "to borrow at interest," is frequent in Plautus: "He got the cash from a
money lender at Thebes on interest — two percent a day" (*Epid.*, line
53); "If I can't get it as a friendly loan, I'm resolved to borrow it at
usury" (*Asin.*, line 248).

95/33 furs . . . Russians] According to Herberstein, *Rerum Muscoviticarum Commentarii*, the Russians exact a high price for skins they
have purchased cheaply elsewhere: "I have sometimes heard of sable
skins being seen at Moscow, some of which have been sold for thirty,
and some for twenty gold pieces. . . . Fox skins, and especially black
ones, which they usually make into caps, are valued highly, for
sometimes ten of them are sold for fifteen gold pieces" (1, 114-15).

96/3m Politian] The person referred to is Angelo Poliziano (1454-94),
but I cannot find this saying in his collected works.

96/6-7 feed . . . herb] Besides the people in Lucian's *True Story* who live
on smoke (see note to 54/29), Pliny describes natives in India who
"live only on the air they breathe and the scent they inhale through
their nostrils" (*HN*, 7, 2).

96/12-13 Topia-Waralladore] Though Hall glosses it only as Spanish
for "discoverer," the name is obviously meant to suggest Sir Walter
Raleigh, the man who introduced tobacco to Europe. The name
may also be rearranged to form the phrase "ador[e] all war," especially fitting for Raleigh in view of his eventual end.

96/16 blackened . . . insides] One of the galleries at Sir Robert Drury's
house in Hawstead (where Hall lived from 1601 to 1608) contained
the picture of a blackamoor smoking a pipe with the inscription
Intus idem, "the same inside" (Cullum, *History of Hawstead,* p.
161). During the reign of James I, smoking and blackamoors were
thought to be fit companions for each other since the King despised
tobacco.

96/18-22 nostrils . . . use] Cf. Hall's account in *Vd.,* 5, 2, 67-76:

> Looke to the towred chymneis which should bee
> The wind-pipes of good hospitalitie,
> Through which it breatheth to the open ayre,
> Betokening life and liberall welfaire,
> Lo, there th'vnthankfull swallow takes her rest,
> And fils the Tonuell with her circled nest,
> Nor halfe that smoke from all his chymneies goes
> Which one Tabacco-pipe driues through his nose;
> So rawbone hunger scorns the mudded wals,
> And gin's to reuell it in Lordly halls;

In one of his sermons Hall asks, "Is there not now as much spent in
wanton smoke, as our honest forefathers spent in substantial hospitality?" (*Works,* 5, 418; see also *Works,* 5, 346).

96/24m prostitutes . . . books] Hall's note comes straight from Moresinus: "The famous house of ill repute of Rome reared itself and
served both types of venery, . . . even appropriating some of the
profits from the prostitutes for its own treasury, for the Roman
whores pay Julian money every single week to the stockpile of the
pope, whose annual census exceeds 40,000 ducats, and so much of
that money comes from the leaders of the church that they even
reckon their income from pandering directly proportional to the
increases in the clergy. Paul III had 45,000 whores on his books,
from whom he exacted a tax every month for the privilege of fornication" (*Papatus,* p. 94). Hall repeats his charge in *Christian Moderation:* "What should I mention the toleration and yearly rent of
public stews? These known courtezans in Spain and Italy pay to
their great landlords [the Church] for their lust" (*Works,* 6, 408). Cf.
Vd., 4, 7, 27 ff., and Stubbes, *Anatomy of Abuses,* pp. 344-45.

97/10 Fortune] According to Plutarch (*De Fort. Rom.,* 317-18), when
Fortune—having resided everywhere in the world—finally crossed

the Tiber, "she took off her wings, stepped out of her sandals, and abandoned her untrustworthy and unstable globe. Thus did she enter Rome, as with intent to abide, and in such guise is she present today." To Hall, of course, Rome is anything but a fortunate place, except for the Roman church.

97/10m Fortune . . . simpletons] According to Henderson (*Latin Proverbs*, p. 132), this saying is a Latin proverb from about A.D. 150. It appears in Erasmus's *Moriae Encomium* (4, 486; tr. p. 116), and then in English as "Fortune fauours Fooles" in Googe, *Eglogs*, p. 88.

97/18m We . . . insane] From Mantuan, *Eclogae*, 1, 118 (in *Adolescentia*, p. 9). "Semel insanivimus" is the motto of *Vd.*, 6, 1.

97/20-21 Lady of Loretto] "According to an extravagant legend, the house of Joseph and Mary in Nazareth was transported by angels, on the night of the 9th-10th of May 1291 to Dalmatia, then brought to the Italian coast opposite (Dec. 10, 1294), till, on the 7th of September 1295 it found rest [at Loretto on the Adriatic]. The pilgrimage thither must have attained great importance as early as the 15th century; for the popes of the Renaissance found themselves constrained to erect an imposing pilgrim church above the 'Holy House'" (*EB*, 21, 609). In "The Defeat of Cruelty" (*Works*, 5, 265-66), Hall ridicules its peripatetic nature, calling the chapel at Loretto "a greater pilgrim than [its visitors], that hath four several times removed itself, and changed stations."

97/21 God of Compostela] "Here the attraction for the pilgrim was the supposed possession of the body of James the son of Zebedee. . . . At the beginning of the medieval period it was believed his body was laid to rest in Palestine. . . . But in Spain belief in this cherished possession was universal; and, step by step, the theory won credence throughout the West. . . . In England, indeed, the shrine of St. James of Compostela became practically the most favoured devotional resort; and in the 12th century . . . a pilgrimage thither was ranked on a level with one to Rome or Jerusalem" (*EB*, 21, 609).

97/21 Parathalassia . . . Desiderius] Of all the English sanctuaries of Our Lady, that of Walsingham in Norfolk was the most celebrated. It was even called the Holy Land of Walsingham, and pilgrims flocked to it from all parts of England and the Continent, making its priory one of the richest in the world (*Cath. E.*, 13, 760-61). Erasmus, in "Peregrinatio Religionis Ergo" (*Colloquia*, 1, 774-87; tr. pp. 285-312), satirizes this shrine in particular (and the religious pil-

grimage in general) under the name *Parathalassia*, "By-the-sea."
Hall ridicules it too in one of his epistles (*Works*, 6, 148): "Blessed
Mary should be a God, if she could at once attend all her suitors.
One solicits her at Halle; another at Scherpen-hewel; another, at
Lucca; at our Walsingham, another; one in Europe; another in
Asia: . . . ten thousand devout supliants are at once prostrate before
her several shrines. If she cannot hear all, why pray they? if she can,
what can God do more?"

97/25 Good Goddess] Bona Dea ("Good Goddess") was a Roman goddess of unknown name, protective of women. Rites in her honor
were celebrated annually in December in the house of the chief
magistrate, under the leadership of his wife and with assistance of
the vestal virgins. No man might be present at this rite (*OCD*, p.
172). Hall's use of this name is clearly ironic, for the goddess is far
from a benevolent deity.

97/29 Madonna Scooperta] "Our Lady is revealed."

98/16–17 ascend . . . knees] "Very likely a reflection on the relic known
as the Scala Sancta, the supposed steps of Pilate's palace in Jerusalem, ascended by Christ on the day of his passion, now in the building by that name opposite the Lateran Palace in Rome, and climbed
by the faithful on their knees, even to-day" (Brown, *Discovery*, pp.
187–88).

98/36m inscription . . . Sannazaro] *Epigrammata*, "Ad Marinum Carac-
ciolum," lines 27–28 (*Opera*, p. 173).

99/10 flamen] "A kind of priest so distinguished in the Roman religion,
as witness the conical cap, that they had only three flamens assigned
to three divinities" (August., *De Civ. D.*, 2, 15).

100/7 most . . . chamber] This practical joke, which makes up the induc-
tion to *The Taming of the Shrew*, comes from an epistle of Juan
Luis (Ludovico) Vives (*Opera Omnia*, 7, 144–46), who relates the
trick as having actually been played by Philip the Good upon a
drunken man in Brussels. Heuterus, in *Opera Historica* (4, 19 [p.
119]), repeats the story. Though the prototype of the tale is undoubtedly "The Story of Abou Hassan; or, The Sleeper Awakened,"
in the *Arabian Nights* (11, 1–38), Hall probably received the story
from Vives, since Vives—a good friend of More and Erasmus—had
his epistles printed with theirs, and Hall obviously knew More's
and Erasmus's writings well. Burton (*Anatomy*, 2, 2, 4) retells it in
an abbreviated version.

100/9m Plautus] *Pseud.*, lines 146–47.

100/12-13 new Endymion] A youth distinguished for his beauty and renowned in antiquity for the perpetual sleep in which he spent his life.

100/19m Ovid] *Met.*, 10, 264.

100/21 clothed . . . ornamented] Hall's marginal note refers to Plaut., *Epid.*, apparently to line 231 where *indusiatam*, "clothed," and *patagiatam*, "ornamented," appear as the invented names for new garments.

100/27m Virgil] *Aen.*, 3, 630.

101/1 "We were Trojans"] *Aen.*, 2, 325. Hall uses the same phrase as the motto for *Vd.*, 4, 3. In both cases the speaker looks back to a better time, acknowledging how much has been lost.

101/11 Credulium] From the Latin *credulus*, "easily believing," "credulous."

101/20 day . . . Venus] There were two Roman festivals that eventually became associated with Venus: the *vinalia urbana* (when the wine from the previous year was first opened), celebrated on 23 April, and the *vinalia rustica* (when the grapes were first pressed), celebrated on 19 August. To what occasion in the Catholic calendar Hall is sarcastically referring I cannot be certain, but I suspect he is making a connection between Venus and the Virgin Mary and thus probably means the Assumption of Mary, celebrated on 15 August, whose octave extended to 22 August.

101/22m Hospidale . . . Garzoni] It is not exactly clear why Hall disparages this work, especially when he borrows from it four times in the *Mundus*. My guess is that Hall may feel Garzoni is merely amused by mankind's folly, when the proper response ought to be indignation.

101/29-31 cloisters . . . land] Perhaps elicited by Lambarde's description of the Valley of Motindene: "What number of buildings, varietie of sectes, and plentie of possessions, Poperie was in olde time prouided for. . . . No corner (almoste) without some religious house, or other: their suites and orders were hardly to be numbered: and as for their landes and reuenues, it was a worlde to beholde them" (*Perambulation of Kent* [1576], p. 230).

101/30-31 Westphalian . . . Lipsius] "Hall is here alluding to the singularly vivid account which Lipsius gives of his unpleasant experiences in Westphalian inns in the month of October 1586. . . . It is to be found in the four letters, afterwards suppressed, which were printed as 13-16 of his *Epistolarum Centuria Secunda*" (E. Bensly, "A Note on Bishop Hall's Satires," *Modern Language Review*, 3

[1907], 169-70). For example, in epistle 15 Lipsius writes: "To be certain, I am suffering in this Westphalian journey. . . . Every misfortune attacks me violently, from the air, from the water, from the food. Perpetual winds and rains: meals, I do not proclaim barbarous, but scarcely human. . . . At the inns (so I call them, though, in fact, they might preferably be called a stable or a pig-sty), as you enter you will be offered a mug of some foul or watery beer, often still warm from being freshly brewed; nor is it possible to refuse it, or proper to throw it up" (*Epistolarum*, p. 12). In *Vd.*, 5, 1, 69-70, Hall also refers to "nice [i.e., fastidious] *Lipsius*" and his "lodging in wild *West-phalye.*"

102/14-15 Roman . . . Varro] In *De Lingua Latina* Varro names most but not all of the Roman gods.

102/21-22 Egyptians . . . dead] In his prefatory poem to Donne's *Anniversaries*, Hall repeats his belief (probably based on the pyramids) that the Egyptians cared more about tombs for the dead than houses for the living:

> . . . the wise Egyptians wont to lay
> More on their Tombs, then houses: these of clay,
> But those of brasse, or marble were;
>
> (*Poems*, p. 146)

In *Vd.*, 3, 2, 5, he refers to a stately tomb as being erected "Egyptian wise."

102/22-23 800 . . . wax] Hall's reference to *Sac. Caerem.* is correct, but he understates the amount of wax expended on a cardinal's funeral by a factor of about ten: "Normally there are six or eight *thousand* pounds of wax in tapers around the church alone, the space of a lance between them, and one lance away from the platform containing the bier; above the pews are placed twelve or eighteen tapers, arranged wherever it pleases" ("De Morte, & Exequiis Reverendissimorum Cardinalium," *Sac. Caerem.*, fol. 102v).

102/30-34 Two . . . body] "On both sides two attendants stand near the dead Cardinal, who, with two flyswatters of black silk, decorated with the arms of the Cardinal, are on guard to drive away flies, even if it be winter" (*Sac. Caerem.*, fol. 103r). Cf. Hall's description in *Vd.*, 4, 7, 53-56:

> To see a lasie dumbe *Acholithite*
> Armed against a deuout Flyes despight,

Which at th'hy Altar doth the *Chalice* vaile
With a broad Flie-flappe of a *Peacockes* tayle.

102/35-36 water . . . salt] "What holiness do [Papists] write in religious
cowls, altars, relics, ashes, candles, oils, salts, waters, ensigns, roses,
words, grains, Agnus Dei, medals, and a world of such trash! . . .
How do they drive out devils out of good creatures by foolish exor-
cisms!" (*Works*, 5, 62).

102/36-103/1 bless . . . roses] "At the end of his speech, with balsam [the
cardinal] anoints the golden rose, which is attached to its own
branch, and in addition sprinkles on ground musk, . . . places incense in a censer according to the usual fashion, then sprinkles the
rose with holy water and burns the incense. . . . Thereafter he gives
it to the hand of the Cardinal's deacon, . . . and he in turn gives it to
the . . . Pontiff, who, holding the rose in his left hand, and blessing
it with his right, proceeds to the chapel" (*Sac. Caerem.*, fol. 59r).

103/1 baptize ensigns] "Omnipotent and eternal God, who art sacred
above all, . . . regard favorably our humble prayers and this vexillum,
which is prepared for the discipline of war, sanctify it by heavenly
benediction so that it might be powerful against adversaries and
rebel nations . . . and be terrible to the enemies of Christian people"
(*Sac. Caerem.*, fol. 61r-61v).

103/2-3 stones . . . blood] Cf. Hall's description in his character of "The
superstitious": "If he hear that some sacred block speaks, moves,
weeps, smiles, his bare feet carry him thither with an offering"
(*Works*, 6, 110).

103/4 Semones] From the Latin *semi*, "half," and *homo, hominis*,
"man," an inferior class of divinities, half god and half man, such as
Priapus, Silenus, and the Fauns.

103/5 Daemones] Powers or spirits which, in an early stage of Greek
religion, were thought to people the world, occupying trees, rivers,
springs, and mountains, giving rise to everything that affects man.

103/11 Chronia] From Χρόνος, the Greek equivalent of Saturn, the god
of time. See following note on the Saturnians.

103/12 Saturnians] Saturninus, a heretic of the early second century,
believed that from one supreme and perfect God there had emanated
a series of aeons, beings of inferior nature who had formed the
heavens. Those who occupied the lowest of the heavens, corrupted
by the inferior matter of our world, endeavored to efface the knowledge of a supreme God from men's minds and set themselves up as

objects of worship in his stead. Hall's marginal reference to Augustine should be *De Haer.*, chap. 3.

103/14 Abraxia . . . Basilidians] "The Basilidians were named from Basilides, who . . . said that there were 365 heavens, this being the number of days which compose the year. For this reason he recommended as a sort of sacred name the word αβρασαξ. In the Greek system of computation the letters of this word add up to the same number, for there are seven: α plus β plus ρ plus α plus σ plus α plus ξ, that is, one plus two plus a hundred plus one plus two hundred plus one plus sixty, which give the sum of 365" (*De Haer.*, chap. 4). Abraxa is the original name of Utopia (*Utopia*, pp. 112, 386).

103/17 Canton . . . Borborites] The name "borborite" comes from the Greek βόρβορος, "mud." Besides what Hall states in his note, Augustine goes on to say that, though the Gnostics boast they are so named because of the excellence of their knowledge, they are actually known for their fantastic and lying fictions: "They . . . attempt to seize upon the weak-minded with frightfully named princes or angels, and they devise many explanations of God which are incredible and contrary to sound truth" (*De Haer.*, chap. 6).

103/17m also . . . Carpocratians] Irenaeus *Contra Haer.*, 7, 25 (*PG*, 1, 685); however, Augustine says the Gnostics merely stemmed from the Carpocratians (*De Haer.*, chap. 6). "The Carpocratians take their name from Carpocrates, who advocated every shameful deed and every experience of sin as the only way to evade and pass through the principalities and powers to whom these things are pleasing in order to arrive at the higher heaven. . . . He considered Jesus merely a man and to have been born of a human father and mother, but endowed with such a mind that He was capable of knowing and imparting the supernatural" (*De Haer.*, chap. 7).

103/17m Valentini . . . Irenaeus] Irenaeus, *Contra Haer.*, 1, 1 (*PG*, 7, 445-52); Augustine also mentions the Valentinian Gnostics (*De Haer.*, chap. 11).

103/20m Eusebius] Eusebius, *Hist. Eccl.*, 6, 38 (*PG*, 20, 598-99). Since Eusebius does not mention that Epiphanius connects the Ebionites with the Elcesaites and Augustine does, the probable source of Hall's note is *De Haer.*, chap. 10: "The Ebionites likewise maintain that Christ is only human. They observe the carnal precepts of the Law, that is, circumcision and all the other burdens from which we have been liberated by the New Testament. Epiphanius unites the

Sampsaeans and the Elcesaites with this heresy to such an extent that he lists them in the same place as one heresy, though he does imply that there are some differences. But he also speaks of them later, ascribing them a place of their own."

103/23 Heracleonites] They received their name from Heracleon, a disciple of the Valentinian Gnostics in the second century. Hall derives his information from August., *De Haer.*, chap. 16.

103/24m Ophites] August., *De Haer.*, chap. 17: "The Ophites get their name from the serpent, for the Greek word for serpent is ὄφις. They regard this serpent as Christ; but also keep a real serpent, which has been trained to lick their bread, and so to sanctify a eucharist for them, as it were. Some people maintain that these Ophites grew out of the Nicolaites or Gnostics, and that it was through their fantastic inventions they arrived at the worship of the serpent."

103/26-104/2 subterranean . . . preserved] August., *De Haer.*, chap. 18: "The Cainites are so called because they honor Cain, who they say was a man of the greatest courage. At the same time they believe the traitor Judas to be of divine nature, and consider his crime a benefit, arguing that he foreknew what a great blessing Christ's passion was to be for the human race, and for that reason had handed Him over to the Jews to be put to death."

104/3 Hygri Pond] From the Greek ὑγρός, "wet," as opposed to More's River Anhydrus in *Utopia*. See note to 74/11m above.

104/4m Severians] August., *De Haer.*, chap. 24.

104/6m Tacians] August., *De Haer.*, chap. 25.

104/7 Montanists] August., *De Haer.*, chap. 26. Besides what Hall mentions in his note, Augustine also says that they use this bread to "perform their eucharist. If the child dies, he is regarded as a martyr among them; but if he lives, a great priest."

104/7m Valesians] August., *De Haer.*, chap. 37.

104/8m Manichaeans] August., *De Haer.*, chap. 46: They believe that men's souls pass "into everything that is rooted in and supported on the earth. For they are convinced that plants and trees possess sentient life and can feel pain when injured, and therefore that no one can pull or pluck them without torturing them. Therefore, they consider it wrong to clear a field even of thorns. Hence, in their madness they make agriculture, the most innocent of occupations, guilty of multiple murder." In *Christian Moderation* Hall says: "Would not that fond Manichee make himself ridiculous that should forbid to gather [grapes and olives], much more to wring them?" (*Works*, 6, 428).

104/8m Euchites . . . Augustine] *De Haer.*, chap. 57. Besides what Hall provides, Augustine continues: "For although the Lord said that we must always pray and not lose heart, . . . this is most sensibly interpreted to mean that set times for prayer should not be missed on any day, yet they go to such extremes in this that they are thereby judged worthy of being named among the heretics." Euchite comes from the Greek εὐχέτης, "one who prays."

104/9m Patricians] August., *De Haer.*, chap. 61.

104/9m Ascites] "The Ascitae get their name from the leather bottle, for ἄσκος is the Greek for what we call 'leather bottle' in Latin. For they are said to dance with Bacchic abandon around a veiled, inflated leather bottle, convinced that they are the Gospel's new skins, filled with new wine" (August., *De Haer.*, chap. 62).

104/9-10 statues . . . Pattalorinchites] "The Passalorinchites are so devoted to silence that they place the finger upon their lips and nose to avoid even breaking silence at all when they judge that they should be silent. This is the reason they are given that name, πάσσαλος being the Greek for stake and ῥύγχος for nose. But why they who invented the name preferred to use the word 'stake' for finger, I do not know. For there is the Greek word δάκτυλος for finger. And certainly they could be called the Dactylorynchitae with greater clarity" (August., *De Haer.*, chap. 63). Harpocrates is the god of silence, represented as a boy with a finger on his mouth.

104/10 cups . . . Aquarians] August., *De Haer.*, chap. 64.

104/13m Rhetorius . . . truly] August., *De Haer.*, chap. 72.

104/15m Abelians . . . Augustine] *De Haer.*, chap. 87.

104/18m Henry . . . David] Henry Niclaes (1502-80) and David Joris (1501?-56) were both members of a group known variously as the Netherland Spiritualizers, Libertines, or Anabaptists—a loosely interrelated antinomian movement of the sixteenth century that attached little or no significance to external sacraments. David Joris turned to Anabaptism in 1533 and—after his mother suffered martyrdom in 1537—began to have visions and the gift of prophecy. These visions led him to claim to be the third David sent to complete the era instituted by the second David: Christ. After years of persecution, in 1543 he found refuge in Basel under the assumed name of Jan van Brugge; however, when three years after his death his true identity was discovered, his body was exhumed and burned at the stake. Why Hall inverts his name and calls him George David is not clear.

Henry Niclaes, through his friendship with David Joris in Amsterdam in the 1530s, also turned to spiritualism and in 1540 began to sign himself by his initials H. N., in calculated reference to his being a new man (*homo novus*). Central to his thought was an insistence on man's actual righteousness and physical holiness—and on God's love dwelling among men of the Spirit. Under Niclaes's ministry a group named *Familia Caritatis*, or "Family of Love," formed, which spread through the Low Countries, and later into France, and then into England, where—much later—it passed into the Quakers (Williams, *Radical Reformation*, pp. 351, 478-80).

104/19 Virginian exiles] "In 1597 some of the Queen's 'faithful Subjects falsely called Brownists' petitioned for permission to settle in Canada, where, as they said, 'we may not onlie worshippe god as wee are in conscience perswaded by his word, but also doe unto her Majestie, and our Country great good service, and in time also greatlie annoy that bloodie and persecuting Spaniard about the Baye of Mexico.' Virginia was, of course, a general term for the North American continent. Two ships which sailed on April 8th to the St. Lawrence for purposes of fishing and discovery carried four members of the sect with them, . . . but they returned with the expedition in September, and ultimately made their way to Holland" (Brown, *Discovery*, p. 228).

105/14 *Il . . . Massimo*] Italian for "the biggest, first-rate buffoon." It was not uncommon for the Pope to be called this; see More, *Responsio ad Lutherum* (*Works*, 5, 53-55): "I will make clear how foolishly [Luther] ridicules the royal majesty's method of disputing, which consists of opposing to the authority of a single buffoon the authority of so many holy fathers." Hall's ridicule of the Catholic church in this chapter closely parallels *Vd.*, 4, 7, 1 ff.

105/15m chamber . . . elected] The chamber of parrots, a room painted with the pictures of parrots and other animals, was used not to elect a pope but to prepare the newly elected Pope for the public coronation marking his elevation to the papacy: "On the appointed Sunday, the Pontifex enters the . . . richly decorated room called Papagalli, to be furnished there . . . with an amice, an alb, a long cingle, a stole, a red pluvial, and a costly mitre. . . . Thus attired, the elected Pontiff . . . marches to St. Peter's" (*Sac. Caerem.*, fol. 20v).

105/28m very . . . Pontiff] The "very words" Hall says appear in *Sac.*

Caerem. (fol. 29v) are those referring to the two thrones of porphyry
outside Saint John Lateran called the *stericoraria,* or "dunghill,"
where the newly elected Pope sits as he distributes silver coins to the
crowd. It was thought that this seat was actually used by the cardinals to ascertain that the Pope-elect was male. This legend arose
because of the belief among enemies of the Catholic church that a
female pope, Pope Joan, was elected between Leo IV and Benedict III
in A.D. 855. Having become pregnant by one of her attendants, she
gave birth to a child during a procession from Saint Peter's to the
Lateran and thus exposed herself (*Cath. E.,* 8, 407-09, s.v. "Joan,
'Popess'"). Hall alludes to both in *Vd.,* 4, 7, 67-70:

> . . . the Female Fathers grone,
> Yearning in mids of her procession;
> . . . the needlesse tryall-chayre,
> (When ech is proued by his bastard heyre)

Hall mentions Pope Joan in *Quo Vadis?* (*Works,* 9, 550) and ridicules those Catholics who claim that "Pope Joan was but a fancy."

105/30-31 carried . . . attendants] See note to Celestini, 71/1*m* above.

105/33 *baldachinus*] "Finally the most holy Pontiff advances astride a
white horse, covered at its rear section by a red canopy called a *baldachinus,* which eight important nobles or Orators carry" (*Sac.
Caerem.,* fol. 20v). From the Italian name for Bagdad, where the rich
brocade for these canopies was first made (*OED*).

106/4-5 He . . . none] "The pope is above the law, like the god Terminus
on the Capitoline, who was punished by Jove, according to Varro's
account. And the pope does not yield to God, is above the law of
God, because according to his interpretation he can prefer unwritten
tradition to written law" (Moresinus, *Papatus,* p. 122).

107/5*m* Horace] *Epist.,* 1, 16, 60-61.

107/5 Ocean . . . Magellan] Marked correctly on the map facing p. 19
and the map facing p. 107 as *Fretum Magellanicum,* "Strait of
Magellan"—running between the tip of South America and the
coast of Lavernia—it is here incorrectly termed an ocean.

107/8-9 Pluto . . . Trinacria] The ancient name for Sicily, from which
Pluto carried off Ceres' daughter to the underworld. See note to
40/6-9 above. Cf. Hall's account in *Vd.,* 5, 2, 77-82:

> So the blacke Prince is broken loose againe
> That saw no Sunne saue once (as stories saine)

> That once was, when in *Trinacry* I weene
> Hee stole the daughter of the haruest Queene,
> And grip't the mawes of barren *Sicily*,
> With long constraint of pinefull penurie.

107/26m Tryphon . . . bandit] Several men appear in classical literature
with that name. Hall's Egyptian bandit is probably that Tryphon
described by Diodorus Siculus as a "violent and impious man" who
seized the throne of Egypt from Osiris, his brother, and murdered
him: he "divided the body of the slain man into 26 pieces and gave
one portion to each of the band of murderers, since he wanted all of
them to share in the pollution and felt in this way he would have in
them steadfast supporters and defenders of his rule" (1, 21).

107/27-28 islands . . . Guiana] The river Hall refers to is the Orinoco,
which Raleigh ascended in 1595 in search of El Dorado ("the gilded"),
the name given by explorers to the fabulous city of Manoa. According to Raleigh, "whatsoeuer Prince shall possesse it, . . . shalbe
Lorde of more Gold . . . than eyther the king of Spayne, or the great
Turke" (*Discouerie of Gviana*, p. 9). Hall's name may have been
influenced by the name Orellana given at that time to the Amazon,
in honor of Francisco Orellana who discovered it in 1540-41. The
Orellana, perhaps partly because El Dorado was also thought to
exist somewhere on its banks, was sometimes spelled Aurelana
(Thevet, *Newfounde Worlde,* fol. 99v). Both in its spelling and its
sound, Aurelana would naturally suggest Raleana to someone like
Hall who enjoyed playing with words. Raleigh describes the islands
of the Orinoco thus: "The great riuer of *Orenoque* . . . hath nine
branches which fall out on the north side of his owne maine mouth:
on the south side it hath seuen other fallings into the sea, so it
desemboketh by 16. armes in al, betweene Ilands and broken ground,
but the Ilands are verie great, manie of them as bigge as the Isle of
Wight and bigger, and many lesse" (*Discouerie of Gviana*, p. 41).

107/29-30 Strabo . . . habitation] "The cities [of the Arcadians], which
in earlier times had become famous, were wiped out by the continuous wars, and the tillers of the soil have been disappearing even
since the times when most of the cities were united into what was
called the 'Megalopolis.' But now the Great City itself has suffered
the fate described by the comic poet: 'The Great City is a great
desert'" (Strab., 8, 8, 1).

108/15m His . . . Lucian] *Dial. D.*, 11, 2. Apollo says this and wonders if
Mercury could "have been practising stealing in his mother's womb,"
since he is so sticky fingered.

108/18 Hercynia . . . Germany] "The breadth of this Hercynian forest
. . . is as much as a nine days' journey for an unencumbered person;
for in no other fashion can it be determined, nor have they means to
measure journeys. . . . By reason of its size [it] touches the borders of
many nations. There is no man in Germany we know who can say
that he had reached the edge of that forest, though he may have gone
forward a sixty days' journey, or who has learnt in what place it
begins" (Caes., *BGall.*, 6, 25).

109/19m Caesar] *BGall.*, 6, 23: "Acts of brigandage committed outside
the borders of each several state involve no disgrace; in fact, [the
Germans] affirm that such are committed in order to practise the
young men and to diminish sloth."

109/20-21 principles . . . Hermetic] "Pertaining to Hermes Trismegis-
tus, and the philosophical, theosophical, and other writings ascribed
to him. Hence, relating to or dealing with occult science, especially
alchemy" (*OED*, s.v. "hermetic").

110/26m Pope . . . Moresinus] *Papatus*, p. 24. The prayer used by the
pope to bless banners is given above in the note to 103/1. Moresinus
says nothing about naming them. Brown speculates that Hall does
not really mean a banner but rather means medals "bearing the
image of the Saviour on one side and of the Virgin and Child on the
other, worn by the loyal Catholics in the Netherlands as a counter-
charm to other medals worn by the Protestant 'Beggars,' which were
stamped on one side with the image of Philip II and on the other
with two clasped hands." However, since Margaret of Parma had
Pope Pius bless these medals in 1567, it is just as possible that he
also blessed the Catholic forces' ensign. According to Brown, naming the banner "Margaret" would serve as a "prognostic of the vic-
tory of the Church over the heretics, after St. Margaret of Antioch,
who, according to the legend, met and overcame the devil" (*Discovery*, p. 192).

110/28-29 I . . . rest] John Cullum, in his *History and Antiquities of
Hawstead* (p. 161), describes the painting of "a bird of prey, in the
air, devouring a small bird," with the legend *Fruor nec quiesco*
underneath. This painting, like the one described in the note to
96/16, was in one of Sir Robert Drury's galleries; Hall was the chaplain to Lady Drury there from 1601 to 1608.

111/4m Egyptian . . . Heliodorus] "This spot is as it were the republic of
all the brigands of Egypt. Some dwell in huts which they have built
upon rising ground above the level of the water, while others live in
boats. . . . The water serves them as a wall, and the reeds, which grow

in abundance, as a palisade. Amongst these reeds they have cut several winding and tortuous paths, easy for themselves to find who know them, but which are difficult of access to others and form a strong defense against invasion" (*Aethiopica*, 1, 1, 5-6).

111/12-13 Crocodilian . . . rower] Probably taken from Peter Martyr, *De Orbe Novo*: "Men and women swim with as great facility as though they lived in that element and found their sustenance under the waves" (1, 315); "When the surviving horsemen strove to attack them, the first barbarians encountered threw themselves quickly into the water,—for, like crocodiles or seals, they swim as easily as they walk on land" (2, 142).

111/15-16 sticking . . . remora] A widespread belief: "With evil purpose it meets a vessel running at full speed before the wind, and fastening its teeth into the front of the prow, like a man vigorously curbing with bit and tightened rein an intractable and savage horse, it checks the vessel's onrush and holds it fast. In vain do the sails belly in the middle, to no purpose do the winds blow" (Ael., *NA*, 2, 17).

112/5 sons of Boreas] Calais and Zetes, represented with wings. They delivered their brother-in-law Phineas from the continual persecution of the Harpies, who had been sent by Jupiter to hound Phineas and spoil the meat served him—his punishment for unjustly blinding his children. Calais and Zetes drove the Harpies as far as the Strophades Islands, where Iris stopped them by promising that Phineas should be tormented by the Harpies no longer (Ap. Rhod., *Argon.*, 2, 240 ff.).

112/9-10 Aristotle . . . Isle] "They say that in the island of Diomedeia in the Adriatic there is a remarkable and hallowed shrine of Diomedes, and that birds of vast size sit around this shrine in a circle, having large hard beaks. They say moreover that if ever Greeks disembark in the spot [these birds] keep quiet, but if any of the barbarians that live round land, they rise and wheeling round attack their heads, and wounding them with their bills kill them" (*Mir. Ausc.*, 836a).

112/9m dog . . . epitaph] Schrader, *Monumenta Italiae*, fol. 76v.

112/27 historians . . . Herodotus] I am uncertain what Hall's exact criticism is, but he seems to be claiming that the ancient writers are often forgotten and that newer authors are therefore successful in passing off what they have read in earlier writers as their own. Or he may be criticizing Pliny and Herodotus for their gullibility in accepting patent falsehoods as truth.

112/28 Mercurius Gallo-Belgicus] *Mercurius Gallo-Belgicus* was a "book

written in Latin and published half-yearly, first at Cologne and
later at Frankfurt [by] . . . a Dutch priest who signed his name 'M.
Jansen of Doccum in Friesland.' This 'periodical' book purported
to give news of what had happened in most of the countries of
Europe during the period 1588 to March 1594. It was known in
England, but . . . not much esteemed for its accuracy" (Berry and
Poole, *Annals of Printing*, p. 112). Donne's epigram "Mercurius
Gallo-Belgicus" accuses the author of overstatement, a charge that
fits with what Hall says here:

> . . . I confesse
> I should have had more faith, if thou hadst lesse;
> Thy credit lost thy credit: 'Tis sinne to doe,
> In this case, as thou wouldst be done unto.
> To beleeve all: Change thy name: thou art like
> *Mercury* in stealing, but lyest like a *Greeke*.
> (*Satires, Epigrams*, p. 53)

112/29 Cardinal . . . historian] Caesare Cardinal Baronio (1538–1607),
who wrote *Annales Ecclesiastici* (12 vols., 1597–1608), covering the
history of the Catholic church from the birth of Christ to 1574. Hall's
unflattering view of this work's truthfulness stems in part, no doubt,
from Baronio's vigorous denial of Pope Joan. See note to 105/28m
for Hall's beliefs concerning this female pope and the anonymous
work entitled *A Dialogue betweene a Protestant and a papist. Mani-
festly proving that a woman called Joan was pope of Rome; against
the surmises and objections made to the contrarie, by Robert Bellarmine and Ceasar* [sic] *Baronius Cardinals* (London, 1610).

113/10 Golden Prince] Compare Chrysius Deus, 117/7–8 below.

113/10 Furtofrancheça] Besides Hall's derivation in the Index of Proper
Names, Furtofrancheça is meant to suggest the German city of
Frankfort, at this period the foremost trading city of Swabia.

113/19 Palatium] From the Latin *palatum*, "palate," and also with
oblique reference to the *Palatium*, the Palatine of Rome where the
imperial buildings were.

113/20 Fripperia] Though glossed in the Index as "a certain section in
Paris," Hall is actually borrowing Stow's name "Fripparia" for the
Cornhill ward of London where cheap cloth, secondhand goods,
and lost articles are for sale (*Survay of London*, p. 219); from "frip-
pery," "tawdry finery," or "a place where cast-off clothes are sold"
(*OED*).

113/23m Plautus] *Poen.*, lines 586-87: "The very framers of lawsuits are no more learned in matters of the maw than these chaps. If they have no litigation on hand, they buy some."

113/26-27 seems . . . Lynceus-like] Lynceus, one of the Argonauts, famed for the sharpness of his sight: "If the report is true, that . . . hero could easily direct his sight even beneath the earth" (Ap. Rhod., *Argon.*, 1, 151-53). Hall mentions his keen sight in *Vd.*, 4, 1, 25.

113/28-31 For . . . poor] Hall says this more strongly in *Vd.*, 2, 3, 15-18:

> Wo to the weale where manie Lawiers bee,
> For there is sure much store of maladie.
> T'was truely said, and truely was forseene,
> The fat kine are deuoured of the leane.

113/34-35 clothes . . . two-toned] In *Vd.*, 2, 3, 30-32, Hall claims essentially the same thing—that lawyers are willing to take either side in a dispute. But there he asserts that which side they take is determined by who can afford to pay the most:

> But still the *Lawiers* eye squints on his fist:
> If that seeme lined with a larger fee,
> Doubt not the suite, the lawe is plaine for thee.

114/6 Argyranchen] From the Greek ἄργυρος, "silver," and ἄγχειν, "to choke." Hall's note gives the Latin equivalent as *argentangina*, from *argentum*, "silver," "money," and *angina*, "choking." The disease, as Hall's reference to Demosthenes makes clear, is one contracted from being bribed. Demosthenes, who at first spoke out against accepting Harpalus, Alexander's treasurer who had fled from Asia to Athens, suddenly lost his voice the day after receiving from him a gold cup filled with 20 talents (Plut., *Dem.*, 25). In English the disease is known as "silver quinsy," "quinsy" being an inflammation of the throat.

114/15m Claves . . . *Chrysopoeia*] According to Gaston Claves, in *Apologia Chrysopoeiae et Argypoeiae*, "Chrysopoeia is the art which teaches how to transmute by natural means matter resembling gold . . . into [true] gold" (p. 9). He claims that "the matter which can produce silver and gold as easily as possible will be the very matter approximating gold and silver in its accidental properties," properties that "we can observe with our eyes" (p. 18). But the context in Hall demonstrates that the merchants of Fripperia use the very similarity in accidental properties Claves speaks of to palm off on their buyers gold plate for solid gold.

114/17-19 offers . . . ones] Paracelsus gives instructions for making pearls "that for splendor, and beauty they can hardly be discerned from the true":

> Cleanse the white of Eggs through a spunge, as purely as may bee, then mingle with it the fairest white Talke, or Mother of Pearle, or Mercury coagulated with Tinne, and brought into an Alcool, then grinde them all together on a Marble, so that they become a thick Amalgama, which must be dryed in the Sunne, or behind a furnace so long, untill it be like Cheese, or a Liver. Then of this masse make Pearles as big as thou wilt, which hang upon the bristles of a hog, and being thus boared through, dry them as Amber, and then thou hast finished them. (*De Natura Rerum*, p. 76; tr. fol. 54r-54v)

114/20 Pliny] "[Pearls'] whole value lie in their brilliance, size, roundness, smoothness, and weight, qualities of such rarity that no two pearls are found that are exactly alike" (*HN*, 9, 56).

114/31-33 merchant . . . sense] Even in 1648 in *Resolutions and Decisions of Certain Cases of Profit and Traffic*, Hall is still thinking of the *Mundus* when he writes: "But if the seller shall use art to cover the defects of his commodity, . . . or shall mix faulty wares with sound, that they may pass undiscovered, he is more faulty than his wares, and makes an ill bargain for his soul" (*Works*, 7, 278).

115/2 art . . . Spagyric] "Adaptation of early modern Latin *spagiricus* (used, and probably invented by Paracelsus) . . . pertaining to alchemy" (*OED*). Hall's remark about spagyric being too praiseworthy a name for such a dishonest art might refer to the similarity between the root in the Latin *spargere*, "to sprinkle," in an extended meaning "to bless," and *spargyric*, an alternative spelling for *spagyric*. The *OED* gives no origin for the word, and I offer this without being convinced that this is an adequate explanation of Hall's reference.

115/6 Cyllenius] Another name for Mercury, from Cyllene, a mountain in Arcadia where Mercury was born and raised.

115/9-10 having . . . womb] Lucian, *Dial. D.*, 11, 1-3. The thefts Hall mentions are all included in this particular dialogue, except that Lucian claims Mercury was unsuccessful in stealing Zeus's lightning since it was "too heavy and scorching hot." He also mentions Mercury's "glib and fluent tongue," to which Hall alludes several lines later.

115/16 secrets . . . Cabalists] "One skilled in mystic arts or learning" (*OED*).

115/21-23 besieged . . . again] "Selling for a trifling sum, some their whole property, others their most valuable treasures, [the Jews] would swallow the gold coins to prevent discovery by the brigands, and then, escaping to the Romans, on discharging their bowels, have ample supplies for their needs" (Joseph., *BJ*, 5, 10, 1). Hall mentions this custom again in his *Epistles* (*Works*, 6, 266): "The very basest element yields gold: the savage Indian gets it; the servile prentice works it; the very Midianitish camel may wear it; . . . the covetous Jew swallows it; . . . what are all these the better for it?"

115/26 Plagiana] "Hall's views on literary imitation and plagiarism are well discussed by H. O. White in his *Plagiarism and Imitation in the English Renaissance* (1935). He notes that Hall was apparently the first to anglicize Martial's figurative use of *plagiarius* (man-stealer) for a literary thief, and that 'plagiary' or 'plagiarism' is recorded only three times before 1625. . . . Yet Hall himself imitates Juvenal in *Virgidemiae*, Seneca in the *Epistles*, and Theophrastus in the *Characters*." In Hall's estimation, however, "an imitator is not a plagiarist so long as he treads in the paths of others 'with an higher and wider step,' but he becomes a plagiarist when he servilely copies 'whole pages at a clap'" (Davenport, *Poems*, pp. 259-60).

115/28 Rigattiera] From the Italian *rigattiere*, "a dealer in secondhand goods."

115/29m Scapula] Johann Scapula, an assistant of Henricus Stephanus (Henri Estienne), published an abridgment of his *Thesaurus Graeca Lingua*, entitled *Lexicon Graecolatinum Novum* in 1579. Its popularity pushed aside Stephanus's larger volume and led to his eventual poverty. Hall provides only part of the boast that begins Scapula's dictionary (*Lexicon*, sig. ¶1v):

> Momus says no lexicon may be called new
> I contend this lexicon *is* new
> But to be new is nothing, it is said, unless it is useful:
> This newness is not without its usefulness.

115/33m Homer . . . Gentes] "The poet Homer, by resorting to poetic license and by emulating Orpheus' original belief in polytheism, makes mention of several gods in a mythical way, lest his poetry should appear to differ from that of Orpheus, which he was so intent on imitating that in the very first verse of his Iliad he expressed his partiality toward him. As Orpheus had exclaimed at the beginning of his poem [*Fragments*, in *Argonautica*, p. 383]: 'O goddess, sing the wrath of Demeter, the bearer of fruit,' Homer began his *Iliad* thus: 'O goddess, sing the wrath of Achilles, the son of Peleus.' It appears to me that Homer here preferred to violate the poetic metre rather than be accused of having omitted from the start the names of the gods" (Justin Martyr, *Cohortatio ad Graecos*, chap. 17).

116/2 For . . . woman] This line is identified by Dirk Canter [Theodorus Canterus] (*Variae Lectiones*, 2, 3) as being from Orpheus. He claims that "Homer himself was not . . . entirely free from the blemish [of borrowing], and even pilfered much from Orpheus, Musaeus, and others who came before him" (p. 740). In his marginal note to this line, Hall provides a line from Homer (*Od.*, 11, 427), which is essentially identical to that of Orpheus. Yet he defends Homer from Canter's charge, claiming that Homer imitates rather than steals. Hall sees a vast difference between the two and addresses this matter several times. (See note to 115/26). In the preface to his *Characters* he defends the worthiness of imitation by saying "As one therefore, that, in worthy examples, holds imitation better than invention, I have trod in their paths, but with an higher and wider step; and out of their tablets have drawn these larger portraitures of both sorts" (*Works*, 6, 90). The distinction, then, is between servile borrowing and imaginative imitation.

116/4-5 One . . . Musaeus] Hall (or his printer) mistakenly prints Homer's line from the *Iliad* (6, 149) and identifies it as Musaeus's. Canter gives the line from Musaeus as: Ὡς δὲ καὶ ἀνθρώ του γευεὴ καὶ φύλλον ἐλίοτει, "The generations of men spring up in turn, even as the foliage."

116/6-7 And . . . place] Hall identifies them as coming from the *Iliad*; Canter further specifies that they come from Menelaus's slaying of Euphorbus (*Variae Lectiones*, 17, 53-54). Homer's lines at this point are identical to those Canter gives from Orpheus.

116/10 pages . . . Petrarch] In *Vd.*, 6, 1, 251-52, Hall accuses the English of stealing from "honest" Petrarch:

> Or filch whole Pages at a clap for need
> From honest *Petrarch*, clad in English weed;

116/11 Tuscan poet] The poet is Dante, echoes of whose *Divine Comedy* appear throughout Petrarch's *Canzoniere*. See Nolhac, *Pétrarque et l'humanisme*, 2, 235-37, and Marco Santagata, "Presenze di Dante 'Comico' nel 'Canzoniere' del Petrarca," *Giornale storico della letteratura italiana*, 146 (1969), 163-211.

116/23 Codicia] From the Latin *codex, codicis*, "account book."

116/23 Münster] Hall has apparently written this reference from faulty memory, for not only does Münster report men with dog's heads instead of hog's heads, but he also specifies that they are a completely different race from those who walk on all fours: "Cinomolgi or Cynocephali, which have the head and ears of a dog, readily disclose by their barking that they are more beasts than men. Then there are said to be other creatures called Artapathitae, who go on their hands and feet like quadrupeds" (*Cosmographia*, p. 1319).

116/24 Mandeville] See note to 86/35-87/1 above. Mandeville describes dog-headed people on p. 206 of his *Travels* (Cf. Ael., *NA*, 4, 46).

117/3-4 dine . . . fox] "The wolf is peculiar in that it sometimes eats dirt when it is starving, according to Aristotle, Pliny, and Solinus. Albertus Magnus writes that the wolf does this not for the sake of nourishment but so that in this way—with its weight increased—it may more easily overwhelm whatever animal it attacks" (Gesner, *Historia*, 1, 720).

117/5-6 almost . . . lion] Gesner says that the lion sleeps "with his eyes open because of the smallness of his upper eyelid" (*Historia*, 1, 646).

117/7-8 Chrysius Deus] From the Latin *chryseus*, "golden," and *deus*, "god," with the comparable Greek words provided by Hall in the margin.

117/10 *cloacal*] "Cloacal," which means "pertaining to the sewers," appears in a fragment of Cato's surviving in Festus, a fourth-century Roman grammarian (*Scriptorum Romanorum quae Extant Omnia*, p. 123, no. 10).

117/16 30 years] As Salyer ("Joseph Hall," p. 265) points out, Hall, who was born 1 July 1574, would have been 30 years old from 1 July 1604 to 30 June 1605. Since the *Mundus* was entered in the *Stationers' Register* 2 June 1605, this statement strongly suggests that work on it stopped at some time between July 1604 and June 1605.

118/2-3 Actaeonius . . . dogs] Ov., *Met.*, 3, 229 ff. Palaephatus, *De Incredibilibus*, also asserts that "Actaeon was not literally devoured by his hounds but was eaten up by the cost of his extravagant hunting" (Allen, *Mysteriously Meant*, pp. 58-59).

118/4 Amazonia . . . American] The American region Hall refers to is
the Amazon River in Brazil, named by Francisco Orellana, the first
man to descend from the Andes to the sea, who in his trip of 1541
battled a tribe of Tapuya savages where the women fought along-
side the men. Hall's remark that Amazonia, once located in the
Americas, has now become British [literally "ours"], "thanks to the
manly spirit of our inhabitants," sarcastically refers to the "manishness and monstrous disguisedness" of British women that he complains of in his sermon "The Impress of God" (*Works*, 5, 76).

118/7 Virgil] *Ecl.*, 2, 68.

118/11–12 Amantina . . . Danube] See note to 61/26 above.

118/18 Assagion] From the Italian *assaggio*, "taste."

118/19 Auffzeichner] Cf. the "masters of the wine" in Ath., 10, 425.

118/21 Beachera] In addition to Hall's derivation, the name may refer to
the German town Bacchara, "a place as famous in Germanie for her
generose wines [as] . . . Falernus in Campania. . . . It seemeth by the
name to be a towne of great antiquity. . . . For some make the ety-
mologie of the name to be *quasi Bacchi ara*, the Altar of *Bacchus*.
Because that drunken God *Bacchus* had Altars erected vnto him in
this place in time of the Pagan idolatrie. Others deriue it from *Bacchus* only, which by a Rhetorical figure called *metonomyia* doth
signifie wine" (*Coryats Crudities*, p. 574).

119/2–3 *Sacrarum Caeremoniarum*] Fol. 20v.

119/7 Baveria] From the French *baver*, "to talk drivel"; also suggestive
of the German province of Bavaria.

119/9 בֵּח לָהֶם] See note to 34/14 above.

119/12 Bolsec] Jerome-Hermes Bolsec (died c. 1584), a French theolo-
gian (at first a Carmelite monk and later a Protestant reformer) who
was disliked by Calvin. Bolsec eventually reconverted to Catholicism
and published unflattering biographies of Calvin and Beza, which
earned for him a reputation for treachery and lying among the
Protestants (*Cath. E.*, 2, 643).

119/17 liar . . . memory] Quint., *Inst.*, 4, 2, 91; Eras., *Adagia*, 2, 514; tr.
fols. 33v–34r.

120/1 Horace] *Sat.*, 1, 2, 98.

120/14 Cuillera] Hall's derivation is incomplete. He spells it two ways:
here Cuillera, which suggests, instead of the word he gives, the
much closer French word *cuiller*, which also means "spoon"; and
on p. 23 Culliera, suggesting the Latin *cullearis*, "a measure of a
culleus, or 20 *amphorae*."

120/22 Di-Marza] Despite Hall's statement, the word is not Italian (or French, Portuguese, or Spanish). Possibly he synthesizes Di-Marza from the Greek Δί, a shortened dative form meaning "to the god," and Mars, the god of war, adding the suffix *a* to make the word seem Italian. As a source of blood rather than water, it would be appropriate for such a stream to be named for Mars.

120/28 Pliny] The correct reference is *HN*, 15, 19.

121/5 Fouetta] The word is not French; what Hall means is that he has invented a Latin word from the French *fouetter*, "to whip," (Brown, *Discovery*, p. 222).

121/10 Furtofrancheça] See note to 113/10.

121/26 Hierosule] Jerusalem, whose Latin form is *Hierusalem*.

122/32 Menturnea] "The city of Minturnae was actually not within the traditional boundaries of Samnium, but in southern Latium on the coast, at the intersection of the Liris (modern Garigliano) River and the Appian Way" (Brown, *Discovery*, p. 202).

122/36 Stephanus] Stephanus of Byzantium (*Ethnica*, p. 396) gives several names that Cyprus was called in earlier times, including Μηιο-νίς, the apparent source for Hall.

123/1 Milana] Note the similarity to the Italian city of Milan.

123/16-17 grape . . . Virgil] *Ecl.*, 2.70.

123/30 Plautus] *Aul.*, 3, 2, 32.

124/31 adding an a] The Latin incorrectly reads: "removing both e's."

124/35 Seplasium] Hall "seems to have in mind Livy's account of how the luxuries of Capua undermined the discipline of the Carthaginian soldiers in the winter of B.C. 340 (*History*, 7, 38). Livy makes no mention of the Seplasia, but it is frequently referred to by Cicero and Pliny the Elder" (Brown, *Discovery*, p. 204).

125/6 Spagyric] See note to 115/2.

125/7-8 Strophades . . . Plotoe] The Plotoe are two islands lying off the coast of Messina, celebrated as the famous residence of the Harpies. See also note to 112/5 above.

125/13 Topia-Warallador] Sir Walter Raleigh, who discovered Guiana and had friendly dealings with the king, Topia-Wari, bringing his only son back to England (*Discoverie of Gviana*, pp. 70, 74–81). See also note to 96/12–13.

125/23 Vale-dolium] There is no such Spanish word; the name is actually a play on the Latin words *vale*, "good-bye," and *dolor*, "pain."

BIBLIOGRAPHY AND SHORT TITLES

Ael., *NA*. Aelian. *On the Characteristics of Animals*, tr. A. F. Scholfield, 3 vols. London, 1958–59.

Agricola, Georg. *De Animatibus Subterraneis*. Basel, 1556.

Albertus Magnus. *Opera Omnia*, ed. Auguste Borgnet, 38 vols. Paris, 1890–99.

Alden, Raymond MacDonald. *The Rise of Formal Satire in England under Classical Influence*. Philadelphia, 1899.

Allen, Don Cameron. *Mysteriously Meant: The Rediscovery of Pagan Symbolism and Allegorical Interpretation in the Renaissance*. Baltimore, 1970.

Alumni Cantabrigienses . . . to 1900, comp. John Venn and J. A. Venn, 10 vols. Cambridge, 1922–54.

Alumni Oxonienses, The Members of the University of Oxford, 1500–1714, comp. Joseph Forster, 4 vols. [early series]. Oxford, 1891.

Anderson. H. J. Anderson, ed. *Mundus Alter et Idem*. London, 1908.

Anthon. Charles Anthon. *A Classical Dictionary*. New York, 1848.

Ap. Rhod., *Argon*. Apollonius Rhodius. *Argonautica*, tr. R. C. Seaton. London, 1921.

Apul., *Flor*. Apuleius. *The Apologia and Florida of Apuleius of Madaura*, tr. H. E. Butler. Oxford, 1909; rpt. Westport, Conn., 1970.

————., *Met*. *Metamorphoses, or The Golden Ass*, tr. W. Adlington (1566), rev. S. Gaselee. London, 1965.

Ar. *Aristophanes*, tr. Benjamin Bickley Rogers, 3 vols. London, 1924. Individual works:

    Av.: *The Birds*, vol. 2.

    Eccl.: *The Ecclesiazusae*, vol. 3.

Arabian Nights: The Book of the Thousand Nights and a Night, tr. Richard F. Burton, 17 vols. N.p., n.d.

Arber, Edward, ed. *A Transcript of the Registers of the Company of Stationers of London, 1554–1640 A.D.,* 3 vols. London, 1875–77.

Arist., *Eth. Eud.* Aristotle. *The Eudemian Ethics,* tr. H. Rackham. London, 1935.

————., *Eth. Nic. The Nichomachean Ethics,* tr. H. Rackham. London, 1956.

————., *Gen. Corr. De Generatione et Corruptione,* tr. D. J. Finley. London, 1955.

————., *HA. Historia Animalium,* tr. A. L. Peck, 3 vols. London, 1970.

————., *Long. Brev. Vitae. De Longitude et Brevitate Vitae,* in *On the Soul, Parva Naturalia, On Breath,* tr. W. S. Hett. London, 1964.

————., *Mete. Meteorologica,* tr. H. D. P. Lee. London, 1952.

————., *Mir. Ausc. On Marvellous Things Heard,* in *Minor Works,* tr. W. S. Hett. London, 1934.

————., *Pol. Politics,* tr. H. Rackham. London, 1959.

Ath. Athenaeus. *Deipnosophistae,* tr. Charles Burton Gulick, 7 vols. London, 1941.

August., *De Civ. D.* Augustine. *The City of God,* tr. George E. McCracken, 7 vols. London, 1966.

————., *De Haer. De Haeribus,* tr. Liguori G. Müller. Washington, 1956.

Barreiros, *Commentarius de Ophyra.* Gaspar Barreiros. *Commentarius de Ophyra Regione apud Divinam Scripturam Commemorata,* in *Chorographia de Algvns Lugares que stam en hum caminho.* Coimbra, Portugal, 1561.

Bellarmine, Robert. *De Monachis,* in *Opera Omnia,* vol. 2. Naples, 1856–62.

Bensly, E. "A Note on Bishop Hall's Satires." *Modern Language Review,* 3 (1907), 169–70.

Berry and Poole, *Annals of Printing.* W. Turner Berry and A. Edmund Poole. *Annals of Printing.* London, 1966.

Biographie Universelle, ed. J. F. Michaud and L. G. Michaud, 85 vols. Paris, 1811–62.

Biondo, Flavio. *De Roma Triumphante.* Basel, 1531.

Blacker, Irwin R., ed. *Hakluyt's Voyages.* New York, 1965.

Boccaccio, Giovanni. *Genealogia Deorum Gentilium Libri,* ed. V. Romano, 2 vols. Bari, 1951.

Bright, Timothy. *A Treatise of Melancholie*. London, 1586.

Brown, *Discovery*. Huntington Brown, ed. *The Discovery of a New World*, tr. John Healey. Cambridge, Mass., 1937.

Burton, Robert. *Anatomy of Melancholy*, 3 vols. London, 1932.

Bush, Douglas. *English Literature in the Earlier Seventeenth Century, 1600–1660*, 2nd ed. Oxford, 1966.

Caes., *BGall.* Julius Caesar. *The Gallic War*, tr. H. J. Edwards. London, 1937.

Camden. William Camden. *Britannia*. London, 1590.

_____. *Britain*, tr. Philemon Holland. London, 1610.

Canter, Dirk. *Variae Lectiones*, in Janus Gruterus, ed., *Lampas, sive Fax Artium Liberalium, hoc est, Thesaurus Criticus*, vol. 3. Frankfort, 1604.

Catalogus Universalis. Catalogus Universalis pro Nundinis Francofurtensibus. Frankfort, 1606–07.

Cath. E. The Catholic Encyclopedia, 16 vols. New York, 1907–11.

Cato, Marcus Porcius. *Scriptorum Romanorum quae Extant Omnia*. Venice, 1964.

Celsus, *Med. De Medicina*, tr. W. G. Spenser, 3 vols. London, 1935–38.

Chambers, R. W. *Thomas More*. London, 1935.

Cic., *Fam.* Cicero. *The Letters to His Friends*, tr. W. Glynn Williams, 3 vols. London, 1943.

Claves, Gaston. *Apologia Chrysopoeiae et Argypoeiae*, in Lazarus Zetner, ed., *Theatrum Chemicum*, 2, 6–80. Strasbourg, 1659–61.

Clement of Alexandria. *Stomateis*, ed. John Potter; in *PG*, 9, cols. 9–603; tr. and ed. J. A. Hort and J. B. Mayor. London, 1902.

Coccaio, Merlino [pseud. for Girolamo Folengo]. *Macaronicon*, in *Opvs Merlini Cocaii, Poetae Mantuani Macaronicorum*. Toscolano, 1521.

Colie, Rosalie. *Paradoxia Epidemica: The Renaissance Tradition of Paradox*. Princeton, 1966.

Columella, L. Junius. *On Agriculture*, tr. Harrison Boyd Ash, 3 vols. London, 1941–54.

Commentarius de Ophyra. See under Barreiros.

Corthell, Ronald James. "The Early Literary Career of Joseph Hall." Diss., Cornell University, 1976.

Coryat, Thomas. *Coryats Crudities*. London, 1611; rpt. London, 1978.

Cullum, John. *The History and Antiquities of Hawstead and Hardwick*, 2nd ed. London, 1813.

Davenport. Arnold Davenport. "Interfused Sources in Joseph Hall's

Satires." *Review of English Studies*, 18 (1942), 208-13.

————. Arnold Davenport, ed. *Poems of Joseph Hall.* Liverpool, 1949; rpt. Liverpool, 1969.

Dictionarium Theophrasti Paracelsi, ed. Gerhard Dorn. Frankfort, 1584.

Diod. Sic. *Diodorus of Sicily,* tr. C. H. Oldfather, 12 vols. London, 1933-67.

Diog. Laert. Diogenes Laertius. *Lives of Eminent Philosophers,* tr. R. D. Hicks, rev. ed., 2 vols. London, 1958-59.

Discovery. The Discovery of a New World, ed. Huntington Brown, tr. John Healey. Cambridge, Mass., 1937.

DNB. Dictionary of National Biography, ed. Leslie Stephen and Sidney Lee, 66 vols. London, 1885-1901.

Donne, John. *Donne's Poetical Works,* ed. Herbert Grierson, 2 vols. Oxford, 1913.

————. *The Satires, Epigrams, and Verse Letters,* ed. W. Milgate. Oxford, 1967.

Dorsch, T. S. "Sir Thomas More and Lucian: An Interpretation of *Utopia.*" *Archiv für das Studium der neueren Sprachen und Literaturen,* 203 (1966), 345-63.

Duhamel, P. Albert. "Medievalism of More's *Utopia.*" *Studies in Philology,* 52 (1955), 99-126; rpt. in *Essential Articles for the Study of Thomas More,* ed. R. S. Sylvester and G. Marc'hadour. Hamden, Conn., 1977, 234-50.

Duncan, Douglas. *Ben Jonson and the Lucianic Tradition.* Cambridge, 1979.

EB. Encyclopedia Britannica, 11th ed., 29 vols. Cambridge, 1910.

Elliott, Robert C. *The Power of Satire.* Princeton, 1966.

————. *The Shape of Utopia.* Chicago, 1970.

Eras., *Adagia.* Desiderius Erasmus. *Adagia,* vol. 2 in *Opera Omnia,* ed. John Cleric, 10 vols. Leyden, 1703-06; rpt. Hildesheim, 1961-62; tr. Richard Taverner as *Proverbs or Adagies, gathered out of the Chiliades of Erasmus,* London, 1569.

————. *Colloquia,* vol. 1 in *Opera Omnia;* tr. Craig R. Thompson as *The Colloquies of Erasmus.* Chicago, 1965.

————. *The Correspondence of Erasmus,* tr. R. A. B. Mynors and D. F. S. Thomson, vols. 1-. Toronto, 1974-.

————. *Moria. Moriae Encomium,* vol. 4 in *Opera Omnia;* tr. Clarence H. Miller as *The Praise of Folly.* New Haven, 1979.

Eusebius, *Hist. Eccl. The Ecclesiastical History,* tr. Kirsopp Lake and J. E. L. Oulton, 2 vols. London, 1926-32.

Fendt, Tobias. *Monumenta Sepulchrorum, cum Epigraphis Ingenio et Doctrina Excellentium Virorum.* Breslau, 1574.

Florio, John. *His firste Fruites.* London [1578].

_____. *Florios Second Frutes.* London, 1591.

Frye, Northrop. *Anatomy of Criticism.* Princeton, 1957.

_____. "Varieties of Literary Utopias," in *Utopias and Utopian Thought,* ed. Frank E. Manuel. Boston, 1966.

Fuller, Thomas. *The History of the Worthies of England.* London, 1662.

Galen, *De Simplicium Medicamentorum Facultatibus, Libri 2.* Vol. 5 in *Galeni Librorum Quinta Classis eam Medicinae Partem, quae ad Pharmaciam Spectat, Exponens,* 7 vols. Venice, 1625.

Garzoni, Tomaso. *Discourso,* in *Opere.* Venice, 1605.

_____, *Hospitall. Hospidale di pazzi incurabili;* tr. anon. as *The Hospitall of Incurable Fooles.* London, 1600.

Gell., *NA. The Attic Nights of Aulus Gellius,* tr. J. C. Rolfe, 3 vols. London, 1927-28.

Gesner, *Historia.* Conrad Gesner. *Historia Animalium,* 4 vols. Zurich, 1551-58.

Googe, Barnabe. *Eglogs, epytaphes, and sonettes* (1563), ed. Edward Arber. London, 1871; rpt. New York, 1966.

Grynaeus, *Novus Orbis.* Simon Grynaeus, ed. *Novus Orbis Regionum ac Insularum Veteribus Incognitarum.* Basel, 1537.

Hakluyt, *Principal Navigations.* Richard Hakluyt. *The Principal Navigations, Voyages, Traffiques & Discoveries of the English Nation,* 10 vols. London, 1927-28.

Hall, Joseph. *The Discovery of a New World,* tr. John Healey. London [1609].

_____. *The Discovery of a New World,* tr. John Healey, 2nd ed. London [c. 1613-14].

_____. *The Discovery of a New World,* tr. John Healey, ed. Huntington Brown. See Brown, *Discovery.*

_____(?). *A Modest Confutation.* London, 1642.

_____, *Mundus. Mundus Alter et Idem.* Frankfort, n.d. [London, 1605]; 2nd ed. Hanau, 1607.

_____, *Poems. The Poems of Joseph Hall,* ed. Arnold Davenport. Liverpool, 1949; rpt. Liverpool, 1969.

_____, *Works. The Works of the Right Reverend Joseph Hall, D.D.,* ed. Philip Wynter, 10 vols. Oxford, 1863.

_____, *Vd. Virgidemiae;* in *Poems.*

Harrison, William. See Holinshed, *Chronicles.*

Hastings, *Dict. Bib.* James Hastings, ed. *A Dictionary of the Bible,* 5 vols. New York, 1898-1904.

Healey, John, tr. See Hall, *The Discovery of a New World.*

Heiserman, A. R. "Satire in the *Utopia.*" *Publications of the Modern Language Society of America,* 78 (1963), 163-74.

Heliodorus. *Aethiopica,* anon. tr. Athens, 1897.

Henderson, Alfred, comp. *Latin Proverbs.* London, 1869.

————. *Scottish Proverbs.* Glasgow, 1881.

Herberstein, Sigismund, Baron von. *Rerum Muscoviticarum Commentarii,* tr. and ed. R. H. Major. London, 1851-52; rpt. New York, 1963.

Herod. *Herodotus,* tr. A. D. Godley, 4 vols. London, 1921.

Hes., *Op.* Hesiod. *Opera et Dies; Works and Days,* tr. Hugh G. Evelyn-White. London, 1920.

Heuterus, Pontus. *Opera Historica Omnia: Burgundica, Avstriaca, Belgica.* Louvain, 1643.

Holinshed, Raphael. *Chronicles, first collected by Raphael Holinshed,* augmented by John Hooker [*alias* Vowell] et al., 3 vols. London, 1586-87.

Individual works:

Description of Britaine, William Harrison, vol. 1.

Description of England, William Harrison, vol. 1 (follows and completes Harrison's *Description of Britaine;* the two works are numbered consecutively).

Description of Scotland, Hector Boethius, tr. William Harrison, vol. 2.

Hom., *Il.* Homer. *Iliad,* tr. A. T. Murray, 2 vols. London, 1965.

————., *Od.* Homer. *Odyssey,* tr. A. T. Murray, 2 vols. London, 1930.

Hor., *Carm.* Horace. *Odes,* tr. C. E. Bennett. London, 1968.

————., *Epist.* Horace. *Epistles,* tr. H. Rushton Fairclough. London, 1929.

————., *Sat.* Horace. *Satires,* tr. H. Rushton Fairclough. London, 1929.

Hrabanus Maurus. *Commentaria in Libros II Paralipomenon,* ed. Georgius Colvenerius; in *PL,* 109, cols. 279-539.

————. *De Clericorum Institutione,* ed. Georgius Colvenerius; in *PL,* 107, cols. 293-419.

Hugh of St. Victor. *De Sacramentis,* ed. The Regular Canons, St. Victor, Paris; in *PL,* 176, cols. 183-618.

Huntley, Frank Livingstone. *Bishop Joseph Hall.* Cambridge, 1979.

Irenaeus, *Contra Haer. Contra Haeribus,* ed. R. Massuet; in *PG,* 7, cols. 433-1225.

Johnson, Robbin S. *More's Utopia: Ideal and Illusion.* New Haven, 1969.

Johnson, William. *Lexicon Chemicum, cum Obscuriorum Verborum, et Rerum Hermeticarum, cum Phrasium Paracelsicarum.* London, 1657.

Jones, John. *Bishop Hall, His Life and Times.* London, 1826.

Joseph., *BJ.* Josephus. *The Jewish War,* tr. H. St. J. Thackeray, 3 vols. London, 1928.

———., *C. Ap.* Josephus. *Contra Apionem,* tr. H. St. J. Thackeray. London, 1926.

Juv. *Juvenal and Persius,* tr. G. G. Ramsay. London, 1928.

Lambarde, William. *A Perambulation of Kent.* London, 1576.

———. *A Perambulation of Kent . . . first published in the yeere 1576 and now increased and altered after the Authors owne last Copie.* London, 1596.

Lascassagne, Claude. "La satire religeuse dans *Mundus Alter et Idem* de Joseph Hall." *Recherches anglaises et nord-americaines,* 2 (1972), 141–56.

Lewis, C. S. *English Literature in the Sixteenth Century, Excluding Drama.* Oxford, 1954.

Lewis and Short. Charlton T. Lewis and Charles Short. *A Latin Dictionary.* Oxford, 1966.

Lewis. George Lewis. *A Life of Joseph Hall, Bishop of Exeter and Norwich.* London, 1886.

Libavius, Andreas. *De Judicio Aquarum Mineralium,* in *Commentationum Metallicarum Libri Quatuor de Natura Metallorum.* Frankfort, 1597.

———. *Alchemia.* Frankfort, 1592.

Liddell and Scott. Henry George Liddell and Robert Scott. *A Greek-English Lexicon,* rev. Sir Henry Stuart. Oxford, 1968.

Lipsius, Justus. *De Constantia.* Frankfort, 1590; tr. Sir John Stradling as *Two Bookes of Constancie,* ed. Rudolf Kirk. New Brunswick, N.J., 1939.

———. *Epistolarum Centuria Secunda.* London, 1590.

Lucian. *Lucian,* 8 vols.: vols. 1–5 tr. A. M. Harmon; vol. 6 tr. K. Kilburn; vols. 7–8 tr. M. D. MacLeod. London, 1913–69.
Individual works:
Alex.: Alexander, vol. 4.
Anach.: Anacharsis, vol. 1.
Charon: vol. 2.

Dial. D.: Dialogi Deorum, vol. 1.

Dial. Mort.: Dialogi Mortuorum, vol. 7.

Icaro.: Icaromenippus, vol. 2.

Menippus: vol. 4.

Octogenarians: vol. 1.

Philopseudes: vol. 3.

Timon: vol. 2.

Ver. Hist.: Verae Historiae, vol. 1.

Lucretius. *De Rerum Natura*, tr. W. H. D. Rouse. London, 1937.

Ludewig, J. P. von. *Universal Lexikon aller Wissenschaften und Künste*, 62 vols. Halle and Leipzig, 1732-54.

Ludovico de Varthema. *Novum Itinerarium Aethiopiae, Aegypti, utriusque Arabiae, Persidis, Syriae, ac Indiae*, in Grynaeus, *Novus Orbis*; tr. John Winter Jones as *The Travels of Ludovico di Varthema*, ed. George Percy Badger. London, 1863; rpt. New York, 1963.

Lyly, John. *Campaspe*. London, 1591.

Mandeville's Travels. The Voiage and Travaile of Sir John Maundeville, ed. J. O. Halliwell. London, 1839.

Manilius. *Astronomicon*, ed. A. E. Housman, 5 vols. Cambridge, 1937.

Mantuan. Baptista Mantuanus. *Eclogae*, in *Baptistae Mantuani Carmelitae Theologi Adolescentia seu Bucolica*. London, 1577.

Martinière, *Dictionnaire géographique*. Bruzen de la Martinière. *Le grand dictionnaire géographique et critique*, 10 vols. Venice, 1737-41.

Martyr, Justin. *Cohortatio ad Graecos*, in *Opera quae Extant Omnia*, 8 vols. Paris, 1742; tr. Thomas B. Falls, in *Writings of Saint Justin Martyr*. New York, 1948.

Martyr, Peter. *De Orbe Novo*, tr. F. A. MacNutt, 2 vols. New York, 1912.

McAdoo, Henry R. *The Spirit of Anglicanism*. New York, 1965.

McConica, James K. *English Humanists and Reformation Politics*. Oxford, 1965.

McCutcheon, Elizabeth. "Denying the Contrary: More's Use of Litotes in the *Utopia*." *Moreana*, 31-32 (1971), 107-21; rpt. in *Essential Articles for the Study of Thomas More*, ed. R. S. Sylvester and G. Marc'hadour, Hamden, Conn., 1977, 263-74.

Melancthon, Philip. *Commentarius de Anima*. Wittenberg, 1548.

Mercator, *Atlas*. Gerhardus Mercator. *Atlas*. Amsterdam, 1630; tr. Henry Hexham. Amsterdam, 1636.

―――. *Drei Karten von Gerhard Mercator*. Berlin, 1891.

Mercurialis, Girolamo. *Variae Lectiones*. Venice, 1571.

Meres, Francis. *Palladis Tamia: Wits Treasury.* London, 1598; rpt. New York, 1973.

Middleton, Thomas, and Thomas Dekker. *The Roaring Girle, or Moll Cut-Purse.* London, 1611.

Milton, John. *The Works of John Milton,* ed. F. A. Patterson, 18 vols. New York, 1931–38.

More, Saint Thomas. *Epigrammata.* Basel, 1520.

———, *Epigrams. The Latin Epigrams of Thomas More,* ed. and tr. L. Bradner and C. A. Lynch. Chicago, 1953.

———. *Responsio ad Lutherum,* ed. John M. Headley, tr. Sister Scholastica Mandeville, vol. 5, pt. 1, in *Works.* New Haven, 1969.

———. *Translations of Lucian,* ed. Craig R. Thompson, vol. 3 in *Works.* New Haven, 1973.

———. *Utopia,* ed. Edward Surtz and J. H. Hexter, vol. 4 in *Works.* New Haven, 1965.

———, *Works. The Complete Works of St. Thomas More,* 14 vols. New Haven, 1963–.

Moresinus, *Papatus.* Thomas Morison. *Papatus, seu Depravatae Religionis Origo et Incrementum.* Edinburgh, 1594.

Münster, *Cosmographia.* Sebastian Münster. *Cosmographia Universalis.* Basel, 1572.

Nichols, John. *The Progresses and Public Processions of Queen Elizabeth,* 3 vols. London, 1823.

Nicolas de Lyra. *Biblia Latina . . . cum Glosa Ordinaria: et Litterali Moralique Expositione Nicolai de Lyra,* 5 vols. Basel, 1502.

Nisard, Charles. *Les Gladiateurs de la république des lettres aux xve, xvie et xviie siècles,* vol. 1. Paris, 1860; rpt. Geneva, 1970.

———. *Le triumvirat littéraire au xvie siècle.* Paris, 1852; rpt. Geneva, 1970.

Nolhac, Pierre de. *Pétrarque et l'humanisme,* 2nd ed., 2 vols. Paris, 1907; rpt. Paris, 1965.

OCD. *Oxford Classical Dictionary,* ed. N. G. L. Hammond and H. H. Scullard, 2nd ed. London, 1970.

Ortelius, Abraham. *Theater. The Theater of the Whole World.* London, 1606; rpt. Chicago, 1968.

———. *Theatrum Orbis Terrarum.* Antwerp, 1592.

———. *Thesaurus Geographicus.* Antwerp, 1587.

Ov., *Fast.* Ovid. *Fasti,* tr. Sir James George Frazer. London, 1967.

———., *Met. Metamorphoses,* tr. Frank Justus Miller, 3rd ed. rev. G. P. Goold, 2 vols. London, 1977.

————., *Tr. Tristia*, tr. Arthur Leslie Wheeler. London, 1924.

————., *Pont. Epistulae ex Ponto*, tr. Arthur Leslie Wheeler. London, 1924.

Oxford Dictionary of English Proverbs, ed. William George Smith, 3rd ed. rev. F. P. Wilson. Oxford, 1970.

Paracelsus. *De Natura Rerum*. Strasbourg, 1584; tr. anon. as *Of the Nature of Things*. London, 1650.

Partridge, Eric, ed. *A Classical Dictionary of the Vulgar Tongue*, by Francis Grose. London, 1931.

Pattison, Mark. *Essays*, 2 vols. London, n.d.

Per. *Juvenal and Persius*, tr. G. G. Ramsay. London, 1928.

Petherick, Edward. "Mundus alter et idem." *Gentleman's Magazine*, 281 (1896), 66–87.

Petron, *Sat.* Petronius. *Satyricon*, tr. Michael Heseltine, rev. E. H. Warmington. London, 1975.

PG. Patrologiae Cursus Completus: Series Graeca, ed. J. P. Migne, 104 vols. Paris, 1857–60.

Philostr., *VA.* Philostratus. *Vita Apollonii*, tr. F. C. Conybeare, 2 vols. London, 1912–37.

Pigafetta. *Magellan's Voyage*, tr. and ed. R. A. Skelton. New Haven, 1969.

Pl., *Crit.* Plato. *Critias*, tr. R. G. Bury, rev. ed. London, 1952.

————., *Leg. Laws*, tr. R. G. Bury, 2 vols. London, 1952.

————., *Resp. The Republic*, tr. P. Shorey, 2 vols., rev. ed. London, 1946–56.

————., *Symp. Symposium*, tr. W. R. M. Lamb. London, 1975.

PL. Patrologiae Cursus Completus: Series Latina, ed. J. P. Migne, 221 vols. Paris, 1844–80.

Plaut. *Plautus*, tr. P. Nixon, 5 vols. London, 1916–38.
Individual works:
    Aul.: Aulularia, vol. 1.
    Asin.: Asinaria, vol. 1.
    Epid.: Epidicus, vol. 2.
    Poen.: Poenulus, vol. 4.
    Pseud.: Pseudolus, vol. 4.
    Stich.: Stichus, vol. 5.

Pliny, *HN.* Pliny (the Elder). *Historia Naturalis*, tr. H. Rackham and W. H. S. Jones, 10 vols. London, 1938–63.

Plut., *Mor.* Plutarch. *Moralia*, tr. F. C. Babbitt and H. N. Fowler, 16 vols. London, 1927–69.

Individual works:
>   *Conv. Sept. Sap.*: *Convivium Septem Sapientium*, vol. 2.
>   *De Fort. Rom.*: *De Fortuna Romanorum*, vol. 4.
>   *Inst. Lac.*: *Instituta Laconica*, vol. 3.
>   *Quaest. Conv.*: *Quaestionum Convivialium*, vols. 8-9.
>   *Quaest. Rom.*: *Quaestionium Romanae*, vol. 4.
_____., *Vit. Lives*, tr. B. Perrin, 11 vols. London, 1914-26.
Individual works:
>   *Dem.*: *Demosthenes*, vol. 7.
>   *Lyc.*: *Lycurgus*, vol. 1.
>   *Phocion*: vol. 8.
>   *Sert.*: *Sertorius*, vol. 8.

Polo, Marco. *De Regionibus Orientalibus*, in Grynaeus, *Novus Orbis*. Basel, 1537.

Postellus, *Cosmographicae*. William Postellus. *Cosmographicae Disciplinae Compendium*. Basel, 1561.

Quintilian. *The Institutio Oratoria of Quintilian*, tr. H. E. Butler, 4 vols. London, 1920-22.

Rabelais, François. *Gargantua*, in *Works*, tr. Sir Thomas Urquhart and Peter Motteux, ed. Albert Jay Nock. New York, 1931.

Rainaud, Armand. *Le continent austral*. Paris, 1893.

Raleigh, *Discoverie of Gviana*. Sir Walter Raleigh. *The Discoverie of the Large, Rich, and Bewtifvl Empyre of Gviana*. London, 1596; rpt. ed. V. T. Harlow. Cleveland, Ohio, 1966.

Rhodiginus, Ludovicus Caelius. *Lectiones Antiquae*. Basel, 1542.

Roscher, *Lexikon*. Wilhelm Heinrich Roscher, ed. *Ausführliches Lexikon der griechischen und römischen Mythologie*. Leipzig, 1884-1937.

Sac. Caerem. Sacrarum Caeremoniarum sive Rituum Ecclesiasticorum Sanctae Romanae Ecclesiae, 3 vols. Venice, 1582.

Salyer, Sandford M. "Joseph Hall as a Literary Figure." Diss., Harvard University, 1921.

_____. "Renaissance Influence in Hall's *Mundus Alter et Idem*." *Philological Quarterly*, 6 (1927), 321-34.

Sannazaro, Jocopo. *Epigrammata*, in *Opera Omnia*. Amsterdam, 1648.

Sargent, Lyman Tower. *British and American Utopian Literature 1516-1975*. Boston, 1979.

Scaliger, Julius Caesar. *Exoticarum Exercitationum Liber Quintus Decimus, de Subtilitate, ad Hieronymum Cardanum*. Frankfort, 1582.

Scapula, Johann. *Lexicon Graecolatinum Novum*. Basel, 1580.

Schrader, Lorenz. *Monumenta Italiae*. Helmstadt, 1592.

Sen., *Controv.* Seneca (The Elder). *Controversiae*, in *The Elder Seneca: Declamations*, tr. M. Winterbottom, 2 vols. London, 1974.

———. *Tragedies*, tr. Frank Justus Miller, 2 vols. London, 1917. Individual works:
> *Hippolytus*: vol. 1.
> *Medea*: vol. 1.

Sen., *Dial.* Seneca (The Younger). *Dialogi*, in *Moral Essays*, tr. John W. Basore, 3 vols. London, 1928-35.

Sendivogius, Michael. *A Chymicall Dictionary*, tr. John French. London, 1650.

———. *A New Light of Alchymie*, tr. John French. London, 1650.

Servius. Servius Honoratus. *Commentarius in Vergilii Aeneidos*, ed. George Thilo, 3 vols. Leipzig, 1881-87.

Sigebertus Gemblacensis. *Chronicon ab Anno 381 ad 1113*. Paris, 1513.

Sil. Silius Italicus. *Punica*, tr. J. D. Duff, 2 vols. London, 1934.

Smith, *Classical Dict.* William Smith, ed. *A Classical Dictionary of Greek and Roman Biography, Mythology, and Geography*. London, 1909.

———, *Dict. Bib. A Dictionary of the Bible*, 3 vols. Boston, 1860-63.

———, *Dict. Geog. A Dictionary of Greek and Roman Geography*, 2 vols. London, 1878.

———, *Dict. Gr. & Rom. Antiq. A Dictionary of Greek and Roman Antiquities*. London, 1875.

———, *Dict. Gr. & Rom. Myth. A Dictionary of Greek and Roman Mythology*, 3 vols. London, 1890.

Smith, J. J., ed. *The Cambridge Portfolio*. London, 1840.

Solinus, *Polyhistor.* C. Julius Solinus. *Polyhistor, seu Rerum Orbis Memorabilium Collectanea*, ed. Joannes Camers. Cologne, 1520.

Statius, *Scriptorum Romanorum.* Caius Caecilius Statius. *Scriptorum Romanorum quae Extant Omnia*. Venice, 1965.

Stein, Arnold. "Joseph Hall's Imitation of Juvenal." *Modern Language Review*, 48 (1948), 315-22.

———. "The Second English Satirist." *Modern Language Review*, 38 (1943), 273-78.

Stephanus of Byzantium. *Stephani Byzantii Ethnicorum quae Supersunt*, ed. August Meinekius. Graz, 1958.

Stevenson. Burton Stevenson. *The Macmillan Book of Proverbs, Maxims, and Famous Phrases*. New York, 1968.

Stow, John. *A Suruay of London*. London, 1598.

Strab. Strabo. *Geography*, tr. H. L. Jones, 8 vols. London, 1917–33.

Stubbes, *Anatomy of Abuses*. Philip Stubbes. *Anatomy of the Abuses in England in Shakespeare's Youth*, ed. Frederick J. Furnivall. London, 1877–79.

Suet. *Suetonius*, tr. J. C. Rolfe, 2 vols. London, 1914–30.
Individual works:
    Aug.: *Deified Augustus*, vol. 1.
    Claud.: *Deified Claudius*, vol. 2.
    Dom.: *Domitian*, vol. 2.
    Ner.: *Nero*, vol. 2.
    Vit.: *Vitellius*, vol. 2.

Suidas. *Lexicon, Graece & Latine*, ed. Ludolphus Kusterus, 3 vols. Cambridge, 1705.

Surtz, Edward, S.J. *Utopia, the Praise of Pleasure*. Cambridge, Mass., 1957.

Swift, Jonathan. *The Correspondence of Jonathan Swift*, ed. Harold Williams, 5 vols. Oxford, 1963.

––––––. *Gulliver's Travels*, vol. 2 in *The Prose Works of Jonathan Swift*, ed. Herbert Davis and Irvin Ehrenpreis, 14 vols. Oxford, 1939–68.

––––––. *Swift's Poems*, ed. Harold Williams, 2nd ed., 3 vols. Oxford, 1958.

––––––. *A Tale of a Tub*, ed. A. C. Guthketch and D. Nichol Smith, 2nd ed. Oxford, 1958.

Sylvester, Richard S. "'Si Hythlodaeo Credimus': Vision and Revision in Thomas More's *Utopia*." *Soundings*, 51 (1968), 272–89; rpt. in *Essential Articles for the Study of Thomas More*, ed. R. S. Sylvester and G. Marc'hadour. Hamden, Conn., 1977, 290–301.

Synesius Cyrenaeus, Bp. of Ptolemais. *Opera*, ed. D. Pitavius; in *PG*, vol. 66.

Taunton, Ethelred. *History of the Jesuits in England 1580–1773*. London, 1901.

Ter. *Terence*, tr. J. Sargeaunt, 2 vols. London, 1912.
Individual work:
    Eun.: *Eunuch*, vol. 1.

Theoc., *Id*. Theocritus. *The Greek Bucolic Poets*, tr. J. M. Edmonds. London, 1938.

Thevet, André. *The Newfounde Worlde, or Antarctike*. London, 1568; rpt. Amsterdam, 1971.

Thompson, James Westfall, ed. *The Frankfort Book Fair*, by Henri Etienne. Chicago, 1911; rpt. New York, 1968.

Traugott, John. "A Voyage to Nowhere with Thomas More and Jonathan Swift." *Sewanee Review*, 69 (1961), 534-65.

Turler, Jerome. *De Peregrinatione*. Strasbourg, 1574; tr. anon. as *The Traueiler*. London, 1575; rpt. Gainesville, Fla., 1951.

Val. Flac., *Argon. Argonautica*, in *Valerius Flaccus*, tr. J. H. Mozley. London, 1934.

Valerius Maximus. *Dictorum Factorumque Memorabilium Exempla*. Paris, 1560; tr. Samuel Speed as *Romae Antiquae Descriptio*. London, 1678.

Varro, *Ling. De Lingua Latina, On the Latin Language*, tr. Roland G. Kent, 2 vols. London, 1938.

Vatablus, *Sacra Biblia*. Francisco Vatablus. *Sacra Biblia . . . cum Annotationibus Francisci Vatabli*, ed. B. C. Bertram. Heidelberg, 1599.

Verg. *Vergil*, tr. H. Rushton Fairclough, 2 vols. London, 1969.
Individual works:
Aen.: *Aeneid*, vols. 1 and 2.
Ecl.: *Eclogues*, vol. 1.
G.: *Georgics*, vol. 1.
Moretum: vol. 2.

Vickers, Brian. "The Satiric Structure of *Gulliver's Travels* and More's *Utopia*," in *The World of Jonathan Swift*, ed. Brian Vickers, Cambridge, Mass., 1968, 233-57.

Vives, Juan Luis. *Opera Omnia*, ed. Gregory Majansius, 8 vols. Valencia, 1782-90.

Volaterra, Raphael Maffei. *Commentarii Urbani*. Rome, 1506.

Waite, A. E. *The Hermetic and Alchemical Writings of Paracelsus*, 2 vols. London, 1894.

Wands, John Millar. "The Early Printing History of Joseph Hall's *Mundus Alter et Idem*." *Papers of the Bibliographical Society of America*, 74 (1980), 1-12.

White, Harold Ogden. *Plagiarism and Imitation in the English Renaissance*. Cambridge, Mass., 1935.

Williams, George H. *The Radical Reformation*. London, 1962.

Williams, Harold. *Dean Swift's Library*. Cambridge, 1932.

Winter, Michael. *Compendium Utopiarum, Typologie und Bibligraphie literarischer Utopien*, 2 vols. Stuttgart, 1978.

Wooden, Warren. "Satiric Strategy in More's *Utopia*: The Case of Raphael Hythloday." *Renaissance Papers*, 1977, 1-9.

Xen., *An.* Xenophon. *Anabasis*, tr. Carleton L. Brownson. London, 1968.

————., *Mem. Memorabilia,* tr. E. C. Marchant. London, 1938.

Yeomans, W. E. "The Houyhnhnm as Menippean Horse," in *Swift: Modern Judgements,* ed. Norman Jeffares. London, 1968.

INDEX

Abelians: heretics, 104, 187

Abraxia, city of, 103; derivation of, 103*n*, 185. *See also* Basilidians

Actaeonius Valley, 91; derivation of, 118, 198

Adonis: gardens of, 28, 141

Aelia Loelia Crispis, xvi, 75*n*, 165

Aelian: *On the Characteristics of Animals*, 192, 198

Aesculapius, shrine of, 34, 144

Aetna, Mount: location of Purgatory in, 54, 154

Agricola, Georg: *De Animatibus Subterraneis*, 84*n*, 171

Aitsinger, Michael: *Leo Belgicus*, 175

Albertus Magnus, 140

Alcinous, gardens of, 28, 141

Alexander the Great, 3

Almagro, Diego de, 11, 131

Amantina (also called Erotium), 61, 199; derivation of, 118, 157

Amazonia (also called Gynandria), 57, 61, 63–66, 157; named Land of Shrewes, 63*n*, 118; men in, 64–66; warlike nature of, 65–66; derivation of, 118, 199

Ampelona, city of (also known as Pampinola), 42, 149; derivation of, 123

Anabaptists. *See* Libertines

Anacreon: verses of, 46, 150–51

Antaeus: giant named, 36, 146

Antoia, city of, 94, 96; compared to Rome, 94; derivation of, 118

Anylos, Mount, 74; derivation of, 118

Aphrodysia, region of, 57, 61–62; derivation of, 118

Apicius: glutton named, 25, 29, 138–39; Suidas on, 29*n*, 142

Apollonius Rhodius: *Argonautica*, 174, 192, 194

Apuleius, 23, 32, 49; *Florida*, 32*n*, 142, 143, 152; *Metamorphoses, or The Golden Ass*, 49*n*, 137, 152

Aqua Fortis, Port, 53; derivation of, 154

Aquarians: heretics, 104, 187

Arabian Nights, 135, 181

Archisilenius: glutton named, 29; derivation of, 142

Ardens Chapel, 51; visit to, 54; derivation of, 154. *See also* Bacchus Pyrodes

Argonauts, 88, 174

Argyranchen: disease of misers, 114, 194

Ariadne, 47, 151

Aristophanes, 60*n*; *The Ecclesiazusae*, xxvi–xxvii; *The Birds*, 46*n*, 150, 156–57

Aristotle, 16, 34, 40, 64, 112; on Philoxenus, 28, 140; on barter, 34*n*, 145; *Politics*, 64*n*; on the Harpies, 112*n*, 192; on a Carthaginian island, 134; on a country's ability to support its population, 149; on the barbarians' treatment of women, 159; on the effect of cold on animals, 160; on the polypus fish, 167; on the Tragelaph, 170; on the reaction of opposites, 171; on the advantage of proximity to the sea, 175

Arrebatia, province of, 116; derivation of, 118